BELONGING AND GENOCIDE

Belonging
and
Genocide

Hitler's Community, 1918–1945

THOMAS KÜHNE

Yale UNIVERSITY PRESS
NEW HAVEN AND LONDON

Published with assistance from the foundation established in memory of
Calvin Chapin of the Class of 1788, Yale College.

Yale University Press books may be purchased in quantity for educational,
business, or promotional use. For information, please e-mail sales.press@yale.edu
(U.S. office) or sales@yaleup.co.uk (U.K. office).

Set in Electra LH. type by IDS Infotech Ltd., Chandigarh, India
Printed in the United States of America by Sheridan Books,
Ann Arbor, Michigan
Library of Congress Cataloging-in-Publication Data
Kühne, Thomas, 1958–
Belonging and genocide : Hitler's community, 1918–1945/ Thomas Kühne.
p. cm.
Includes bibliographical references and index.
ISBN 978-0-300-12186-5 (hardcover : alk. paper)
1. Germany—Social life and customs—20th century. 2. Germany—Social
conditions—20th century. 3. Germany—Race relations—History—20th century.
4. Community life—Germany—History—20th century. 5. Fellowship—Social
aspects—Germany—History—20th century. 6. Genocide—Social aspects—
Germany—History—20th century. 7. Antisemitism—Social aspects—
Germany—History—20th century. 8. Shame—Social aspects—Germany—
History—20th century. 9. National socialism—Social aspects—Germany—
History—20th century. 10. Germany—Armed Forces—Military life—History—
20th century. I. Title.
DD67.3.K84 2010
943.086—dc22
2010010469

A catalogue record for this book is available from the British Library.

This paper meets the requirements of ANSI/NISO Z39.48-1992
(Permanence of Paper).

10 9 8 7 6 5 4 3 2 1

There are two means to unite a people—
common ideals and common crime.
—Adolf Hitler,
Party Leader, Munich, 1923

The Germans are "comraded,"
a dreadfully dangerous condition.
—Sebastian Haffner,
Journalist and Émigré, London, 1939

If this Jewish business is ever avenged
on earth, then have mercy on us Germans.
—Major Trapp,
Police Officer, Poland, 1942

For there is a great, bright aspect
to this war: namely a great comradeship.
—Adolf Hitler,
Reich Chancellor, Berlin, 1942

We Germans are the nation that has gone
for this war enthusiastically and will have
to bear the consequences.
—Franz Wieschenberg,
Wehrmacht Private, Eastern Front, 1944

To stick together and to fight side by side
and be wounded side by side, that's our wish.
—Kurt Kreissler,
Wehrmacht NCO, Germany, 1945

CONTENTS

Introduction 1

INTRODUCTION

We must look into the abyss to see beyond it.
—*Robert Jay Lifton*

Genocide is the destruction of a "national, ethnical, racial or religious group," as the United Nations declared in 1948, or, as scholars argue more recently, of any politically, socially, or culturally defined group.[1] Conceptualized as an essay on why and how the Germans committed genocide against Europe's Jews, this book draws attention to the contrary—the constitutive rather than the destructive side of mass murder. Perpetrators and bystanders energized social life and built collective identity through committing genocide. The desire for community, the experience of belonging, and the ethos of collectivity became the basis of mass murder. Perpetrating and supporting the Holocaust provided Germans with a particular sense of national belonging: the German nation found itself by committing the Holocaust.

The feeling of national belonging based on genocide was not unspoiled. The happiness of a grand community was marred by the moral ambiguities and physical fears characteristic of total and genocidal war. It was a diverse German citizenry that maintained an exclusive solidarity in the midst of murder and destruction. Not all Germans experienced belonging based on mass murder in the same way. I am concerned with the different ways Germans felt about and dealt with nation-building by mass crime, with the breadth of a perpetrator society that enabled and facilitated the Holocaust not least by inaction and inattention. Sadistic perpetrators as well as unwilling bystanders, SS killing units and regular army units, well-educated lawyers and blue-collar workers, men at the war front and women on the home front—all participated in community building through mass crime. It was a mass conscript army rather than an elite warrior society that intensified and abused human needs when it blurred the distinction between regular and genocidal warfare. Instead of focusing on one group of perpetrators—the SS death squads, the police troops, a section of Himmler's terror bureaucracy, a certain generation, the occupiers of a region[2]— this book inquires into the interwoven relationships of the entire society that made the Holocaust possible and then was outrun itself by total war. Why did the German nation never break asunder but remain united in the midst of mass murder and mass death until it was defeated? This book offers an answer: the act of practicing mass killing and mass murder and that of suffering from mass death mutually reinforced each other. Both processes fueled an engine of intensified togetherness. Physical death propelled social life.

This view of Nazi Germany takes up questions and results of previous scholarship. Through the late 1980s, social and political history of the Third Reich was, in crucial respects, disconnected from the history of the Holocaust perpetrators. Third Reich history rightly stressed that German society, despite powerful and constant propaganda and the coercive machinery of Nazi terror, never stood united behind Hitler. Although this scholarship asserted that German defiance, nonconformity, and opposition had little effect, it didn't explain why solidarity or social action did not exist on a broader basis on behalf of the Jews. Why could the Holocaust be executed so smoothly, so effectively, and so successfully? Holocaust history, on the other hand, sought an answer to exactly this question and proffered two conflicting arguments. The "Intentionalists" limited responsibility to Hitler and the Nazi elite who had planned the murder of the Jews. The "Functionalists" saw the Holocaust as the result of a political radicalization that was driven by competing power agencies within the Nazi state, such as the Nazi Party, the state bureaucracy, and the occupational regimes in the conquered territories. Each explanation, however, marginalized the social dimension of the Holocaust. Masses of ordinary Germans supported or actively perpetrated it. Thus, in the 1980s both Third Reich history and Holocaust history obscured the agency of ordinary Germans during the Holocaust.[3]

Not until 1990, with demographic, cultural, and political changes, did scholars start to question these blinkered views. Between 1990 and 1995 the last Germans that had experienced and shaped the Nazi period as young adults or adolescents retired, and younger people who had never been personally entangled in the Nazi society would determine which topics and views would be presented in books, classrooms, newspapers, and TV shows. Only then was the subject of ordinary Germans' propensity to violence addressed openly. At the same time, the "Americanization" of the Holocaust drew public and scholarly attention to how ordinary Germans behaved, and to the choices they had. In 1992 Christopher Browning's book *Ordinary Men* left no doubt that even the members of Himmler's murder troops were never completely denied the option of refusing to kill civilians. In 1993 Steven Spielberg's movie *Schindler's List* showed that Germans had options for rescuing Jews—if they wished to do so. Beginning in 1992 the return of mass violence, even genocide, to the heart of Europe—in the former Yugoslavia, until then known as a lovely tourist country—reminded everyone, including Germans, of the potential for cruelty that lies behind the façade of civilization. People perpetrated, enjoyed, and applauded brutal atrocities against those with whom they had lived peacefully together for a long time. These atrocities were watched in living rooms around the world and also inspired a renewed scholarly interest in the roots of war and genocide.[4]

As a result, in the 1990s the Holocaust became the paradigm of inquiry in the Third Reich.[5] Only by shifting the focus to the theaters of genocidal war were historians able to assess ordinary Germans' involvement in the Holocaust and hence distinguish different types of initiative, enthusiasm, compliance, complicity, shared knowledge, qualms, and choices. Furthermore, scholars no longer compared Nazi Germany only to other fascist regimes or to Stalinism but rather saw it as the climax of a powerful continuity of ethnic cleansing and genocidal violence that ran through the "long" twentieth century and had victimized American Indians, indigenous Australians, south African Herero and Nama, Armenians, Ukrainians, Cambodians, Tutsis and Hutus, and Bosnians and other groups in the former Yugoslavia.

Euphemistically introduced by Serb nationalists, the term "ethnic cleansing" made historians aware of the utopian power of genocide. Genocidal regimes derive their dynamic from fears of the "pollution" of the social body and desires for regaining "purity."[6] The only way to rebuild "Us" is to eliminate "Them." To reassure one's own collective identity, it is necessary to get rid of the "Other." Recent scholars have taken seriously the social impact of Manichaean utopias of salvation through extermination; anti-Semitism serves as precisely such an ideology. While Daniel Goldhagen's assumption of an all-German "eliminationist" anti-Semitism has been refuted by most historians, he was certainly right about the crucial role of popular anti-Semitism in the Holocaust. Saul Friedländer has convincingly analyzed the Holocaust as a consequence of a "redemptive anti-Semitism," a messianic vision that made Germans believe that the elimination of the Jews as the most lethal and active threat against the German *Volk* would lead to a grand national salvation.[7]

Although there is no doubt regarding the large role of anti-Semitism in the Holocaust, this book does not focus on Germans' and other Europeans' hatred of Jews. Nor is it primarily concerned with analyzing anticommunism or the German contempt of Slavs, though the impact of these stereotypes is obvious. Rather it considers the flip side of hatred—love. Love and hatred are two sides of a coin. Genocidal violence, the destruction of Them, can also bolster the love between Us.[8] When Germans carried out genocidal war against the Jews and other "undesirables" in order to realize the utopia of a purified nation, they did more than destroy what they considered to be dirty and dangerous. They experienced togetherness, cohesion, and belonging, and they deluded themselves into believing they would attain a homogenous and harmonious social body, cleansed of pollution, conflict, and inner enemies. The Nazis called this social body a *Volksgemeinschaft*, a people's community. The entire nation would feel as a family or a group of friends, providing closeness, safety, and warmth. Nobody would be alone, everyone would be taken care of, all would feel connected to each other—and all would act in concert. Through committing the Holocaust, Germans gained a feeling for this grand utopia of belonging.

Historians have often deemed this vision nothing more than propaganda. In fact, they have argued, German society never really changed its class and religious cleavages, at least not during the Nazi period.[9] Although this view

4

carries some truth, it leaves one question unanswered. If German society really was so divided, if its unity had been only a façade, why, then, did it not fall apart, especially after 1942, when Germany's downfall became obvious? My answer is that the Nazis managed to include and utilize even strong anti-Nazis to support a grand brotherhood of crime—one that left practically no back door for escape. Its crucial social dynamic made complicit even those who did not want to become complicit. And although understood as a community based on criminal conduct, complicity, and cognizance, it was yet presented as morally sacrosanct. The regime propagated a revolutionary ethos that assured Germans that their murderous activities were morally good.

We are used to timeless definitions of moral behavior. Illusions of timeless stability offer us certainty in an uncertain world. However, human culture, including guidelines for what are good and evil, is socially constructed. The guidelines depend on time and space. They can change. And indeed, they do change. Nazi terror was embedded in an "ethical" framework of its own. Contrary to modern universalistic ethics, the Nazis "believed that concepts of virtue and vice had evolved according to the needs of particular ethnic communities" and "promoted moral maxims they saw as appropriate to their Aryan community"—this according to the historian Claudia Koonz.[10] Repudiating the Judeo-Christian traditions of mercy toward the weak and the Enlightenment principles of universalism, individualism, and egalitarianism, Nazi ethics demanded that charity, kindness, and pity be restricted to Aryan Germans. Koonz and other historians have focused on the exclusionary side of pre-1939 Nazi ethics. By contrast, I show how these racially limited ethics worked within the in-group and propelled powerful sentiments of belonging, togetherness, and community even more during the war and genocide that started in 1939.

The Nazis perfected community-building through violence and racist ethics, but they did not invent it. Rather they built on, and radicalized, cultural traditions that already had become powerful earlier in the twentieth century. Chapter One tracks Germany's obsession with community and belonging as a consequence of the aftermath of World War I, the loss of a devastating war that had left the German nation tattered and fragmented.[11] Soldiers' participation in the immense violence of an industrialized war could no longer be categorized in terms of individual guilt and responsibility. The collective memory of these orgies of destruction concealed the "I" in the Us. The Us dissolved personal responsibility. Communities of comrades, resigned to their fate, sanitized their aggression toward the enemies through altruism bestowed on those who belonged, at least according to collective memory. The myth of comradeship went even further. It praised the platoon as the model of a truly united nation, the Volksgemeinschaft. Hence the way was paved for a new moral system that no longer revolved around the conscience of the individual but rather around the social life and reputation of the group—the platoon as well as the nation.

How comradeship was instilled and installed in Germany from 1933 on is elaborated in Chapter Two. Its focus is the paramilitary and military socialization of boys and men in camps, schools, associations, neighbourhoods, and, not least, the military. In Nazi Germany, the state guided community-building by criminal means. Nothing makes people stick together better than committing a crime together. This basic law of the sociology of crime was well known by the early twentieth century. In the Nazi training camps, Germans usually did not commit actual crimes. But they were trained, or trained themselves, to break the rules of middle-class morality collectively in order to sense the joy and security of male bonding. They learned that the male bond was morally superior and morally sovereign. Hence they began to fantasize themselves as a revolutionary master race that would leave Western values and Eastern peoples behind.

Chapter Three shows the variety as well as the intensity of community-building accomplished by progressive norm-breaking. The focus is on the core Holocaust perpetrators—Himmler's elite troops in the death squads and in the concentration camps. These men generated and experienced togetherness in a world that bore no relationship to civilian ways of life. Death and terror were omnipresent. Whether shooting Jews in the occupied territories in the East or pushing them into gas chambers, men, and sometimes also women, competed in performing the Nazis' revolutionary morality that invalidated individual responsibility, human compassion, and human rights. However, not even these perpetrators, men of different personalities, ages, and social strata, found it easy to leave "traditional" ethics behind. Overcoming qualms was the prerequisite for becoming a full-fledged member of an elite troop. Based on close readings of post-1945 trial testimonies and other eyewitness reports, the third chapter examines how the Nazis welded disparate individuals together by energizing a sense of belonging to a monstrous elite that had burned its bridges to the rest of the world.

Chapter Four, relying on private letters and diaries of ordinary soldiers, shows how the strategy of community building through crime was expanded to the bulk of adult German men in the *Wehrmacht*. From the beginning to the end of the war, soldiers, often naively, enjoyed the pleasures and the emotional closeness of comradeship. They still had some sense of right and wrong. Notwithstanding the after-the-fact myths of ignorance of the Holocaust on the part of ordinary Germans, most of these soldiers — seventeen million — had some idea that the war they waged went far beyond anything considered morally acceptable. Many of them had watched or even applauded the beginning of the genocide in summer 1941 all over the Eastern front. Even if they had not personally participated in murder or had even condemned it, they knew they were implicated. This complicity engendered a fear of revenge from the Jews, Russians, or other enemies. Millions of soldiers understood themselves as members of a pariah nation — the primary reason their bonds remained intact until spring 1945. Most of them tried to ignore their scruples by feigning indifference with a devil-may-care attitude. Such bravado not only was at the heart of genocidal warfare, it also strengthened the feeling of "greater" national uniformity.

Zeroing in on the home front, Chapter Five traces the total psychological mobilization of all segments of the German populace, including the practices, emotions, and ideas that also made women complicit in the community of crime. The Nazi war allowed and encouraged crime. German women and even children strengthened this perception by encouraging their husbands, sons, and fathers to fight like the Nazi idea of men. Thus they also approved, though often only reluctantly and to different degrees, the extermination of the Jews. Why was that so? During the Nazi era, women learned to copy, and to become integrated into, manly comradeship. And they appreciated it as a substantial gain of power from pre-Nazi society. Chapter Five illuminates how far and in what ways women worked with each other and with men on nation-building based on mass murder, mass violence, and mass death. It was only in this way that the glorious "greater comradeship," celebrated by Hitler and other Nazis, came to be a warrior nation, but one with men and women as equally aligned comrades. Thus community-building by criminal means was concluded: many different Germans adopted a sense of national belonging that went far beyond any other kind of national sentiment.

ONE
==

Craving Community

World War I and the Myth of Comradeship

rich Maria Remarque's 1929 novel *All Quiet on the Western Front*, a cry for pacificism published a decade after the devastation of Europe during World War I, was undoubtedly the most popular and the most controversial piece of war memory to come out of modern Germany. Following a petition of the Nazi Party, the Prussian state went so far as to censor the movie version produced in 1930 in America.[1] All this attention was not just about a book or a movie. Nor was it just about the past. It was about the future of Germany, its military future in particular. Was there any? Germany had lost the Great War: it was deeply humiliated by the Versailles Treaty and the verdict of guilty the treaty had handed down; it was appalled by the huge reparations it would have to pay; and it was outraged about the enforced demilitarization. Would the country ever regain its former power?

The challenges Germany faced at this time came not only from its former enemies but also from within the country itself. By the mid-1920s, the pacifist movement had lost most of the support it had achieved immediately after the war. Around 1930, though, a pacifist revival, encouraged by Remarque's best seller, seemed to be unstoppable. Remarque ridiculed military officers, and, even worse, his focus on the brutality of war gave credence to the pacifist appeal "never again." The veterans were not the only ones to be affected by Remarque's message. Militarist and right-wing movements in Germany were even more unnerved by the young people who were crowding cinemas to watch the antimilitarist movie and who were fascinated with the book. Opinion polls suggested that, by 1931, half of all German high school students had read the novel, and many more were undoubtedly familiar with the movie.[2]

As it turned out, however, the hopes of the leftists and the worries of the rightists came to naught. Although Remarque may have intended to strengthen the antiwar movement, he ultimately failed. Looking suspiciously at young people watching the movie, Karl Sclutius, a socialist commentator, dubbed it "pacifist war propaganda," suggesting that the novel might easily be read as a war thriller.[3] He was right—in an even broader sense than he knew. Unintentionally, Remarque's novel contributed to a moral conversion, which eventually became the cultural basis of the genocidal war Germany would wage on Europe ten years later. In fact, this moral shift had started before the Nazis came into power.

A key scene in Remarque's book captures the change. The youthful antihero, Paul Bäumer, who had volunteered for the army as a high school student, is under fire and taking shelter in a bombshell hole when a French soldier suddenly drops in. Frightened, Paul stabs him: "I do not think at all, I make no decision." The enemy, gurgling endlessly, dies slowly. Paul has but one desire—"to get away" from that "dark figure." Ongoing machine-gun fire outside prevents him from fleeing. He is condemned to stay with a human being he has just killed. Hours pass. Looking at his bloody hand, he is nauseated. The hand may be literally dirty, but morally his body and soul are even dirtier.

Suddenly, the enemy-victim's eyes open and paralyze the perpetrator. Paul realizes his victim is not an anonymous soldier, but an individual who had hopes and dreams of his own. Paul has killed all that. He looks for the deadly wound, but there is nothing more to do than to whisper: " 'I want to help you, Comrade, camerade, camerade, camerade'—eagerly repeating the word"—even in French—"to make him understand." When the Frenchman finally dies, Paul feels guilty: "Comrade, I did not want to kill you . . . Forgive me." The scene covers more then ten pages of Paul's monologues and reflections. They become darkest when he discovers the wallet of his victim, revealing portraits of his wife and daughter as well as his name and occupation—"Gerard Duval, compositor."[4]

Eventually the battle fire abates and Paul calms down. He remembers his close comrades, a handful of soldiers who had been with him since entering the barracks. Together they had endured their drill sergeant's harassment and had even taken revenge on him by giving him a good hiding one night when he was drunk. Early in their training they had begun to learn what all the suffering was good for: "It awakened in us a strong, practical sense of belonging, which in the field developed into the finest thing that arose out of the war—comradeship."[5] And comradeship was the message of Remarque's story, comradeship as the great experience of community that emerges out of the war's destruction and depression. Comradeship was the code word for the homoerotic fabric of military male bonding. A comrade would not only demonstrate masculine toughness but also express tender feelings and share his buddies' worries. This was not to generate naive happiness. Developed by a group of men thrown together by fate, it countered terror and destruction. Belief in fate and comradeship helped soldiers to cope with the moral burdens of their lethal job. Killing was never based on individual choice, according to this way of thinking. It was never the "I" but always the "We" who killed, beyond individual responsibility. In Remarque's novel, comradeship fights the amorality of war, and at the same time it keeps the war machine running. The good comrade goes into battle with his buddies. He would never stay behind to try to save his own life. He knows, "They are more than my life." Wherever they are "is where I belong."[6]

After long hours in the shell hole with the man he has killed, Paul eventually gets out, hurrying back to his comrades. They take care of him, comfort him, offer him food and cigarettes, and calm him down. Paul feels relief. "I listen to them and feel comforted, reassured by their presence. It was mere driveling nonsense that I talked out there in the shell-hole." Back with his comrades, breathing their emotional warmth, Paul overcomes the confusion his conscience had engendered. And so the reader learns the lesson of the story. Forget your individual conscience. Stick together. Switch off personal desires, scruples, and worries. Living up to the group's ethos, experiencing the emotional and moral stability of the We helps you to overcome the confusion of the I. Soon a comrade's "rifle cracks out sharply and dry." The war goes on. It will be waged together.[7]

"Everyone Is Out for Himself Alone"

Remarque was neither the first nor the only German to glorify the relief of comradeship in the midst of devastation. Comradeship as a military virtue has a long universal tradition. Everywhere fighting morale depends on esprit de corps and social cohesion. However, during World War I and more so afterward, when Germany had to deal with its catastrophe, the idea of comradeship became widespread in civilian life, too. By attracting all the major, mutually hostile sociopolitical camps of Germany, it gave the entire nation a common cultural basis that had not existed previously. This was the result of an entwined history of public debates, societal struggles, and political disasters that had begun as early as 1900.

From the late nineteenth century, Germany had suffered, like other rapidly industrializing countries, from a cultural crisis often referred to as "atomization"—the sense that society was disintegrating into an agglomerate of isolated individuals. When they moved from the countryside to the big cities, people lost their traditional relationships and communities. In the city, they compensated by joining associations fighting for political ideals or economic interests. But such associations did not always provide new stable identities; instead they often burdened people with new conflicting pressures. Catholic blue-collar workers, for instance, felt obliged to show deference toward their Protestant bosses. At the same time, they were developing anticapitalist class consciousness. Yet they still belonged to the Catholic church, which despised both Protestantism and class struggle. And often people couldn't even find a group they wanted to join. In short, life in urban and industrial centers did not provide the warmth of their old life. They might live "peacefully alongside one another," but they were "essentially detached," observed the German sociologist Ferdinand Tönnies. In fact, he said, "everyone is out for himself alone and living in a state of tension against everyone else." Published in 1887, Tönnies's book *Community and Society* (*Gemeinschaft und Gesellschaft*) became popular around 1900. It identified the widespread fear of modernity and idealized a lost, supposedly intact world. What distinguished true communities from the complexity of modern society was, Tönnies suggested, "concord or family spirit," that is, "reciprocal binding sentiment," a naive and spontaneous "mutual understanding or consensus." Such mutuality rested upon "similarity of background and experience" as well as on "intimate knowledge of another and willingness to share in his or her joys and sorrows." Everything was common—"possession and enjoyment," good and evil, friends and enemies. According to this romanticized view, community did not need negotiation, agreement, reflection, or effort. It was just there, never confused by outside communication. But confusing communication, facilitated by commerce, travel, and social mobility, caused permanent confrontation with the Other and was exactly what shaped the modern world. Old-fashioned community, in a strict sense, was no longer possible.[8]

People's longing for community and their anxiety about the complexity of modern social life were not confined to Germany. Like Tönnies, the American sociologist Charles Horton Cooley looked at the opposition of "primary" face-to-face groups and anonymous "secondary" groups. In France, Emile Durkheim contrasted "organic solidarity and contractual solidarity."[9] And in neither America nor Europe was the discourse on the change of social life limited to academia; political institutions and social movements were deeply concerned with it as well.

The German case, however, was different from other Western nation-states. As a nation, Germany was a latecomer. France and Britain had successfully finished building their nation-states long ago and were blessed with unlimited economic resources in their colonies. Germany's domestic and foreign politics had a weaker basis. As Kaiser Wilhelm II pushed the nation's claim for colonies beginning in the 1890s, Germans feared that enemies, who would not allow Germany to enjoy its rightful "place in the sun," encircled their country. At the same time, they felt threatened by the lack of national unity. In a political climate shaped by social Darwinist obsessions with the "survival of the fittest," they felt they were missing the inner strength and unity needed to guarantee that Germany would not be one of the losers. Internal disruptions were perceived as a lethal threat. At its eastern border, Polish separatism challenged Germany's military strength. At the western border, the annexed provinces of Alsace and Lorraine were suspected of longing for reunification with France. At the northern border, the Danish minority seemed to present a similar challenge. In the 1870s and 1880s, cultural and political wars against supposed "inner enemies"—the

Catholics and the socialists—had established the sharpest conflicts all over the Reich. By around 1890, as a result of these domestic battles, the German nation was splintered into three political camps, each of them amounting to roughly one-third of the population and of the voters: the Protestant middle class, itself divided into a mostly liberal urban and a conservative rural branch; the Catholics, who comprised a broad range of social groups and classes; and the socialist Protestant working class.[10]

The "Spirit of 1914"

Liberal and conservative middle-class Germans at this time, seeing themselves as the heart of the nation, placed the vision of a truly united nation on the political agenda. This vision merged with old longings for harmony and the wish that modernity's anonymous and splintered society be rebuilt as a community of shared concerns—the nation as family. One might wonder how that was supposed to happen. But people did not seem to care much about how. They just wanted a *Volksgemeinschaft*, a "people's community," that would pour warmth and harmony into the cold and disrupted nation-society. Germans of all ideological camps began promoting that vision; the liberal and conservative middle class took over the leadership.[11]

Soon after World War I broke out in August 1914, any doubts about how to make a real Volksgemeinschaft became obsolete. The "spirit of 1914" seemed to wipe away the splintered atmosphere. Mass marches in favor of the war spilled onto streets, pubs were crowded with people singing patriotic songs, and throngs of volunteers joined the army. The Social Democratic Party supported the Reichstag's request for war loans and abandoned its previous opposition to the monarchy's authoritarian nation-state. Thus, the *Burgfrieden*—the truce, a "peace within the fortress"—was established. The grand national consensus seemed to be realized.[12]

But the Burgfrieden proved to be a chimera. Neither domestic unity nor war enthusiasm lasted very long. In truth, the "spirit of 1914" only momentarily concealed the real tears and worries of most Germans. The Burgfrieden could not overcome ineradicable social and economic conflicts. The longer the war went on and the more the lower classes suffered from its consequences, the stronger the dissenters became, especially in the socialist movement, whose party leaders realized that the Burgfrieden offered little for them. They had counted on getting closer to the monarchy's levers of power by supporting the government and cooperating with the bourgeois parties, but these groups had not given up the idea of taming the socialist movement. The government proved unwilling even to democratize Prussia's three-class voting system, which was widely seen as the most outrageous symbol of political unfairness in Wilhelmine Germany.

Social fairness seemed to elude the working class on both the home front and the battlefront. Access to officer rank remained limited to the members of the upper middle class and aristocrats. Thus, the class gaps of civilian society were extended to the battlefront. At home only lower classes suffered from undernourishment, especially during the winter of 1916–17. The middle and upper classes had good shelter and enough food, and when rumors surfaced about their profiting from the war, discontent spread even faster. Even in their private letters—which were censored—working-class soldiers from 1916 on wrote of their hopes for a socialist revolution. It broke out in November 1918.[13] Thus the war led not to a splendidly united nation but to even greater national dissension. And the revolution was followed by civil war and a democratic constitution that fostered party and class struggles instead of overcoming them. After 1918, political and social disruptions were exacerbated. The three political camps continued their war with one another, but now, thanks to the legacy of the lost war, they were even less able to compromise, let alone develop a common sense of national belonging. The nationalist camp came to be composed of conservatives and those liberals who identified most strongly with Bismarck's empire. It had a base in the veterans' and paramilitary associations. Leftist liberals and Social Democrats who had lost their radical wing to the Communists formed the leftist war-weary opposition. The Catholics, split between the moderate Center Party and the staunchly conservative Bavarian People's Party, oscillated between left and right.

"Unity, Whose Sense We Shall Never Lose"

The German revolution in 1918 had evolved out of community, though not the one envisioned by the nationalists. The revolutionaries' community was based on class solidarity, which was inherently linked to class struggle—exactly what the nationalists wished to eliminate. How such confusion? Already in late 1918 the nationalists knew the answer. According to them, the mutineers and revolutionaries in 1918 were led by egoistic demagogues acting out of selfish class interests instead of complying with national needs. Socialist and Jewish ringleaders, cheered on by treacherous women, had stirred up the German people at home and stabbed the heroic army in the back. Nationalists spread this infamous back-stabbing legend all over the country. It did not accord with the historical truth—that the German army had capitulated to the Allies' overwhelming materiel superiority. The legend, though, ignored the facts and blamed a lack of moral resources in explaining Germany's defeat. If only there had been more willpower, if only Germans had stuck together, if only the Socialist-Jewish conspiracy had not undermined the "spirit of 1914," Germany would have won the war.[14]

Evidence of such analyses was to be found in soldiers' memories, often regarded as a source of holy truth. Only the combat soldiers had successfully preserved and practiced what was supposed to unify the whole country—the "spirit of 1914." Out there at the front was a better world, filled with social harmony and altruism, in sharp contrast to civilian "egoism" with its class struggle and political factions. Walter Flex's novel *The Wanderer Between Two Worlds*, published immediately after his death, became enormously influential. The hero of the novel, Ernst Wurche—like the author the son of an educated middle-class family—maintained "good comradeship" with artisans, workers, and other lower-class men. As a perfect comrade, he always took care of his men, would even give his life to save them. And vice versa. His men always stood ready to follow him into battle.[15]

Such distortions of facts were told and retold from 1918 on. Feverishly, rightists praised the military leaders they saw as comradely and charismatic and denied what really had poisoned the German military—the persistence of civilian class gaps. According to such stories, in the trenches previous civil conflicts between peasants, blue-collar workers, and educated middle-class men no longer mattered. Only in the trenches had the model of a new society, the Volksgemeinschaft, come into being. The German nation had survived solely at the front, claimed Franz Schauwecker, a former front officer. Amid all the devastation, "We found one another, we who had for so long longed for another. . . . But it has come at last. Here we have it, unity, whose sense we shall never lose, unique unity—the nation."[16] According to such myths, in the trenches status no longer relied on differences of wealth or birth but was based instead on competence, ambition, and performance, all of which strengthened the kind of community that was the model for future German society. This society would then willingly thrive under the authority of a charismatic leader, also born in the trenches, thought Johann Wilhelm Mannhardt, a former front officer, already in 1919.[17]

Immediately after the war, most Germans were shocked by the damage the war had caused. Civil war and runaway inflation did not let them rest. Above all, two million soldiers had died, and many more had come home physically or mentally crippled. Hundreds of thousands of German pacifists marched against war. Even men who still believed in soldierly virtues doubted whether these virtues would ever regain the esteem in which they were once held. According to Siegfried von Wegeleben, a former officer like Schauwecker and Mannhardt, the idea that the "holy war" had given birth to "pure altruism" was a phantasm; he considered any effort to use the moral and social resources of trench experience a losing battle.[18] He articulated the resentments felt by many former soldiers, as the investigations of Joseph Schneider, a Bavarian pastor, revealed. In asking homecoming soldiers for their most striking war experiences, Schneider got depressing answers. About one in three referred to individual suffering from fighting, to fear of death or of being injured. Even more just wanted to forget what they had felt or seen. A significant number—about 10 percent—remembered primarily the unfairness of army life and dearth of comradely behavior. Just one in fifty said he actually had experienced comradeship![19]

Schneider was a conservative who believed in soldierly virtues. Had he published the results of his inquiries without comments, he would have handed a gift to the antimilitarists, who denied what nationalist war memory praised: the comradeship between officers and enlisted men. The political left rubbed salt into the German military's wounds by castigating the officers' privileges and arrogant habits. No wonder, they said, that hardly anyone recalled comradeship. Virtually everyone knew it, including nationalists, but it wasn't easy to admit. Theodor Bartram, the cofounder of the *Stahlhelm* (Steel Helmet) paramilitary organization, asked frankly in 1919:

Who had *not* suffered from bad experiences with comrades? At the same time, he pointed to the risk of talking too openly of bad experiences. They might be "misused" by the socialists and pacifists. Instead, Bartram sought to "present a positive, viable ideal."[20]

What Bartram suggested, Schneider did, when he published the results of his opinion polls in 1926 as an appendix to a moral breviary. Even though his accurate statistics were a testament to the emotional and social turmoil of war, he understood that in the crisis of the 1920s Germans did not want the truth of turmoil but a vision of order. What did all that suffering, mass death, and the continuing misery add up to? And above all, what was the way out? Statistical truth of frustration and isolation did not provide an answer. Mythical truth of eternal comradeship did seem to. In the early nineteenth century Ludwig Uhland had written a poem—"The Good Comrade" ("Ich hatt' einen Kameraden")—that was then set to music and sung by Germans whenever it came time to mourn fallen soldiers. The poem is about two soldiers who fight side by side until one takes a bullet and dies. The other is filled with grief. He has lost "a part of myself."[21] By the 1920s, every German knew this song. Schneider merely had to allude to it in order to paint a recognizably "true" picture of soldierly life in the recent war. "Outside there"—in the trenches—"was the world of the good comrade," Schneider claimed. That his statistical data gave evidence to the contrary did not bother him. As he put it, the negative voices represented only exceptions to the rule, whereas those "thousands" of soldiers who knew about comradeship at the front would just remain silent. They would commemorate their comrades "who had saved their lives" in their hearts, not with their lips.

People need mythical truth to cope with their burdens and to establish collective identity.[22] For Germans after World War I, the myth of comradeship performed both functions. Having experienced brotherly, selfless, and uniting comradeship, one of Schneider's interviewees claimed that he would now spread peace and harmony whenever he met quarrelsome people. He articulated the core message of the myth of comradeship. The trench soldiers had not been aggressive or destructive but instead peace-loving, not just in a political sense, but also morally and emotionally. Amid all of the destruction of the war machine, the soldiers had strengthened the "forces of compassion" and actually had become true "apostles of peace," emphasized Schneider.[23]

Schneider's picture of companionable soldiers who had carried out Europe's first industrial war was not original. Germans in the 1920s were deluged with images presenting the soldier as the epitome of everything a civilized society regarded as "humanity." "Sneered at by the horror of all the mass deaths, despised, and degraded," the soldier had nevertheless been pulled from this hell by "the supporting, compensating, alleviating coun-terweight of his comrades," said a speaker in front of ten thousand people attending a veterans' meeting at Lake Constance in 1925. "It was they"— the comrades—"who had loyally shared with him all the suffering and the meager joys as well. . . . That was comradeship—that *is* comradeship." The secret of comradeship, so the Catholic vicar of Constance added, lay in the "enduring awareness of what is human." Returning from the firing line, "in the company of dear comrades, soldiers were able to recover their sense of what it means to be a human being."[24]

According to the myth, soldierly brotherhood guaranteed intense social life, security, and emotional warmth in the midst of the cold bleakness of mass death. Comrades always took care of each other; they shared food and cigarettes, worries and happiness, risks and danger. The good comrade would never hesitate to give his life to save that of his buddy. Such a com-rade possessed a holy aura, sanctified by Christian tradition. The Gospel according to John (15:13 and 3:16) promises the Lord's strongest love to the person who sacrifices his own life for that of his brothers. In this sense, the soldier had become Christ-like. Oral tradition as well as war monuments all over the country reminded Germans constantly of the sacred dimension of comradeship.[25]

A person did not have to be either a Christian or a nationalist to be fasci-nated with this myth. Although the socialists opposed exaggerating soldierly virtues, they also spread the myth. Already in late 1918, the socialist organiza-tion *Reichsbund der Kriegsbeschädigten und ehemaligen Kriegsteilnehmer*, or National Association of Disabled Soldiers and Veterans, claimed that each of its hundreds of thousands of members would never forget "the one comrade who had rescued him from the line of fire when he was lost there helpless, his limbs destroyed."[26]

There was a difference between nationalist and socialist war memory, however. While nationalist war myth praised the brotherhood of officers and enlisted men, the leftists reminded the public of the snobbery and privileges of the officer "caste," as they put it. True comradeship existed only between ordinary soldiers, who were suppressed by their superiors, the officers, declared the *Reichsbanner Schwarz-Rot-Gold* (Imperial Flag Black-Red-Gold),[27] founded in 1924 to provide left-wing Germans with an alternative veterans' forum to those of nationalist associations. The unity of ordinary soldiers, the Social Democrats explained, evolved out of mutual resistance to war itself and to the officers, who lived it up in wartime and who misused their enlisted men in order to earn medals of honor. In Constance, the Reichsbanner provoked the nationalists by staging a play that showed a group of officers, far from the front, amusing themselves with women and wine while enlisted men were dying for the fatherland.[28]

By renouncing the paternalistic meaning of comradeship, the socialists did not refute the myth in general. They rather established a counter myth of comradeship, understood as solidarity among equals against superiors, which might even include "officercide."[29] And they took this perception one step further, relating the myth of frontline comradeship to their own internationalist roots. They understood comradeship as the military version of what had been established long ago by the working-class movement: class solidarity. The mistreated soldiers, they suggested, had developed a sense of solidarity with the ordinary enemy-soldiers, who had suffered from war and had been oppressed by their superiors just as the Germans had. Paul Bäumer, in Remarque's novel, calls his victim, the French Duval, "comrade," pointing out: "If we threw away these rifles and this uniform you could be my brother just like Kat and Albert."[30]

Like the myths that were held by their nationalist opposite, such fiction was presumed to be authentic. In 1932, the socialist Reichsbund reported euphorically that German war stories and movies were warmly welcomed in France. They would remind French veterans of their own parallel memories of shared trench experiences. According to this interpretation, German and French socialist worker-soldiers had, in the trenches of World War I, anticipated the Franco-German reconciliation, which had culminated in the Locarno Treaties of 1925.[31]

"Soldiers Are Murderers"

In the 1920s, the idea that comradeship across the lines during the war had anticipated peace politics could only provoke rightists in Weimar Germany. They praised battlefield comradeship not to stimulate international conciliation but to build national unity and power. Yet the opposing versions of the myth of comradeship overlapped in crucial ways. They both insisted that the soldier-comrade had preserved his humanity in the midst of the inhumanity of war. The leftists saw the fraternizing of soldiers with their enemies as a lesson against any further war, but this very lesson also offered relief for the future warrior. He could think of himself as human, regardless of what he had done in war—or what he would do in a future war.

More than any previous war, the Great War had horrified European societies. War had become a mass phenomenon. Whole societies were mobilized and huge numbers of men *had* killed, violating one of the civilized world's strongest moral rules: "Thou shalt not kill," in the Christian tradition; "Thou shalt not commit murder," in the Jewish tradition. The soldier did kill; so what was the true definition of murder? Modern states and nationalist ideologies might provide some moral justification by putting the soldier into a sophisticated framework of duty and order. In an era of liberalism and democracy, however, notions of obedience were weak arguments against the freedom of action imputed to every moral agent. The soldier in battle had choices—even if only by just not aiming properly.[32]

What did the soldier do in battle? Wasn't he burdened with the guilt of killing when he came back home? Was he truly the same person as before? Was he even still a human being? Or had he fallen into barbarism, brutality, and inhumanity forever? There were no satisfactory answers to these questions. "For four years, there were entire square miles of land where murder was mandatory . . . Did I say: murder? Sure, murder. Soldiers are murderers," declared the antimilitarist Kurt Tucholsky in 1931.[33] His goal was to discredit the military and its leaders, not the ordinary soldier, but he touched on a sore point for them, too. Already during the war they had been terrified by their own "brutalization," as they said themselves. Being forced to commit "mass murder" had left them traumatized.[34] When the war was over, the "brutalization" of millions of men would not be forgotten. It kept people in a state of moral confusion, to which the myth of comradeship offered at least some relief.

Only a small circle in Germany after 1918 drew a different conclusion from the soldiers' qualms—the most radical one. Enjoy the pleasure of war, said Ernst Jünger. Enjoy killing in battle. The future will be nothing but horrible war, and thus the future belongs to a revolutionary new morality. Only the true warrior will share it. He is a man of steel who has no scruples about killing. He comes into being only by killing. In the 1920s, this type of warrior was still seen as a cold and lonely hero who despised the social warmth of comradeship. At that time, none of the radical apologists of brutality preached comradeship. Comradeship came with a human touch, which the elitist martial circles despised—exactly the human touch that attracted major parts of German society still in need of reconciling the horrors of war with a normal life. Around 1930, they were not yet ripe for the "battle in its most horrible way." They did not listen to Jünger but yearned instead for stories of community, togetherness, and social harmony in combat, in order to make their peace with the war experience.[35]

The myth of comradeship built a bridge over the abyss between civilian morality and war. Whoever had experienced comradeship in war had been taught humanity by the inhumanity of war; that was the message of the myth. And after the war the warrior-student of humanity could teach the same lesson everywhere. As with all such myths, the myth of comradeship needed implementation, not just verbal reiteration. Myths revolve around eternal truths—values, virtues, and wisdoms that never change. Those who listen to the story know how to live according to it, so many veterans set about making it real. Right after the war, veterans in local Stahlhelm branches invited their families to Christmas festivities to give proof "to our wives and children that we, even if 'brutalized' during the war, still harbor a true German sense of home-love and domesticity." Even more significantly, all veterans' associations feverishly built up private social security systems to support their needy members. Fund-raising events for them also included an important symbolic message. As the *Kyffhäuser*, the news magazine of the oldest and most popular German veterans' organization, put it in 1929: "Practicing comradeship by providing social security" gives the lie to the "thoughtlessly spread untruth according to which the past war had brutalized people, dismissing them as being something like robbers and murderers."[36]

"The Frontline Community Will Give Birth to the Volksgemeinschaft"

The ambition of the veterans' associations went even further. They envisioned the rebirth of the German nation based on the experience of wartime comradeship. To prove that such vision was viable, they staged their meetings as an anticipation of the desired Volksgemeinschaft. When the mayor of Constance, Otto Moerike, opened the veterans' meeting in August 1925, he gave a lecture about its true meaning. It was by no means only about joy. This event was to serve as a model for how to cope with Weimar Germany's own moral, social, and political disorder. The veterans' convention, Moerike said, would demonstrate to the "entire fatherland" how to overcome the misery the war had produced. A Catholic priest echoed the message: "We need to reform and infiltrate the entire public life with the spirit of comradeship" in order to make the shattered nation whole again. "Our fatherland is filled with the spirit of factions, so disunited, so full of sharpest hatred," he said. As the local papers proudly reported, the meeting itself united "weatherworn peasants from the Black Forest and their wives and children" with people from the big cities, as well as with locals from the villages speaking a broad range of German dialects. Both supporters and opponents of the democratic government were included. The supporters of the Weimar constitution carried their black-red-gold banner. The monarchists waved the old black-white-red imperial flag. Yet both positioned themselves "peacefully side by side." Thus the meeting could seem to anticipate the united nation that Germans were longing for.[37]

In Constance in 1925, however, such consensus was limited. Not all social groups and political camps had even been allowed to join that grand meeting. Former army chaplains represented both Protestants and Catholics, but their Jewish counterpart was excluded, notwithstanding that Jewish Germans had served in the Baden regiment, that almost half of the German Jewish soldiers had been decorated for bravery, that Jewish soldiers had died on the battlefield alongside their gentile comrades, and that Jewish veterans felt comradely just as non-Jews did. While the Jews were rudely excluded from the Constance meeting, the strong Social Democrats and the Reichsbanner, the left-wing veterans' association, did not even wish to participate. Months before the meeting the local socialist paper had prophesied doom: veterans' organizations would not care about former enlisted men but only about the officers, who all had reactionary and militarist tendencies.[38]

Not surprisingly, the Volksgemeinschaft that the Constance festival was to embody remained incomplete. So it was in the whole country. All nationalist veterans' organizations despised Jews and Social Democrats. Like the future Nazi Volksgemeinschaft, the Stahlhelm and other right-wing veterans' organizations treated Social Democrats differently than they did Jews, however. Racist fears of Jews contaminating the purity of German "blood," and völkisch essence had fueled nationalist thought already before the war. And during the war it had precipitated the infamous "Jew count" (Judenzählung) in the military in 1916. After the war, the legend of the stab in the back further propelled anti-Semitism. Long before 1933, the Stahlhelm took the lead in rigidly excluding Jews on the basis of an explicit Arierparagraph in its statutes.[39] In fact, veterans' meetings often anticipated a racially purified Volksgemeinschaft.

Rightist veterans' associations didn't welcome Social Democratic blue-collar workers either. Unlike Jews, they were not excluded axiomatically but were pressured to abandon their party affiliations. The Stahlhelm offered benefits through its social security system, and some employers told their socialist employees to join the Stahlhelm if they did not want to lose their jobs. Statistically, none of these efforts produced meaningful results. Probably fewer than 10 percent of the Stahlhelm's members were blue-collar workers, even though they constituted approximately 50 percent of the German population. But statistics did not matter where myth was available. For the Stahlhelm, each laborer who switched from a socialist network to a nationalist veterans' organization was seen as a tiny but nonetheless significant addition to the great mosaic of the envisioned Volksgemeinschaft.[40] In fact, the veterans' movement succeeded in bringing together a broad variety of social groups—artisans, peasants, teachers, shopkeepers, entrepreneurs, nobles, and Catholics and Protestants—though, of course, no

Jews. "One day, the Stahlhelm's frontline community will give birth to the Volksgemeinschaft," announced the *Stahlhelm* journal in January 1925.[41] It would need just eight years to make that vision real, although it was not the Stahlhelm but the Nazis who were to establish it.

To be sure, the vision of a harmonious Volksgemeinschaft intrigued Social Democrats as well. But to them, the Volksgemeinschaft would not abandon the ideals of tolerance, democracy, and peace. While the rightists wanted to overcome democracy, revise the Versailles Treaty, and prepare for another war, the Social Democrats, the left Liberals, and the Center Party wanted Weimar's democracy to succeed. Reconciliation with the former enemies of Germany, such as France, was high on their agenda, and they opposed racist fantasies of national purification: Jews were welcomed in the Social Democratic Party as well as in the Reichsbanner.[42] Notwithstanding such deep political differences, groups on the left confronted the same problem as those on the right: how to heal the violent traumas of the mass of former soldiers and how to reconcile the experience of mass death and mass killing with the ethics of civil society. Left-wing thinkers could not easily buy into the glorification of the front experience. To them, the war was the consequence of imperialist capitalism and the political ineptitude of the former monarchy. Yet they could not ignore the pressure to reconcile war veterans to the civilian present. Thus they, too, tried to use the front experience as a model for resolving the conflicts of the Weimar Republic. In 1926, only one year after the rightist veterans' meeting in Constance, the leftists, including the Reichsbanner, held a different—pacifist and pro-republican—veterans' meeting in the same city. Its speakers denied the nationalist and patriarchal version of the myth of comradeship. At the same time, the principal speaker at this republican assemblage, a leader of the Catholic Center Party, reminded his public of the holy meaning of comradeship. Whoever had observed comradeship, he said, thereafter was always compassionate, never egoistical. The speaker had in mind not least the comradeship between enemy soldiers. Whereas any rightist speaker wanted to extend front comradeship into *national* unity, the leftist preached the contrary: comradeship was to be used as a model of *international* conciliation. On such a basis, the Reichsbanner could always start singing Uhland's "The Good Comrade" at its meetings.[43]

"The I Is Gone"

The myth of comradeship became so popular because it was so ambiguous. The myth did not offer one message but many. It could be understood in various and even contradictory ways. Its ambiguity was its strength. The myth presented countless stories of tenderness and humanity in the trenches and at the same time praised male toughness and fighting spirit. Even pacifist war novels extolled soldierly values like discipline and courage. In *All Quiet on the Western Front*, resting in a shell hole under fire, Paul Bäumer contemplates staying there—and saving his life. But, afraid of looking cowardly, he jumps out to rejoin his comrades.[44] He acts exactly in the way military training manuals advised recruits: "The soldier *has* to live in peace with his comrades. He may not abandon them in battle, distress, or danger but has to support them as far as possible, whenever they are in need of him."[45] And Paul does more than fulfill his duty; he pressures his fellow soldiers to abide by the code. His former drill sergeant Himmelstoß is eventually ordered to the front and becomes Paul's trainee. Not surprisingly, the torturer in the barracks turns out to be a coward in battle; he hides in a dugout "pretending to be wounded." It is up to Paul to teach him the other side of comradeship, as cold pressure takes the place of warmth and empathy: " 'Get out!' I spit. . . . 'You lump, will you get out—you hound, you skunk, sneak out of it, would you?' . . . I push him forward to the door and shove him out head first."[46]

The right-wing novelist Hans Zöberlein was more vehement. The hero of his best-selling war novel *Belief in Germany* (1931) warned against "the idea of the shame of falling behind, of being called a shirker," and so he ran into battle again and again, even with a high fever and close to physical breakdown. Zöberlein, who published his novel soon after Remarque, was a Nazi. But the ideology of self-sacrifice bridged the gap between Nazis and leftists. Antimilitarists and militarist nationalists both championed a cultural framework that celebrated group ethos and conformity rather than individual decision making and personal responsibility—in the words of military trainers, "de-individualization." The boyish civilian would become a manly soldier by realizing: "I am no longer I, the I is gone."[47]

Beginning in Germany soon after the war, the military concept of de-individualization was advocated as desirable social training for civilian society by all ideological camps—all rendered homage to a moral code that required subordination of the individual to the will of the group. Pacifist war novels around 1930 despised the coward just as the military's official teaching did. Whoever was unwilling to sacrifice the I on the altar of the We was threatened with an "unbearable existence," as an officer put it.[48] Even socialists agreed that the individual who violated the laws of comradeship was to be shamed and isolated. In 1929, the *Reichsbanner* journal published a war story targeting the "egoist" in a group of working-class soldiers. The "egoist" in this story was a peasant who refused to share the gift boxes full of butter, ham, and sausages his relatives had sent. His starving comrades tried to teach him comradeship by kicking him out of their shelter and violently forcing him to give some of his food to them, but he proved unwilling to learn. One day, when food shortages compelled his comrades to eat the meat of a horse killed in battle, the "egoist" mockingly started singing the song of the good comrade, well aware that soldiers looked on their horses as comrades as well. The unit took revenge by confiscating the "egoist's" food supply and making *him* eat the entire horse roast.[49] The message of such stories was always the same: stick to the group and forget about your individual needs and desires if you don't wish to be ostracized. The story also carried another message: the group of comrades made its own rules and enforced compliance with them. The group was sovereign, independent from the rest of the world.

Yet, alternative lessons from the war experience were presented as well. Siegfried Kracauer, later a prominent film critic, had served briefly as a soldier and never saw action. At the end of the war he wrote a philosophical comparison of friendship and comradeship. Friendship thrived on the individual's way of life and was based on personal choices—in Kracauer's view the only truly modern social relationship. Comradeship, on the other hand, was a nightmare. It "de-personalizes the individual mind, kneads it again and again, until it parallels the rhythm of the others." Many liberal intellectuals in the 1920s agreed with Kracauer. When the young philosopher Helmut Plessner in 1924 diagnosed Germans' craving for community, he was filled with disgust and advocated the right to intimacy and individuality. In the same year, Leopold von Wiese, an influential sociologist, published a memoir about his life as a young cadet, a member of an elitist military college in imperial Germany. The story paints a nasty portrait of the rituals of torture, pressure, and social isolation awaiting the individual who was either unable or unwilling to accept his peers' social rules. Wiese's conclusion was as decisive as Kracauer's and Plessner's: the individual carries a much higher moral value than does any community.[50]

"The Community Recognizes the Outsider"

In 1931, another sociologist, Alfred Vierkandt, summarized his and many of his colleagues' shared belief: modern society revolves around the individual. Since the early nineteenth century, class conflicts and middle-class ideologies had been liberating the individual from age-old social shackles. Modern meritocracy fostered personal ambition, personal responsibility, personal achievements, and personal sovereignty. In tribal societies in Asia, Africa, and the Americas these values simply did not exist, according to Vierkandt's studies. These people constantly lived under public control; their communities did not allow individual differences.[51]

Fifteen years later the American anthropologist Ruth Benedict popularized similar findings with her book on Japan, *The Chrysanthemum and the Sword*. Benedict described the Japanese as "the most alien enemy the United States had ever fought in an all-out struggle," characterizing the Asians in terms similar to Vierkandt's for tribal cultures. As Benedict wrote, the Japanese people rejected the idea "that the pursuit of happiness is a serious goal of life," characterizing it as "immoral." Their morality instead revolved around ideas like obedience, duty, and suffering—elements of shame culture, as Benedict put it. In contrast, Western ethics, and those of nontribal Americans in particular, grew out of a guilt culture. "A society that inculcates absolute standards of morality but also relies on men's developing a conscience is a guilt culture by definition." There, "a man who has sinned can get relief by unburdening himself." But where "shame is the major sanction, a man does not experience relief when he makes his fault public, even to a confessor. So long as his bad behavior does not 'get out into the world' he need not be troubled and confession appears to him merely a way of courting trouble. . . . A man is shamed either by being openly ridiculed and rejected or by fantasizing to himself that he has been made ridiculous."[52]

In guilt cultures, people are responsible for their own actions. They experience guilt individually and in dialogue with God or the superego. In shame cultures the community sets itself up as the highest moral authority. Shame is grounded in the fear of exposure, disgrace, and exclusion, with which the community threatens the individual who does not submit to its rules. Shame culture trains one to be inconspicuous, to conform, to participate—and to be happy by being in the good graces of the group, by enjoying security and relief within the community. Deviating from Benedict's dichotomous view, scholars more recently have stressed that both moral paradigms arise in every society. The question is, in what ratio? In Germany around 1930, shame culture, propelled by the myth of comradeship, attained a level that was unusual for an industrialized society.

What caused Germany to shift from a guilt culture to a shame culture? To rightist and militarist milieus and the liberal and conservative middle classes, the military defeat of 1918, and even more the Versailles Treaty, had been a massive national degradation. Article 231 had declared Germany's war guilt. She lost all of her colonies, one-eighth of her territory, and her conscripted army, and she was burdened with huge reparations. She lost power, sovereignty, pride, and honor. The nation felt ashamed and humiliated. Thinking and feeling about honor and its opposite, shame, had already been deeply rooted in the German middle classes and aristocracy in the nineteenth century.[53] But the trauma of 1918 inflated shame culture and based it on much broader social strata.

After 1918, the question of responsibility for mass death, economic disaster, social dissolution, political disruption, and national humiliation could not be answered in terms of individual guilt. The idealized war community, with its myths and its visionary extension into a national Volksgemeinschaft, healed the wounds of the past and overcame the turmoil in the present. If only we had more comradeship, as we once had, suggested many papers and speakers, we could solve all of our problems, explained the popular version of the myth of comradeship. Not all Germans believed it entirely, and many of them did not believe it at all, but these Germans remained silent. The myth of comradeship ruled Germany's public discourse, especially the veterans' movements of all major political camps representing the older generations. And young people became even more fascinated with it.

The German youth movement came into being around 1900, a time when middle-class youth felt anonymous in urban society and wanted to escape the world of the adults. So they got together in small groups and left their urban homes for the countryside—even if only for weekend trips. Of course, adults were upset about their male and female children off hiking together and even camping together overnight. The middle class had always strictly separated girls and boys except when supervised by parents. Many of the youths, though, rejected their parents' anxieties about premarital sex (which certainly did not happen very often) and even homoerotic excursions. Because of adult disapproval, they could feel rebellious.

These young people also longed for community. Community in the early 1900s, however, still allowed for a good deal of individualism—not the individualism of lone wolves but that of like-minded friends who also were looking for alter egos. Sitting around a campfire or staying overnight in a barn, they enjoyed communal life on a voluntary basis; everybody was free to join or leave a group or to start another one. They did not devalue comradeship, though. Instead, they merged the concepts of friendship and comradeship into one, or used them interchangeably. This kind of naive togetherness became obsolete during World War I, when young people were no longer preoccupied with the freedom of a hiking trip but with the order of military marching. Once the war was over, in the overheated political climate of postwar Germany, it was not surprising that the youth movement never cohered but instead splintered into rival camps, segmenting along ideological lines and increasingly falling under the influence and guidance of the adult parties, pressure groups, veterans groups, and the military itself. Before long, whether socialist, Catholic, or nationalist, young people might still worship a common cult of friendship and individuality. But as the 1920s passed into the 1930s, these concepts were replaced by comradeship and its commanding ingredients.[54]

Although many I's came together at a campfire, the We ruled the postwar youth groups. Of course, the risk of death did not challenge them as it had the trench soldiers, but even so, duties had to be shared on a fair basis. Whoever preferred to look for some solitude instead of joining the crowd was seen as uncomradely and was shunned.[55] Mommy's boy, the "chicken" who was solely concerned with his "private" longings, was destined to be an outcast.[56] The community would always "recognize the outsider and know how to defend itself," threatened the *Reichsbanner*, looking to its own socialist youth associations.[57] The tone of such language is very much to the point. The youth movement succumbed to the pressure of the mythical community, which required subordination and denied individual freedom. Before 1933, nobody was forced to join the young people's communities. Many youths, however, wanted to be "pressed" into a "community which was afraid of neither death nor devil."[58] The activities of these groups were seemingly harmless—boyish games and tests of courage—but in the broader political context they were part of the obsession with enforced community-building in Germany around 1930 that was far from harmless.

In the 1920s and early 1930s, there was still much ambiguity in the youth movement, as there was in Remarque's Paul Bäumer, whose thoughts switched back and forth between comradeship and conscience. Franz Matzke has left us a sensitive and concise account in his *Confessions of the Youth* (1930). "Silently we make ourselves subordinate, even if we know better and feel differently. Such subordination, however, will be limited to the outer districts of our selves, and never intrude into the nucleus of our mind, which always will be individual and distant to the community, even if longing for the community."[59] Matzke's distinction between the true inner mind and its external mask was extremely popular in the age of two total wars.[60] It allowed people to preserve the illusion of being able to save their consciences, even as they violated the essence of these ethics, that is, when they were ruled by the fear of shame. How the latter would prevail was up to the training camps of Nazi Germany.

TWO
===

Fabricating the Male Bond

The Racial Nation as a Training Camp

In early 1939, trying to adjust to his London exile, Sebastian Haffner was disgusted when he thought of Germany. He had recently left his home country with his Jewish fiancée. As an Aryan whose closest friends in Germany had been Jews, he was appalled by the Nazis' brutal harassment of and violence against the Jews. Even more frightening to him was how rapidly the Nazis had awakened the "readiness to kill" among his compatriots. According to his assessment, the "whole nation, Germany," was infected "with a germ that causes its people to treat their victims" as if they were "wolves." The Germans were not "subjugated" (to Hitler and the Gestapo), they were "something else, something worse," Haffner wrote, "they are 'comraded,' a dreadfully dangerous condition. . . . They are terribly happy, but terribly demeaned; so self-satisfied, but so boundlessly loathsome; so proud and yet so despicable and inhuman." "Widely praised, harmless male comradeship," Haffner said, "completely destroys the sense of responsibility for oneself." And as such, he believed, comradeship had become "demonic" as well as pandemic in Germany.[1]

"The Life of an Individual Must Not Be Set at Too High a Price"

No Nazi would have agreed with Haffner's devastating evaluation, but all of them would have proudly confirmed that the Third Reich had elevated comradeship to a state virtue. In truth, the Nazis glorified precisely what

Haffner condemned. What Haffner took as a horrible pathology was the moral foundation of the Third Reich. The National Socialist movement understood itself as born in the trenches, with the goal of transferring the frontline comradeship to the entire German *Volk*. In 1933, that vision seemed to become reality. The veterans' movement welcomed the apotheosis of comradeship as "the basis of the new *Reich*." "Our yearnings are fulfilled," exclaimed the *Kyffhäuser*; "finally, the bridge from frontline experience to state building is complete."[2] Even Catholics, though opposing the Nazi movement, were swept along by the "feeling of national and German emotion" that "has seized our people," as the Catholic Teachers Organization exulted. "We have succeeded in breaking through the un-German spirit that prevailed in the revolution of 1918."[3]

The term *comradeship* was ubiquitous in the Third Reich. All Hitler Youth and Labor Service units were called "comradeships," or *Kameradschaften*. College students would meet in comradeships instead of in fraternities. Apprentices for all kinds of occupations were to be trained in comradeships. Even artists would come together no longer in art colonies but rather in comradeships. Nazi Germany presented itself as a great "national comradeship," with a broad range of institutions and aids to overcome party struggle, class divisions, the lacunae of an unfinished nation, and any appearance of "egoism" and loneliness.[4]

But despite the euphoria of 1933, Nazi leaders, thinkers, and propagandists understood that the Volksgemeinschaft—the national comradeship—was far from complete. The Nazis may have called their "seizure of power" and the nazification of state institutions in 1933 a revolution, but they knew that a "transitory period" would be needed to "re-educate" their countrymen, as Heinrich Himmler once admitted. "National Socialism is not at the end of its days but only at the beginning," Hitler said in 1938, explaining why the Nazi state forced its youth into various organizations. Ridding them of "class consciousness or pride in status" and educating them "to think as Germans and act as Germans" would require thorough training.[5]

In fact, Hitler's "social revolution" was to lead to "something completely new and totally revolutionary," as the historian Yehuda Bauer has stated. Rooted in social Darwinist obsessions that saw history as a constant struggle between peoples for dominance and in the conviction that Germans were superior to any other nation, the Nazi revolution was planned and carried out as a racial rather than as an economic revolution. In other words: it aimed at a new class structure which went beyond any Marxist category. Despite its ongoing propaganda against class divisions, the Nazi state did not seriously touch the gap between middle and working classes. But millions of people seen as racially inferior were to be annihilated or enslaved—a revolution that would have changed class hierarchies far more profoundly. Nazi racial politics intended to distribute the properties and homelands of these people among Aryans. Those "subhumans" that would be spared from annihilation were to be installed as a new underclass beneath the real Aryan society. Hitler's Germany would thus become a welfare state based on the expropriation and exploitation of "inferiors." Millions of slaves from all across Eastern Europe would provide "the menial labor that would allow Aryans to pursue higher pleasures."[6]

Before the war, the brutal basis of glory was not subject to public announcement; the people's comrades, or *Volksgenossen*, received a foretaste of the glorious future of the Volksgemeinschaft in seemingly harmless ways. Nazi Germany discarded the burdens of the Versailles Treaty, regained its national pride, and reclaimed its military power. With the economy recovering, full employment, mass consumerism, and a comprehensive welfare program came within reach. The state tourist and leisure agency, *Kraft durch Freude* (literally Strength Through Joy) announced the production of an inexpensive car for the masses, the *Volkswagen*, which promised happiness for every citizen in the near future. Until then, relatively inexpensive radios and tourist trips anticipated what would come. Everyone, or more precisely, every *Volksgenosse*, would live better than before.[7]

But in the Nazi utopia, the promise of the Promised Land was not milk and honey. Rather it was liberation from the selfish dynamic that burdened modern societies with endless conflicts. Material well-being and private happiness were promoted in the Third Reich only so long as they oiled the engines of national harmony. No pleasure without indoctrination was the law that governed mass consumerism and leisure activities. Radios transmitted the speeches of Hitler and Goebbels, Nazi spies sniffed out the ideological conformity of Germans relaxing on tourist trips, and the Volkswagen driver, traveling through the country, was to internalize the grandeur of the German fatherland. All these activities served the same goal as the huge national rallies that the Nazi Party held in Nuremberg: to reinforce the unity and harmony of the Volksgemeinschaft.

Understood as a national regeneration, the Nazi revolution aimed at the ethics, minds, and hearts of the Aryans to overcome their ideological divisions rather than their economic ones. Whereas Karl Marx had argued that being impacts consciousness, the Nazis based their revolution on the reverse assumption: consciousness was to determine being.[8] Winter Aid, or *Winterhilfswerk*, was established in 1933 to solicit donations for the needy and to replace the welfare organizations of the Weimar Republic, the trade unions, and the Christian churches. Hundreds of thousands of Germans committed themselves to helping. "With the aid of this tremendous society," Hitler said in 1937, "countless people are . . . regaining the firm belief that they are not completely lost and alone in this world, but sheltered in their Volksgemeinschaft—that they, too, are being cared for." As Hitler explained, this statewide charity would give Christian and socialist traditions "practical life." Such charity would not drop from heaven. "People are not born socialists, but must first be taught how to become them." Winter Aid served as not only a shelter for those in need, but also an "insurance against lack of common sense," Hitler announced. It was a program to turn the Volksgenossen into "practical" socialists.[9]

Donating to Winter Aid was mandatory. "YOU too must SACRIFICE," propaganda posters reminded Germans continuously. Pressure and control were omnipresent. Landlords issued forms to make householders report what they had donated, and teachers encouraged students to collect contributions from their parents, so as not to be listed on a classroom display board as a black sheep. Whoever did not contribute ran the risk of public denunciation and ostracism. In Flensburg, businessman Otto Schrader failed to contribute to Winter Aid and was immediately taken into "protective custody," as the local newspaper reported. Thus publicly outlawed, he promised to integrate himself "fully and wholly into the Volksgemeinschaft" through significant contributions to Winter Aid. "Finally the training program was effective," the paper stated smugly.[10]

Rather than putting Christian and socialist ideals into practice, Nazi welfare in fact abandoned them. Neither voluntary as a matter of individual empathy nor universally addressed to all persons in need, charity

in the Third Reich reeked of compulsion—and exclusion. No non-Aryan
benefited, and whoever did not contribute was considered an enemy of the
fatherland. Becoming a "practical" socialist, that is, a National Socialist,
meant to absorb the rigid dichotomies of racist distinctions between Them
and Us. Whether applying for a marriage loan from the state or for a vacation trip with Strength Through Joy, virtually every activity was meant to
reveal, and to make one think about, one's racial origins. The Nazi welfare
program aimed simultaneously at the ideological elevation and the racial
purification of the German nation. In the schools, students now learned
about the nation as a "community of blood," a "community of mind,"
"a community of fate and struggle," and a "community of work."[11] The
envisioned Volksgemeinschaft would be rid of Jews and other supposedly
racially inferior groups, and at the same time insiders would be converted,
reformed, and made uniform—not just outwardly but inwardly, in their
thinking and habits.

Winter Aid and other welfare programs in Nazi Germany promised charity to achieve conformity. They demanded self-sacrifice and attempted to
erase "egotism" and selfishness, the mental conditions that were blamed
for the divisions of Weimar society and for Germany's surrender in 1918.
As one pedagogue said, "What an individual is worth is to be measured by
the yardstick of the people, i.e., he will be measured by his achievements
for the totality."[12] The virtues of individual life had no place in the Nazi
utopia. Addressing his military entourage in late 1941 and considering the
massive losses of German soldiers in the aborted drive to reach Moscow,
Hitler explained: "The life of an individual must not be set at too high a
price. If the individual were important in the eye of nature, nature would
take care to preserve it. Amongst millions of eggs a fly lays, very few are
hatched out—and yet the race of flies thrives." So the end goal was a state
in which every citizen knew he lived and died solely for his species—the
Aryan Volksgemeinschaft.[13]

Hitler's martial rhetoric was directed to his military audience and its
bloody environment. Military power relied on unity and self-sacrifice; egotism and selfishness, synonyms for individuality and private group interests,
were seen as the most decisive detriments to it. The war on Europe, the
expansion of *Lebensraum* in the East, and the subjugation of millions of

people were inconceivable without domestic homogeneity, attainable only by ideological regimentation. And vice versa: war forged unity and strengthened community. In 1927 Hitler had outlined the basics by conjuring a mythical past "where there was no class division. This was in the platoons at the front line. There must be a chance to establish such unity at home as well. Why did it work at the front line? Because opposite was the enemy, and you were aware of the threat he constituted." Hitler's conclusion was: "If you want to amalgamate our people into a unity, the first thing you have to do is to create a new front line with a mutual enemy, so that everybody knows: We have to be united, because the enemy is the enemy of all of us."[14]

"The Aim Is Always the Same, Namely to Declare an Enemy"

No community and no unity exists without the "other": those who do not belong, who really or supposedly threaten the community either physically or just by looking different, by pursuing different ways of life, by harboring different experiences and visions—thus by challenging the identity of those who belong. If there is no enemy, one has to be invented. The larger and the more complex the in-group (as in industrial societies), the more difficult it is to obtain uniformity.

In 1932 Carl Schmitt, later a major political philosopher of the Nazis, outlined what a state had to do to reach "internal peace." It had to decide "upon the domestic enemy"—the enemy within. "Whether the form is sharper or milder," he explained, "explicit or implicit, whether ostracism, expulsion, proscription, or outlawry are provided for in special laws or in explicit or general descriptions, the aim is always the same, namely to declare an enemy." The inner enemy was to be considered "the other, the stranger . . . he is, in an especially intense way, existentially something different and alien."[15] Thus, the cohesion of the people's community was based not just on threatening clichés about imperialist England or subhuman Slavs, but even more on tracking down, identifying, persecuting, and terrorizing "domestic enemies."

Combining established anti-Semitic traditions, popular eugenic discourse, and anticommunist resentment, the Nazis chose "the Jew" as the racial paradigm of a "domestic enemy" and painted a frightening picture of a conspiracy being planned and executed inside and outside Germany. Endless propaganda, decisive legislation, constant harassment, and brutal terror transformed assimilated Jews into a German menace. "The Jew" served to unite the Aryan Volksgemeinschaft. In Osnabrück, the Nazi Party county leader (*Kreisleiter*) Münzer spoke in August 1935 to a crowd of twenty-five thousand people about the "Jewish question." It was not just about "anti-Semitism in a traditional sense," he said. It was "not just a fight against Jews as such, but a fight for the German soul. . . . The Führer wants each German to be really aware of the Jewish menace and to recollect his own German identity in order to understand that any softness toward the Jew damages the German people."[16]

Many Germans agreed; they fabricated a widespread sense of national belonging by excluding the Jews. In 1937, the Jewish Victor Klemperer saw a picture in the *Stürmer*, the radical anti-Semitic Nazi newspaper, which showed "two girls at a seaside resort. Above it: 'Prohibited for Jews,' underneath it: 'How nice that it's just us now!' " Klemperer, who strongly identified himself as a German and had long taken pride in being a World War I veteran, understood the "horrible significance" of these words. To Germans, being "just us now" meant to live without Jews. "I have not only outwardly lost my Fatherland. . . . My inner sense of belonging is gone," noted Klemperer in his diary.[17] Ousting Jewish citizens strengthened the Aryans' sense of belonging. Clients boycotted their Jewish shopkeepers, patients boycotted their physicians, and students ostracized their Jewish classmates and professors. The Nazi government and party agencies dissolved Jewish associations and escalated into destroying houses and synagogues, Aryanizing businesses, and, long before the Holocaust started, forcing Jews to emigrate after stripping them of most or all their possessions.

To be sure, not all Germans acted alike. Relatively few used violence, and not all ostracized their former Jewish colleagues, neighbors, and friends. Many Germans felt uneasy about openly attacking them, and some continued to shop in Jewish stores, much to the displeasure of the Nazi leaders. Consequently the Osnabrück Kreisleiter, in his 1935 speech, agitated not only against Jews but also against those Germans who still kept in touch with Jews. Such Germans were branded as *Volksverräter*, traitors of the German people. In covering its local issues, the *Stürmer* publicly denounced the names and addresses of those Volksgenossen who still shopped with Jews. Very few non-Jewish Germans were able to resist such pressure. Most of them conformed one way or another, not always hating Jews yet modifying their behavior in ways that propelled the vision of a Volksgemeinschaft "cleansed" of the Jews. Beginning in 1933 the German Jews lived in a state of constant fear.

One of these Jews was Lilli Jahn, who did not emigrate and was murdered in Auschwitz. Raised in a Jewish family in Cologne, well educated in the arts, theater, and music, she studied medicine and fell in love with a non-Jewish fellow medical student, Ernst Jahn. In 1926, they married and moved to Immenhausen in Hesse to set up a medical practice. They missed urban life but enjoyed "some refined company . . . the local clergyman, their colleagues . . . and the local landowner, a highly cultivated man," observed Lilli's closest friend, Lotte Paepcke, also a Jewish woman married to a gentile. The Jahns were welcome—so they thought. Until 1933. "Just imagine," wrote Lilli to friends on 2 April, the day after the infamous nation-wide boycott of Jewish shops, lawyers, and physicians, "they also boycotted my Amadé [her husband] because he has a Jewish wife!" All of a sudden, the Jahns were ostracized by their neighbors and even their friends. One day the local landowner appeared with a minor cut and asked the doctor to take care of it. "Purely in passing," he also wanted to "make it clear that he and his wife would, alas, be temporarily compelled to sever relations with the doctor and his family." The doctor shouldn't take it personally, his patient added. So did a colleague, excusing himself for no longer socializing with Ernst. " 'Nothing could ever detract me from my respect for you and your lady wife, but circumstances . . .' . . . Six months later the clergyman came to say that he had now received his third warning from Party headquarters and that their pleasant chats at the doctor's home must unfortunately cease." And another half year later, Lilli wrote in a letter to friends: "Our ostracism here in Immenhausen is now more complete than anyone could have dreamt. SA [the Nazi paramilitary group] headquarters has forbidden Bonsmann to cross our threshold!! The fact that he had obeyed this prohibition requires no comment." Bonsmann had been Ernst's friend and colleague. Now he was an SA man.[18]

Again, not all Germans followed Nazi boycott appeals. Shortly before November 1938, when Nazi thugs destroyed synagogues all over Germany, murdered scores of Jews, and sent thirty thousand to concentration camps, Lotte Paepcke's father, Max Mayer, stated that some Aryans readily accepted the "relentless expulsion" of the Jews from the body politic and "mindlessly" recited the slogans supplied by the propagandists. To a large extent, however, Max Mayer said, "people reject this persecution, aware of the falsity and injustice of such slogans, but unable to assist their victims." Mayer's diagnosis was quite right. The Security Service of the SS, the *Sicherheitsdienst* (SD), came to the same conclusion by "x-raying" ordinary Germans' opinions. Many of them inconspicuously or even demonstratively ignored the Nazi appeals to boycott Jewish shops, doctors, and lawyers. And when anti-Jewish violence escalated into the Kristallnacht pogrom in 1938, many Germans were shocked. To be sure, the motives of such discontent were disparate. Embarrassment of the educated middle class about the disgrace of German civilization was paralleled by concerns of workers "calculating the number of extra hours they will need to work to repair the damage done to German national property."[19]

The Germans' attitude toward the Jews during the Nazi era cannot easily be reduced to a common denominator, as historians have often attempted. Lilli Jahn's fate is a particularly tragic example. Her husband Ernst did what so many Germans did—yield to the anti-Semitic pressure. In 1942, he divorced his wife and left her unprotected; in fact, he handed her on a plate to the death machinery. It was not so much the hatred of Jews but indifference toward them—a silent or passive complicity—that established mass support of Nazi racial politics in the 1930s. Most Germans accepted the pseudo-legal measures that led to the exclusion of Jews from social life and to their expropriation. At the same time, many Germans despised the violent acts perpetrated by radical Nazis. Such ambivalence rarely alleviated the terror experienced by the Jews. But it troubled the regime. While symbolic gestures and concerns of Aryans about the fate of the Jews grew fainter, the Nazi leaders knew that the Volksgemeinschaft was not as united and ideologically synchronized as they wanted it to be. And the Germans' attitude toward the Jews was not the only thing that did not satisfy the regime's desire for totalitarian control. Throughout the 1930s Gestapo and Nazi block wardens, charged with supervising their neighbors, reported from all over Germany on the many former Social Democrats and Communists who continued to spread discontent with the regime by word of mouth. Discontent could not be tolerated. While propaganda wrapped the utopia of a grand community in the tinsel of consumerism and charity, a different notion of Volksgemeinschaft took on ever sharper shape, one that was welded together by violent terror outwardly, but also by psychic terror inwardly.[20]

Learning community in the way Hitler envisioned it meant becoming sensitive to anything and anybody who did not conform or who did not fit the standards of a racially and ideologically homogeneous society. The Volksgemeinschaft was threatened not only by racially alien elements such as Jews or Sinti and Roma, but also by biologically and hereditary defectives, and by a broad range of "asocials" or "community aliens" (Gemeinschaftsfremde) like homosexuals, whores, alcoholics, tramps, beggars, who, though not clearly criminal, were considered as unable to adapt themselves to the community. These were to be eliminated, sterilized, or taken into "preventive detention."[21] The hunt for the enemy within was so insidious because it spread uncertainty. What exactly was "asocial" behavior? Some categories were established, but only to open a vast gray area. "Whoever challenges our unity, will end up at the stake," announced Baldur von Schirach, the national leader of the Hitler Youth, in 1934. What precisely challenged the unity of Hitler Youth? The very boy who, instead of enjoying the pleasure of comradeship in the Hitler Youth, wasted his time with a stamp collection at home or with spontaneous adventure trips with his friends was suspected of being a social outcast. Nazi propagandists, jurists, doctors, and pedagogues worked ambitiously to categorize all kinds of "community pests" in order to make the Volksgenossen detect the slightest deviance. Among these categories were the "coward," the "shirker," the "grind," the "troublemaker," the "griper," the "peacock," the "uncontrolled," the "schemer," and the "loner." Although the lone wolf was not necessarily a criminal, as a military psychologist noted uneasily, his behavior could be considered a "preliminary stage of desertion." Desertion, though, from any unit was the epitome of treason, the ultimate betrayal of one's comrades and community. And whoever did not conform or obey but just tried to be himself was considered a possible deserter—a traitor of the Volksgemeinschaft.[22]

"Their Comrades Are Their Conscience"

Not all carriers of social pathogens were automatically deemed hopeless. Unlike the persecution of the Jews, the treatment of Aryan outsiders was flexible. Preparing for total war, the *Wehrgemeinschaft*, or martial community, needed to mobilize as much manpower as possible.[23] Thus, the rhetoric of extermination that threatened "community aliens" or "community pests" left the door open for converting the troublemakers into useful Volksgenossen, or at least into cannon fodder. In a 1935 lecture on how to build comradeship the physician Horst Buchholz drew on an extreme case of "egotism" to show what the right social setting could achieve. Three years earlier he had treated a man who suffered from a severe case of asthma as well as extreme myopia. Solely concerned with himself, the patient had sought refuge in Indian mysticism and Schopenhauer's solipsist philosophy. Overall, he had "completely disowned the real world and any real people." A hopeless case of egotism, Buchholz's audience might have concluded at this point. The specialist, though, knew of a therapy that would work a miracle. Instead of wasting time with medicine or sanatoria, Buchholz, a psychiatrist and specialist in internal medicine, sent his patient into a "strong school of community—the SA." There, his patient found what he needed: "duties and engagement on the one hand, comradely support for his many little disabilities on the other hand." Proudly, Buchholz added: "The patient has been healthy for three years." Buchholz left no doubt about the point of it all. Egotism was not to be treated for the individual's ailments but to remove the obstacles on the road to "our grand mutual goal, the German Volksgemeinschaft."[24]

To cleanse Germans of "egotism," to construct a new people and a grand community, the Nazi state forced young boys and also, less insistently, girls, into a sophisticated, life-long training program. As Hitler explained in a speech in December 1938, "Boys join our organization at the age of ten." Four years later, "they move from the *Jungvolk* to the Hitler Youth. . . . And then we are even less prepared to give them back into the hands of those who create class and status barriers, rather we take them immediately into the Party, . . . into the SA or into the SS," after which they "are polished for six or seven months" in the Labor Service. And if there "are still remnants of class consciousness or pride in status, then the Wehrmacht will take over the further treatment for two years" and after that, "to prevent them from slipping back into old habits once again, we take them immediately into the SA, SS etc., and they will not be free again for the rest of their lives."[25]

German boys from the age of ten to eighteen joined the Hitler Youth. In 1933 one of three did so, from 1939 on almost everyone joined. As part of their training, usually a couple of weeks per year, they spent some time in a camp. Adults also were asked to join a training camp for a certain period. From 1933 through 1939, about 70 percent of German teachers participated in at least one training camp. From 1935 on, the compulsory camps of the National Labor Service—*Reichsarbeitsdienst*, or *RAD*—enforced a six-month work schedule on all males between the ages of eighteen and twenty-five. And from 1935 until 1945, the Wehrmacht drafted about seventeen million men for military service, which began with a training period in the barracks—a special kind of camp. The *Waffen-SS* added another million.[26]

Unlike the pre-Nazi youth movement, which had allowed any boy or girl to leave camp whenever he or she liked, the Nazis organized camps militarily. Youths were subjected to a hierarchical structure and to a strict and uniform daily schedule of education, training, and service. Housed in tents or barracks, they were separated for weeks, months, or even years from what had been their normal life; jobs, possessions, friends, and relatives were no longer of importance. Initially strangers, once isolated from the rest of the society in a "community of fate," these young people had to get along, whether they liked it or not. Whereas in modern society an individual lives, works, plays, and sleeps in different places with different people, Nazi camps were organized as "total institutions." This is the label the sociologist Erving Goffman coined for prisons, hospitals, monasteries, and military barracks where all of these activities occur in the same place, with the same people answering to a single authority.[27] And so it was in Nazi youth camps. All camp members wore uniforms as the symbol of their equality, all were required to work, sleep, and play together, and all were subjected to a tight daily schedule that included exercises, classes, meals, sleeping, but very little leisure time.

What did young Germans learn in these camps? Total institutions can serve different goals. Whereas prisons or concentration camps are purported to save the "good" society from "bad" people, military-like barracks or train-ing camps were supposed to "improve" people's ideological dispositions, mental conditions, or social skills. Separation from relatives and friends also "condensed" social interaction in the camp, providing the optimal prerequi-sites for brainwashing or "assimilation," as a leading Nazi pedagogue, Ernst Krieck, wrote. The camp brought together youths so that they would "all adopt the same type [of personality] and a similar lifestyle."[28]

Sebastian Haffner took his own experience as a paradigmatic example of how such "assimilation" worked in National Socialist Germany. In early 1933 he had just finished law school and was preparing to establish his pro-fessional life. After the Nazis came into power, though, he learned that civil service candidates like him had to join a training camp for some weeks before being permitted to take their legal exams. After receiving his call-up papers, he traveled to Jüterboog, a village on the plains of Brandenburg, quite a distance from Berlin, where he had grown up. The camp was located outside of Jüterboog. Not knowing how to get there from the train station, he and some prospective comrades deliberated about whether to order limousines. Some SA men, who looked forward more eagerly to the camp than Haffner, ultimately decided for them. They knew that entering a training camp in comfortable cars was not an appropriate option. Instead, they ordered the crowd to "form up in threes" and to march. And out of the deep uncertainty that would never leave him in the weeks to come, Haffner remembers, "we obeyed."

Surprisingly to Haffner, ideological indoctrination did not play a major role in the Jüterboog camp. There were no lessons on anti-Semitism, Nazi eugenics, the "Lebensraum" ideology, the leadership principle, or on the heroic past of the NSDAP. Slowly Haffner learned that the lessons were much more subtle than mere indoctrination. Camp life fostered togeth-erness, military order, and, most important, the practice of comradeship, which was to replace the security of family and friends Haffner had been used to in civilian life. If one's feet smelled, one was obliged to wash them "every morning and every evening. That is a rule of comradeship." And it was not just about personal hygiene. More important were fitness exer-cises and paramilitary drills, bellowing "Heil Hitler," marching around the camp, and singing military songs.

And beyond obeying orders, even without supervision, the comrades practiced comradeship on their own. "Civilian courtesy" was scorned with the abundant use of crudities and profanity. The "ritual reciting of lewd songs and jokes" served to vilify bourgeois love. Comradeship "actively decomposed" both "individuality and civilization" and elevated men above "civilized tenderness." A highlight of such decomposition was the boyish prank "of attacking a neighboring dormitory at night with 'water bombs,' drinking mugs filled with water to be poured over the beds of the defenders. . . . A battle would ensue, with merry 'Ho's and 'Ha's and scream- ing and cheering. You were a bad comrade if you did not take part. . . . It was taken for granted that comradeship prevented those who had been attacked from telling tales."

The group did not need a superior authority to run its internal affairs but restored order on its own. Individuals were powerless, but comrade- ship offered empowerment. The night after a dormitory raid "we had to be prepared for a revenge attack." Revenge restored order just as ostracism did. "If someone committed a sin against comradeship" by acting superior or showing off or exhibiting "more individuality than was permissible, a nighttime court in the barracks would judge and condemn him to corporal punishment. Being dragged under the water pump was the punishment for minor misdemeanors." Someone who "favored himself in distributing butter rations," however, suffered a "terrible fate." He was "dragged from his bed and spread-eagled on a table. 'Every man will whack Meier once, no one is excused,' the judge thundered." And the victim was well advised to accept what the group did to him. "By the dark laws of comradeship that governed us, independently of our individual wills, a complaint would have put him in danger of his life."

In his memoir Haffner drew ambivalent conclusions about what all this meant. Comradeship, he wrote, "can become a means for the most ter- rible dehumanization" as it "relieves men of responsibility for their own actions, before themselves, before God, before their conscience. They do what all their comrades do. . . . Their comrades are their conscience and give absolution for everything." This analysis reveals the rage of an individu- alist who had been compelled to betray his personal identity and illustrates what Siegfried Kracauer had described fifteen years earlier. Comradeship "de-personalizes the individual mind." In the camp, Haffner had no privacy. Friends and relatives were cut off. With the young men isolated from these securities, uncertainty ruled the camp and could be overcome only by merging into the community of comrades. In the training camp, young men replaced their previous individual identities with a new group identity, one that pertained exclusively to a male society. On the other hand, Haffner also wrote that in the camp, he began to partake of the "happiness of comradeship. . . . It was a pleasure to go for a cross-country run together in the morning, and then to go naked into the communal hot showers together, to share the parcels that one or another received from home, to share also responsibility for misdemeanors that one of your comrades had committed, to help and support one another in a thousand little ways."[29]

"A Feeling of Absolute Superiority"

From time immemorial the cultural codes for men have been drastically different than those for women. In preindustrial societies, boys participated in initiation rites that separated them from women and initiated them into becoming men—to think, feel, and behave like other men, to adopt and internalize manly social qualities. Boys were sent to the men's hut to learn male conformity and male solidarity. How that happened varied from one culture to another. Sometimes homosexual practices were included, sometimes not. Usually, these rites were dramatically framed, torture and humiliation playing a major role. Only these activities seemed to guarantee the desired result.[30]

According to cultural anthropologist Victor Turner, male initiation rites are embedded in a "liminal" period of intended uncertainty, during which the characteristics of the ritual subject are ambiguous. "He passes through a cultural realm that has few or none of the attributes of the past or coming state." Social conventions are decisively disregarded during this transitional state, and even social hierarchies, authorities, and inferiorities are confused. The neophytes have left the "society as a structured, differentiated, and often hierarchical system of politico-legal-economic positions." They enter a new society—actually an antisociety. The "anti-structure," as Turner names it, "emerges recognizably in the liminal period as an unstructured or rudimentarily structured community."[31] Similar patterns of male initiation were still at work in modern societies, and so also in Nazi Germany. Crucial is how they relate to their political context. Nazi Germany inflated these traditions and deployed them to fabricate a Volksgemeinschaft of its own.

To become a real man, a "momma's boy" needed to erase any infantile, egocentric identities that were rooted in the female world of his family. To knock out his private identity and to give him a new, truly male identity, he was sent to "schools of manliness"—the military, the Labor Service, or the Hitler Youth. Educators in interwar Germany justified and organized such training as a "period to break up the wrong consciousness," to reshape completely the entire personality of a youth. Max Momsen, a college director in Cottbus, explained in 1935 how camp training worked. "When camp service seizes the body and compels it to a certain concise performance, it also forces the body into certain mental and emotional habits, which consist first of all in relinquishing all that is individual and selfish. . . . The private self, the individual, will be broken. This might be a hard and painful procedure. It is inevitable, though, for the sake of a higher and larger community."[32]

The boy who was to become a full member of this larger community had to start from scratch. Accepting status as lowest on the pecking order was the first step.[33] The new recruit was made to do "things he would have decisively refused to do as a pampered mother's boy"—cleaning, mending, darning, making beds, peeling potatoes, folding the wash, all the things that "mama" had done for him and that were "not at all a man's job."[34] Thus, ironically, for a boy to become a real man, he had to become a woman first. For the moment, he lost any gender identity. The dramatic humiliation rite followed the "principle of the lower service."[35] Only there, at the lowest step of the ladder in the hierarchical structure of male bonding, could a new identity be ascribed to him. Mother's boy had "to go through an entire system of tortures" executed by his comrades or his superiors in order "to be acknowledged as a real man and no longer be considered just a young whippersnapper."[36]

Although the camp or barrack was devoid of women, its "anti-structure" was not without the symbolic power provided by the dichotomies and hierarchies of a gendered system. Although cleaning, darning, and cooking were not ordinarily valued as men's work, "female jobs" still had to be done in an exclusively male institution. "A man has to do things by himself. So does the soldier. When in the battlefield, he also is on his own."[37] Embedded in this popular appeal is the kernel of a powerful idea: in an all-male society, the male bond is independent of the rest of the world, in particular from women. It is sovereign. It creates the world from scratch. Humiliation, thus, was designed as the starting point of a period of suffering, which would eventually lead to redemption.

It was all about community—the sovereignty of the community but also its collective responsibility. If one comrade failed in some task or merely stepped out of line, the entire group was blamed and penalized. To handle collective responsibility, the group sought inner conformity. "Comradeship entails strong discipline and oppresses the malicious, unreliable and uncomradely elements," as military pedagogue Erich Weniger stated. The outsider represented the "other"—the needed enemy for those who wanted to belong, just as cohesion of the good society "needs" its criminals, as George Herbert Mead wrote in 1918. "The attitude of hostility toward the lawbreaker has the unique advantage of uniting all members of the community in the emotional solidarity of aggression." Observing that "nothing unites the members of a group like a common enemy," the sociologist Albert Cohen has concluded that external and internal enemies are, in a way, exchangeable. Either of them "arouses the sentiments of community and revives a waning solidarity." This, again, is the reason why communities need the deviant. He may "function as a 'built-in' out-group, and contribute to the integration of the group in much the same way as do witches, devils, and hostile foreign powers."[38]

If there was no outsider, one had to be fabricated. Often a smart superior chose an outsider whom the group could terrorize. A Wehrmacht tank gunner received a symbolic burial for his failures in formal drill. His sergeant made him lie in a hole and pull his steel helmet over his face. Then, his comrades covered him with a sheet of corrugated iron. Eventually, the sergeant shot three blank cartridges over the "grave." The next time the gunner made mistakes in shooting, he had to hold a cigarette that the sergeant pretended to shoot out of his hand. The sergeant did not need to be afraid of any problem with army regulations. His men were on his side. They showed little sympathy for the "sniveler" who at the slightest reprimand started "trembling and howling" and "wouldn't join in anymore." When someone fell in on parade with a dirty neck and his superior told him to wash, his comrades took it as encouragement to drag the bawling young man into the washroom and "scrub him down."[39]

Anybody who failed to adapt to the mood of his group and resisted demands to sacrifice himself on the altar of the "Us" was almost sure to find himself in the outsider role. In the military, your superior was at hand not only as the teacher of comradeship but also as its catalyst. He tortured the recruits with mud baths, locker room and dormitory roll calls, masquerades, and confinement to barracks. But shared hatred of the tormentor ensured a certain harmony within the group, even collective joy and collective power. "We have imperceptibly grown together into firm comradeship" through the harassment they suffered in the first weeks of serving together, wrote a Wehrmacht recruit to his friend in the Hitler Youth. Now they felt like "nobody can get to us."[40] Another recruit, Kurt Kreissler, was enthusiastic about "an iron comradeship" that had grown out of his and his roommates' hatred of their superiors. "Almost nothing can shake us anymore, not even when our first lieutenant bawls us out," he noted in his diary.[41] Former Wehrmacht soldier Hanns Karl Vorster recalled the nasty trick he and his comrades played on a malicious superior. After their sergeant got drunk and fell fast asleep one night, his soldiers secured a padlock around his testicles and kept the key. The next day was awful for him, as he had to carry out his duties with his hand in his trouser pocket to try and minimize his discomfort. His recruits, though, were delighted, and they stuck together when the sergeant demanded that the culprit reveal himself. Together they got through the inevitable punishment with conspiratorial indifference.[42]

Amid uncertainty, loneliness, and powerlessness, comradeship provided security, togetherness, and strength. It often took the form of little "conspiracies," even as it protected the culprit trapped in the workings of the military or paramilitary obedience and subjugation machine. While Hans Lorenz and his comrades were at a pub—their first such excursion after three weeks in the military—his belt and his gun were stolen. Three days of detention awaited him; a soldier was responsible for his gear, and there were no excuses. His comrades, however, held "a council of war" and decided that one of them would report sick every day so that Hans could borrow the "sick" soldier's gun and a belt. They continued this scheme until they were permitted another pub visit, at which time Hans managed to procure a gun and a belt in the same way he had lost his own.[43]

Those who achieved a sense of security through comradeship amid the insecurity of a totalitarian state and the reins of a "total institution" shared an exceptional feeling—the "feeling of absolute superiority," as Klaus Ewald, a former student in one of the *Napolas*, the paramilitary Nazi elite schools, put it. There, war games fostered an even stronger sense of togetherness than did the hunt for outsiders or little conspiracies against superiors elsewhere. "Over there is the enemy," students were told as they were introduced to field exercises. "We are going to attack. First we have to get through that hollow, then approach the hill over there: we'll fan out and move forward to face the enemy and provide each other with fire protection. I'll be shooting, you'll jump; together we keep the enemy down, then another one will take over protective fire, he moves forward, and so on— that is total working together." [44]

A new social order was emerging. Who was in and who was out, who was above and who was below, what was to be done and what was to be left out—all this was to be redefined. Middle-class ethics and customs no longer counted. "We really had to swelter and freeze, we had to get soaked in our tents. We might curse about it, and it might bring out our nastier side, but we always came back to the communal group," said Wilfried Glatten. This atmosphere lent itself to a "conspiratorial community," which Nazi propaganda loved to conjure. It radiated an aura of revolt, upheaval, and protest, not against the political regime but against a supposedly outdated social climate—the musty smell of bourgeois privacy, security—and boredom.[45]

"We All Knew That Something Dreadful Had Happened"

Although not all boys did equally well in switching from bourgeois boredom to hooligan-like conformity, most of them eventually made the change. One of them was Jost Hermand, born in 1930 in Berlin into a typical Aryan lower-middle-class family. His mother, being proud of her "inner dignity," kept some distance from the "too vulgar" Nazis. Jost's father had different concerns. He struggled to support his family by selling fabrics during the day and playing piano in bars in the evening. Jost was betwixt and between. Other boys mocked him because he stuttered. But he wanted to belong, so before joining the *Jungvolk* in summer 1940, when he was ten years old, he memorized its dogma: "Boys of the Jungvolk are tough, discreet and true: Boys of the Jungvolk are comrades. The Jungvolk boy's highest ideal is his honor."

In the Jungvolk, Jost's training started in spontaneous brawls that would convert "dishrags" and "mama's boys" into "real guys." Jost served as the perfect butt of such brawls. Physically weak and awkward, Jost failed miserably. When it came to exercise on horizontal or parallel bars, he earned the name "spider monkey."[46] From late 1940 on, Jost spent most of his time in various camps of the child evacuation program (*Kinderlandverschickung*, or *KLV*). Though officially established to save the children in the big cities from the Allied air raids, these camps also served to isolate the kids in the hothouses of social vacuums and thereby enable them to work intensely and exclusively on male bonding.

Most of the boys had respect only for those of their peers who constantly boasted, could show budding biceps, could get their way by brute force, and who mercilessly tyrannized the weaker boys—in short, for boys who were "sturdy," "swift as the greyhound, tough as leather, and hard as Krupp steel," as the slogan of the Hitler Youth had it. Believing in the Nazi social-Darwinist ideology, the camp authorities encouraged this performance. Showing "any pity for our 'opponents' " was not acceptable. Instead, the platoon leaders urged the boys "to bring down anyone who opposed us with a hook to the jaw, or to hold him in a headlock until he ran out of steam or gave up." Jost himself climbed some steps in the pecking order when he one day proved his toughness by "unsheathing the dagger we all wore at our left side and plunging it deep into my right thigh," as he wrote in a memoir.[47]

Jost Hermand's camp experience took effect quickly. Back in Berlin in 1942–43, he voluntarily joined one of the street gangs, "as a protest against my mother's efforts to turn me into a 'sissy.' " These gangs were illegal and "met secretly in order not to be discovered by the Hitler Youth patrols." But "conspiratorial community" was exactly what the boys were seeking. "We began to smoke, cursed obscenely, and played 'doctor' with the girls; we also suspended condoms filled with water from tree branches, and as soon as someone looked up, puzzled to see these things hanging in the trees, we would shoot at the condoms with BB-guns and give the unsuspecting pass-erby a cold shower. When our leader, Walter, felt especially full of beans, he ordered us to capture other boys and girls and drag them to our den. There he would torment them, sexually and sadistically, taking their clothes off and fiddling around with their private parts. Afterward, with his pants down, he would jerk off under the lustful eyes of Lilo, one of the gang members."[48]

At the age of thirteen, Jost joined the KLV camp Gross-Ottingen in the Warthegau. There, sexual sadism became even more relentless. "Dorm parties" were the prelude to torture, as when "the 'big guys,' the sports aces, would take one of the 'delicate and sensitive' boys and strap him down naked on a table. Next he was either smeared with shoe polish and 'polished' with brushes or forcibly masturbated until—after the first climax—he cried out in pain." The pecking order would always remain unstable. "Later, as some of the boys had their first ejaculations . . . weaker ones like me were even raped, and we suffered painful anal bleeding as a result. Over the months, as more boys had ejaculations, the entire ranking system changed. From now on those who could already 'come' belonged to the select and tormented 'little boys' in truly mean ways."[49]

Jost Hermand's frightful experiences were perhaps exceptional; he did not face the same brutality in all the camps he joined. But his descriptions of sexual boasting and sexual sadism shed light on the grammar of male bonding. That grammar would not change in the military or in any other military-like setting. Male bonding was about negotiating and demonstrat-ing male dominance and power—the power of strong and "male" men over weak and "feminized" men—and over women as well, of course. Crucially, male bonding exercised and demonstrated the gender hierarchy sexually, too, with or without females. Any kind of sexual intimacy, including with women, was as obsolete as the individual conscience was. Admitting tender feelings toward loved ones at home would have provoked the mockery of comrades. Public sex in the brothel and obscene jokes fueled comrade-ship, not the intimacy of individual love.[50] A comrade was someone with whom "you could get up to something now and then," as police lieutenant Gerhard Modersen put it in his diary in 1943.[51] For countless soldiers, "get-ting up to something" meant one thing: adventures with women. Modersen was married. But it was precisely adultery, which he constantly practiced along with his comrades, that made the life as a soldier attractive to him. Beyond a matter of sexual needs, at least as important was the ability to boast of sexual adventures to your comrades. Showing off about sex was as much a part of assimilation into a community of male buddies as was affectionate homo-eroticism. Both demonstrated the social sovereignty of the leagues of males, their superiority over women, family, and home—over civilian society and civilian morality. An important requirement for boys to become men was never to question these basics of the gender order.

But even for those inside the male bond, male power never provided certainty. The laws of comradeship produced fear—the fear of becoming an outsider.[52] The outsider would be left alone. Nobody would help him. "Each of us was grateful not to be the one being beaten and would rather pull the covers over his head than let the victim's whimpering 'soften' him," observed Jost Hermand. The basic rule of the male bond's grammar was that whatever happened, it was always better just to stand by or to look away than to become a victim yourself.

Once in the Warthegau in occupied Poland, Jost and his comrades had a chance to test their moral apathy. "One afternoon we were in the school court-yard when we saw an SS man on a bicycle coming from Standau (Straszewo), his dog running alongside." He suddenly stopped and ordered his dog to "jump at a very pregnant Polish woman walking on the village street." The dog did as ordered; the woman screamed and fell to the ground, cowering in fear. "The SS man got off his bicycle and stomped on the woman's belly with his boots until she died from internal injuries." Jost and his comrades stood and watched "fatalistically. . . . It did not occur to us to rush over to help the woman." Only afterward were they embarrassed. "We all knew that something dreadful had happened." But no one would talk. Everyone was "discreet," as the Jungvolk's dogma had it. He who followed it felt at least some security—the security of comradeship, which by now was far more important than revulsion at what the comrades had seen. He who stuck to the group knew that the group would defend him, the brother-in-crime.[53]

The Nazis did not invent violent group culture or male initiation rites. Long before 1933, informal hierarchies in proletarian subculture and urban gangs had been based on strong biceps and rude behavior. Whoever wanted to belong to such cliques had to be prepared to violate middle-class norms. To be accepted, the applicant had to commit a few crimes such as holdups or break-ins. Only then would the group believe that he would not betray them. Crimes, pranks, and roguery strengthened social cohesion. Juvenile delinquency and denigrating the respectable culture established masculinity—not only in Germany.[54] And when it came to making men from boys in modern Western or other societies, it was not only about gangs and delinquency. Male initiation rites exist in most traditional and modern societies. Military service, praised as the "school of manliness," has been not only the most widespread initiation rite in modern societies but also an example of how the state orchestrates male initiation. As much as such rites vary, they all serve the same goal—making sure that boys acquire the social qualities of what is considered masculine. Maleness, though, in almost all of these societies means to rule over civilian society and thus over women. Eventually, "liminality" does not destroy the gender regime as the civilian society's basic principle but guarantees its permanence. Thus, as Albrecht Erich Günther, a dedicated supporter of radical militarist and nationalist circles, put it in 1934, sending young boys into all-male training camps would by no means alienate them from family life but rather would make them fit for their role as strong rulers over wives and children.[55] "Liminality" and "anti-structure" (Victor Turner) are limited in time and space, both in tribal cultures and in modern societies. Even when such boundaries evaporate as in rogue youth gangs, civilian society and state authority still exist and are called to counteract and to control delinquency and liminality. They are the "structure" to which "anti-structure," delinquent gang culture, and liminal male initiation are in opposition.

What, then, was the peculiarity of "liminality" in the Third Reich? The Third Reich abolished exactly the polarity of "structure" and "anti-structure," notwithstanding Günther's rather traditional considerations. When the Nazi state sent boys to training camps and military or paramilitary service, no return to civilian society was planned. Once the war began, there was no longer any civilian society. That is what it meant to build a state on comradeship, and that is precisely what frightened Sebastian Haffner in 1939. In Nazi Germany, "liminality" and "anti-structure" served as a model to reorganize—that is, to revolutionize—the entire society. Anti-structure became structure, liminality the basis of a genocidal society.

THREE

Performing Genocidal Ethics

Togetherness in Himmler's Elite

After having committed mass murder throughout southern Russia in summer and fall 1941, Police Reserve Battalion 9 was allowed a rest in Poland. At a fellowship evening of the Fourth Company in early January 1942, the men traded war stories. Police officer Karl Schiewek amused his comrades with an original poem titled "The More or Less Funny KdF Trip to the Southeast" (Nazi Germany's official tourist and leisure agency, *Kraft durch Freude* [Strength Through Joy], was abbreviated KdF). In thirty stanzas, the poem conjured Operation Barbarossa and the adventures of Schiewek unit as a KdF excursion. The parallelism was part irony, part bravado, as its author intended.

> Soon we traveled through Saxonia
> In a dusty convoy
> Sudetenland, Protectorate,
> What a pleasure!
> All the girls welcoming us,
> If our "old dears" knew about that.
>
> From Iglau to Engerau
> The second day went on.
> In Vienna, the SD[1] got nicely drunk
> Not only once . . .
> Through the Marusch valley, where

Already two thousand years ago
The Vandals romped toward the East
And tested their strength as we did,
We zoomed to Mühlbach, Reussmarkt, and
    Hermannstadt,
To Schässburg with the Saxons
There many cops heard
Their little hearts beating faster.

However, there was no time for that!
War was approaching fast . . .
In a rush three platoons departed . . .
To join the *Kommandos*
In Czernowitz, Falesti, Barlad . . .
Pietra Neamt is named the dump,
Where the shabby rest find accommodation.
When the job finally is done,
We have the shits!
And if a guy gets a break from that,
You see him running to the bars.

In Czernowitz, however, Schneider's men,
Like the Turks, really are at work.
They make a big haul, suuuch piles . . .

The poem goes on to recall the siege of Odessa and other battles. Neither hardship nor boredom, danger nor cruelty, had dampened the good mood of the troop, at least according to the poem. Rather, the troop kept itself busy with boozy pleasures, sexual adventures, living like the Vandals—and terrorizing the local population.

And then Kinne's big moment comes,
Who goes to Babtschinzy
To carry away Jews
Partly into a gutter, partly over the Dienester.
There, the scythe is also at work,
And some songs of harvest are sung . . .

56

The staff moves on with the car,
At some point even to Nikolayev!
Another command is already waiting there;
They enjoyed themselves splendidly
And get hold of lots of stuff.
Who would that be? Well, it is 11a!

Meanwhile, you won't believe it,
10b fought against partisans
It cracks—this is not a lie—30 bunkers a day . . .

From Yalta to Sevastopol
Around Simferopol
There we wreak havoc like the titans,
Quite powerful. And the partisans
Have their large asshole tanned.
Furthermore, the Jews and the Krymchacs
Rapidly forget how to crack nuts.
The war goes wild at all front lines.
We are all there,
We are showing what we can achieve,
And nobody missed the target . . .

Suddenly, close to Christmas
They send us back home . . .
The KdF is now over.
All in all, it wasn't that bad . . .[2]

A poem generates fictional distance. This one merges irony, sarcasm, and cynicism. It also mirrors reality. First is the reality of the facts. Murder, deportation, rape, and all kinds of terror against civilians had filled the daily life of the detachments of Einsatzgruppe D, one of four mobile killing units that carried out the Holocaust in Russia. Called *Einsatzkommando* or *Sonderkommando*, they were numbered 10a, 11a, 11b, 12, as in the poem. At Babtschinzy, Police Battalion 9 murdered about one hundred Jews of both sexes, including children, in August 1941. The Germans had charged these Jews with interfering with the harvest—the poem recalls songs of harvest—and with serving as Communist spies. Soon thereafter, Sonderkommando 11a arrived at Nikolayev at the Black Sea, as described in the poem: it started shooting Jews—227 in total—and registered about five thousand more to be killed soon after with the support of Einsatzkommando 12. Then, within a few days in September, both units murdered thousands more Jews, first the men and then the women and children. And so it went, just as the poem recounted. In December 1941, Sonderkommando 11b and other units murdered 1,500 Krymchacs and 13,000 Jews "around Simferopol." Right after having participated in this "action," the fourth company of PRB 9 was indeed sent "back home."[3]

The poem reveals another reality, the social climate of the police troop. According to the poem, committing mass murder provided the police officers with boyish pleasure and amusement—just as chasing women did, or boasting of sexual adventures or continuous boozing followed by bouts of diarrhea. Such "adventures" reflected collective joy and allowed the men to demonstrate masculine endurance, toughness, and power. Doggerel like this isn't meant to be entirely realistic, of course. By simplifying, exaggerating, and harmonizing a chaos of facts and moods, remembered pleasures ameliorated the horrors of mass executions and instigated collective joy on a new level.

In truth, not all police officers had shared collective joy based on mass murder. Police Reserve Battalion 9 was not composed solely of born killers and sadists. Some experienced moral qualms; some men backed off when their comrades started shooting civilians; some vomited during or after these "actions." One of the police officers, Otto Eichelbaum, was troubled when he had to aim at a boy of seven or eight. "When we were about to fire," he recalled later, "the boy looked at me seeking help. At that moment I felt as if I were about to kill my own child. Confused as I was, I shot only some time after we got the order to fire. The shot missed its target. Then I had a nervous breakdown and had to be relieved immediately from the execution command. . . . As a result of that breakdown I became gray within a couple of months."[4]

This account was retrospective. Eichelbaum testified in 1964 when West German investigators took the perpetrators to court. We do not know if he truly had the serious qualms in September 1941 that two decades later he claimed to have had. But a broad array of documents and testimonies confirms that not all men were equally willing to participate in mass murder. However, none of the perpetrators' qualms, worries, or breakdowns helped the victims. PRB 9 did its job in the way it was supposed to do. The unit did not break apart. And PRB 9 is only one of innumerable examples of groups of men who fueled the Nazi death machine. What enabled them to carry out mass murder despite all of their internal differences and dissonances?

Focusing on the SS, the SD, the Gestapo, and other police units as the major institutions of the Nazi death machine, this chapter explores how terror merged into togetherness; it tracks how performing acts of brutality generated a sense of belonging; it inquires into the Nazi ethics that justified and even required mass murder; and it shows that committing genocide enabled the perpetrators to build, to change, and to revolutionize social frameworks. They created a new "society"—with new boundaries, new inner hierarchies, and new values.

"No Pity, No Nothing"

Humans are used to ordering their lives and all of humanity through binary categories—life and death, men and women, old and young, right and wrong, beautiful and ugly, good and evil, Us and Them. Universal ethics aim to transcend these polarities. All people are created equal, and all should be given equal chances and opportunities; a bond exists between all kinds of human beings, as different as they may be. Universal ethics detach moral categories from other polarities, so that they can be applied, potentially, to anybody. Thus, good and evil transcend the fundamental division between Us and Them. Everyone is potentially good or evil and deserves to be treated according to how he or she acts. If one examines slavery, colonialism, imperialism, and the racial discrimination that was still alive in the twentieth century, or the practices of warfare throughout the modern era, one can argue that even liberal Western societies only imperfectly adopted these universal ethics.[5] The Nazi failure, however, stands uniquely because it combined two things. First, the Nazis developed a sophisticated ideology of antiuniversalistic, dichotomist ethics that not only justified genocide but required it. Second, the regime made significant parts of the entire nation stick to these ethics, and even attracted other national entities to support them.

In the Third Reich, only the We of the Aryan Volksgemeinschaft was recognized as "good," whereas They could not be other than "evil." "Our ethics," declared Heinrich Himmler in a speech in January 1939, "comply solely with the needs of our people. Good is what is useful for the people, evil is what damages our people." Nazi propaganda had spread this message since 1933, denouncing "false humanity" and "exaggerated pity," the essentials of Christian (and Jewish) ethics, as a crime to the German Volk. But nobody put it as drastically as Himmler in his infamous speech to SS generals in Posen on 4 October 1943. Looking back on the successful course of the murder of the Jews, he outlined the moral grammar that invalidated both the Judeo-Christian tradition of human compassion and pity for the weak, with its the command of mercy for a defeated enemy and the notion of natural, equal, and universal human rights. The "holiest laws of the future," he said, were that "our concern, our duty, is to our people, and to our blood. That is what we must care for and think about, work for and fight for, and nothing else." And, he continued, "It is basically wrong for us to project our whole harmless soul and heart, all our good nature, our idealism, onto foreign peoples. . . . Whether other people live in prosperity or starve to death interests me only insofar as we need them as slaves for our culture. Otherwise, it is of no interest to me. The SS man follows only one principle: we must be honest, decent, loyal, and comradely to members of our own blood, and to no one else. What happens to the Russians, the Czechs, does not matter a bit to me."

To worry about "foreign people" was a "sin against our own blood," said Himmler. To give them "ideals," he explained, would mean "that our sons and grandchildren will have a harder time with them." The moral pathos here is worth noting—concern for other people was a "sin." In this speech, Himmler only briefly addressed the reasons for that rigid dichotomy. He did not need to dwell on its ideological background. The SS elite already knew it. It was the basic law of social Darwinism, according to which people and human beings are fundamentally and irreconcilably different, are engaged in a life and death struggle—only the fittest survive. The idea of racial difference did not allow for pluralist harmony but required a fight to the death. The superior race was fundamentally threatened by the inferior race and its (supposedly) immoral attacks—the conspiracies of the Jews, for instance.[6]

As Hannah Arendt has noted, the Nazis actually believed in their own racist obsessions and acted accordingly, as though the Jews did indeed control the world and the world thus "needed a counterconspiracy to defend itself." Wondering about the "Jewish question," Joseph Goebbels noted in his diary in August 1941, "We need to approach this issue without any sentimentality. We only have to imagine what the Jews would do to us if they were in power to know what has to be done as we are in power."[7] Consequently, Himmler too, in his 1943 speech, reminded listeners of the national disaster of 1918 and the supposed threat of the Jewish conspiracy: if "we still had Jews today in every town as secret saboteurs, agitators and trouble-mongers, we would now probably have reached the 1916/17 stage when the Jews were still in the body of the German people." The annihilation of the Jews was justified as the only way to save the Aryan race. Such ideas were common sense in Nazi Germany. A German police officer said after the execution of two hundred Jews in Memel in late June 1941, "Good heavens, damn it, one generation has to go through this so that our children will have a better life."[8] This comment of an ordinary German echoes the heroic sacrifice invoked in Himmler's Posen speech, which continued by "referring to . . . the extermination of the Jewish people. . . . Most of you here know what it means when 100 corpses lie next to each other, when 500 lie there or when 1,000 are lined up. To have endured this and at the same time to have remained a decent person—with exceptions due to human weaknesses—has made us hard. This is a page of honor in our history which has never been and never will be put in writing." As cynical as equating mass murder with "honor" may seem, seen through the lens of Nazi ethics it made perfect sense. "My Honor is Loyalty," was the motto of the SS. The SS men's honor went far beyond mere obedience to the *Führer*, Adolf Hitler. Rather it included "loyalty to the German people . . . as well as loyalty to its blood, to our ancestors and grandchildren, loyalty to our comrades." Thus, it also meant rigorous devotion to the community of Aryans and the abandonment of any concerns that troubled this devotion.[9]

Felix Landau was one of those able to "endure" facing piles of corpses and still remain "decent." Born in 1910, he joined the Austrian Nazi Party in 1931. As an SS man he participated in the attempt to assassinate Austria's Chancellor Dollfuss in 1934. After his imprisonment and Austria's annexation to Nazi Germany, Landau worked with Himmler's Security Police and was awarded the *Blutorden* (Blood Order), one of the most prestigious Nazi decorations. As of July 1941 he served with an Einsatzkommando in the Lemberg (Lvov/Lviv) area in the General Gouvernement in Poland. There he kept a diary: a document of his private worries and intimate affairs, but also of his murderous job. On 14 July 1941 he wrote, "Report for an execution. Fine, so I'll just play executioner and then gravedigger, why not? Isn't it strange, you love the battle and then have to shoot defenseless people. Twenty-three had to be shot, amongst them the above-mentioned women. . . . We drove one kilometer along the road out of town and then turned right into a wood. . . . The death candidates assembled with shovels to dig their own graves. Two of them were weeping. The others certainly have incredible courage. What on earth is running through their minds during those moments? . . . Strange, *I am completely unmoved. No pity, no nothing.* That's the way it is and then it's all over. My heart beats just a little faster when involuntarily I recall what I felt and thought when I was in a similar situation." This was when Landau, on 24 July 1934 in the Chancellery in Vienna, was confronted with the machine-gun barrels of the Austrian militia, which defeated the SS assassins of Chancellor Dollfuss. "Then there were moments when I came close to weakening. I would not have allowed it to show, no, that would have been out of the question for someone of my character."[10]

Landau had internalized the SS ideal of hardness, though he was still concerned with the confusion of military ideals and the murderous ethics of an SS man. Hardness and toughness were traditional military virtues; the SS filled them with different meaning. Whereas the military praised virtues that made soldiers disregard their own *physical* health and their own life in battle, the SS values made men — "political soldiers," as they put it — disregard their ideas of *moral* health as rooted in the Judeo-Christian tradition. The perfect SS man was not the one who sacrificed his physical well-being, but the one who abandoned the moral world which asked for pity for others, for mercy, and forgiveness, and which made those who fail feel guilty. The ideal SS man did not need to feel guilty for having acted mercilessly.[11] According to the new Nazi ethics, mercilessness to the putative enemies served Aryan survival; thus, performing mercilessly was "good."

"The Outlaws"

Neither Himmler nor any other Nazi leader invented the morality of immorality. These ethics emerged as a response to the experience of mass destruction in World War I. While the majority of German society tried to come to grips with the burden of mass killing by escaping into the myth of comradeship, a few warriors preached or even practiced eternal war. Ernst Jünger took on the literary part of the task. As he confessed in 1922, he had always felt horrified by looking at the corpses and mutilated bodies after battle. Such views not only stirred fear for one's own body. Jünger found even more confusing the qualms they set off: that is, the question of "guilt." The warrior was well aware that he not only had risked his own life but also had destroyed other lives. Jünger, however, boasted of having immunized himself against such qualms. He had elevated himself above Christian and bourgeois morals that ask for mercy and pity. "Overcoming" served as the key term of Jünger's war ethics; it was not the fear of being killed that needed to be overcome, but the fear of killing itself.[12]

Jünger anticipated Himmler's ethics only partially. The trench fighter still thought and acted within the categories of regular warfare. He did not praise the murder of civilians. It was only when the war was over that the Freikorps and other radical nationalists started war against civilian political enemies. Although it was not the Freikorps alone that gave birth to the Nazis and the SS, some continuity is obvious.[13] Rudolf Höss, who became the commandant of Auschwitz, had lost his parents during the war. He joined the Freikorps and "found a home again, and a sense of security in the comradeship of my fellows." In his memoir, written after World War II, he described himself, with some discomfort, as having been a "lone wolf" who kept his thoughts and feelings to himself. However, he had "felt continually drawn towards that comradeship which enables a man to rely on others in time of need and of danger." Höss's discomfort reflects the uneasiness of an entire society. Belonging had become less stable than ever before. "Danger" was required to regain emotional stability. Belonging was granted best by identifying an enemy to fight against. "In fact the more we were pushed around by the government in office, the more firmly did we stick together. Woe to anyone who attempted to divide us — or to betray us! . . . Treachery was punished with death, and there were many traitors so executed." Höss acted accordingly when it came to punishing a supposed Communist spy whom the group blamed for being responsible for the death of the Nazi martyr Leo Schlageter. As "no German court would have convicted him, so it was left to us to pass sentence in accordance with an unwritten law which we ourselves, according to the exigencies of the times, had laid down."[14] Regarding established jurisdictions and codes of ethics as insufficient, the group created its own. The group claimed moral sovereignty and knew that it would stick together.

In the early 1920s, other elements of the extreme nationalist subculture also fostered rigid ideas of belonging based on terrorizing insiders as well as outsiders. Consider the sensational *Feme* murders by the Black *Reichswehr*, a hidden branch of the German military that was founded in 1923 and that dissolved in that same year. *Feme* is the medieval German word for sentence. In the 1920s the notion was used to burnish vigilante justice by alluding to Germany's mythical past. When the state dissolved this reserve army, some of its members were killed in cruel ways by their own comrades, who accused them of treachery, mostly without any substantial reason, and passed sentence. In fact, the victims had just attracted attention by committing minor misdemeanors.[15] The Feme murders are best understood as a radical version of how the military carried out its own justice against those who had sinned against the group. By executing Feme justice, the group elevated itself above the rules of the civilian society and the democratic state. Although the Feme murderers tried to hide their misdeeds, their real success began when they were caught and brought to trial. Thanks to the publicity they received, the Feme murderers acquired a heroic image among radical nationalists.

In 1930 Ernst von Salomon published his memoir, *The Outlaws*, which became one of the most popular paeans to the ethics of terror. *The Outlaws* perverted the influential genre of the German *Bildungsroman* (coming-of-age novel), which had begun around 1800, and told how an adolescent youth gradually becomes a valuable citizen and family man by accepting individual sovereignty, sociability, and responsibility for others. In his memoir Salomon described himself as a young man who grew into a valuable, tough, and merciless member of a criminal gang. Born in 1902, Salomon entered an elite military academy in 1913. Too young to fight in the war, he joined a Freikorps unit to fight against Communists in Silesia and the Baltic in 1919. In 1922 he took part in the plot to assassinate Walter Rathenau, the Jewish-German industrialist, politician, and advocate of "fulfilling" the Versailles Treaty. Later, Salomon was involved in a Feme murder. He spent years in prison for both crimes but had no regrets. Murder served an exclusive goal. "We felt that we embodied Germany. We believed that we were entitled to have that power."

Desperately seeking a feeling of belonging, Salomon praised "man's lust for destruction," dwelt on the soul as an "emanation of blood," and celebrated the revelry of violence. It was never just about physical destruction or even sadism. Murder, lynching, and terror reflected moral destruction, the destruction of whatever civilization praises as good—securing order, providing stability, saving life, protecting the weak, feeling pity. And at the same time, the terrorists promulgated a new ethic. Dedicated not to mere destruction but rather to the "will to create" through destruction, they garnished themselves with a mythical tradition. "The appearance of these troops," Salomon wrote, "recalled the days when the Teutonic knights had brought a new faith and new race into the land." The "outlaws" followed their own laws. They "obeyed none of the ordinary military laws." They refused to recognize any rules but those of their own choosing. The "commander's will" was based not on defined authority but solely on his ability to strengthen the "dynamic forces that animated the whole company." It was all about cohesion and unity. If ever one of the members "sinned against the rigid laws of the clan," the company would hold a "short court-martial," send him to death, and move on, singing their pirate song.[16]

Salomon's autobiography offered a mythical explanation of the social and ethical dynamic of political violence in late Weimar Germany, as practiced by the Stormtroopers of the Nazi Party. From late 1929 on, the Stormtroopers (SA) waged civil war on Communists and socialists. Dance hall battles, brawls, and knife fights became a daily routine in German cities. Unleashing brutality in bar brawls, fighting together furiously in the streets, and committing murder together served as social "cement," as Joseph Goebbels said. It was not just standing together against an enemy, as soldiers do in battle, that created comradeship. Moral transgression forged bonds as well. In fact, the SA popularized the myth of revolutionizing society by violating civilian, humanitarian norms. SA men did not hide murder; they staged it. Inflicting ruthless violence guaranteed public attention. When they marched in Charlottenburg, a Berlin suburb, they sang, "We are the Nazi guys from the murderer unit of Charlottenburg." To the SA, comradeship meant fighting civilian establishment. If you wanted to become an SA man, you would change your identity. You would not just switch into a uniform but adopt a new antibourgeois name, copied from the criminal underworld, like "Revolver Gob" or "Submarine." Participating in collective violence was the ticket to enter the group. When they met in "storm bars" to relax, they dwelt on war stories and granted the most brutal comrade the greatest respect.[17]

Committing murder on behalf of the "movement" was the best way to become a hero of the movement. On 10 August 1932, several SA men attacked a Communist family in Potempa, Upper Silesia, and murdered the father in front of his wife and his children with extraordinary savagery. The murderers were sentenced to death soon after. The Nazi Party now had new heroes. Hermann Göring immediately sent money to the murderers' families, and the SA leader, Ernst Röhm, visited them in jail. On 22 August, Hitler himself honored the murderers in a sensational public telegram: "My Comrades! This outrageous blood sentence unites me with you by unlimited loyalty. From now on, your freedom will be a matter of honor for us. Fighting this government, which has allowed this, will be our duty." Soon thereafter, the conservative Franz von Papen, Reich Commissar in Prussia, commuted the death sentence to life imprisonment. When Hitler came into power, the murderers were freed.[18]

Following the Nazi seizure of power in January 1933, concentration camps were established as part of Himmler's empire of terror. They served not only to exclude domestic enemies but also to instill moral hardness and mercilessness among the SS guards. Dachau camp commander Theodor Eicke was the model. His "disciplinary camp regulations," issued on 1 October 1933, decreed that prisoners should be treated as brutally as possible, although with discipline and control. "Tolerance means weakness. This means, whenever the interests of the Fatherland are at stake, only ruthless measures are appropriate." As a "political soldier," any camp guard was to be completely devoted to Nazi ideology; traditional legal standards shouldn't matter to him. Any pity whatsoever for the "enemies of the State" was unworthy of an SS man. As Paul Neurath, who was imprisoned in Dachau and Buchenwald in 1938 and 1939 before he managed to immigrate to Sweden and then to the United States, observed, the sentinels watched not only the prisoners but also one another. "Apparently," wrote Neurath, "the individual guards wanted to show off to their friends and comrades, sometimes to their superiors, and prove what tough guys they were. . . . Some of the guards didn't beat prisoners unless they knew they were being watched by their comrades."[19]

Not even Eicke's order from 1933 issued a carte blanche to sadists, however. "Decent" torture and murder were required, not torture with relish. Obvious sadism was even prosecuted, although only rarely. The sadist who gave free rein to his personal needs could never be accepted where only the community counted, as the Nazi jurist Friedrich Grimm explained in 1938 in justifying a Feme murder. Feme may have been committed to exacting revenge, but that was still consistent with national interests. Never, though, was murder to be justified as a consequence of "hate, blindness, or ambition"—that is, of individual dispositions. Establishing a culture of brutality did not mean satisfying the needs of psychological pathologies but engineering a totalitarian community, for which nothing but communal life and social cohesion mattered. "Normal" men were to rid themselves of restrictions, to embody mercilessness and to perform (rather than to enjoy) brutality on behalf of the racial ideology. In practice, the boundaries between discipline and sadism were often blurred. Usually, a senior SS man would take the beginner into a barrack and assume the role of a teacher by torturing or harassing prisoners. Then it was up to the recruit to show what he had learned. "Kick him in the stomach," might be the order. If the beginner hesitated, he would be dressed down. "What, you are shit-scared of that Jewish bastard? You pretend to be a soldier of the Führer? You are a coward!" Back among his comrades, the "coward" was again humiliated, this time in front of them.[20]

Flogging, too, was to be exercised in front of and under the control of the comrades. As Rudolf Höss recalled, "Eicke had issued orders that a minimum of one company of troops must be present during the infliction of these corporal punishments." Initially Höss felt "compelled to watch the whole procedure" and to listen to the screaming prisoner. "When the man began to scream, I went hot and cold all over." However, he managed to rid himself of empathy. "Later on, at the beginning of the war, I attended my first execution, but it did not affect me nearly so much as witnessing this corporal punishment." Afraid of being shamed as a "weakling," Höss would never have admitted any "sympathy" for prisoners. "Outwardly cold and even stony, but with most deeply disturbed inner feelings," he fulfilled his duties no matter what. Precisely this dutifulness made him an exemplary SS man. "My stony mask" convinced the superior "that there was no need to 'toughen me up.' "[21] Höss had internalized the rules of shame culture just as Felix Landau had. It was all about the mask, about outward performance of brutality. Everybody wore a mask; many, maybe most, eventually forgot that it was a mask. With or without a mask, they all acted accordingly.

"Everyone Wanted to Be the Best"

From 1941 to 1944, some twenty to thirty officers of the Border Police Station in Nowy Sącz (in German, Neu-Sandez), fifty miles southeast of Kraków in West Galicia, murdered thousands of Jews and sent another fifteen thousand or more to Bełżec and other death camps. Although these policemen were by no means equally eager to perform genocide, they did not need orders to do so. They developed a murderous dynamic that created a microcosm of the Holocaust, located between mobile death squads and stationary camp guards.

When Germany attacked Poland in September 1939, the population of Nowy Sącz was about 38,000, and the city was the capital of an administrative district that included six smaller towns and twenty-six villages — overall 315,000 inhabitants, mostly ethnic Poles. At that time, ten thousand Jews lived in the city, with another seven thousand spread over the rest of the district. By August 1942, due to the enforced concentration, the total number of Jews in the city had grown to more than fifteen thousand. Any one of them was the potential target of SS-Obersturmführer (First Lieutenant) Heinrich Hamann and his men. Hamann came to Nowy Sącz as deputy chief of the Border Police Station — a branch of the Security Police (SiPo) and the

Security Service (SD)—in September 1939. In early 1940, he was promoted to chief. Even before the Final Solution became a matter of official orders, Hamann was known as the "master of death and life" in Nowy Sącz.[22]

Starting in 1940, the Jews were registered and forced to move into the then still open ghetto, where they suffered from want and insufficient food. The black market began to flourish. Any Jew caught black marketing risked being shot on the spot or incarcerated and tortured to death in the police prison. Murderous whipping was common, but the Gestapo's favorite torture was a medieval apparatus by which victims were hanged in iron shackles over a cross for hours. Often blood and pus collected over the floor below and produced such a stink that even the guards felt nauseated. Hamann's men knew well that such torture "did not help to establish the truth" in any investigations—"on the contrary," admitted one of them later. Terror and torture were not conducted to produce information but to build a community of violence.[23]

On one occasion, Hamann and some comrades were in the local prison square and for enjoyment told two Jewish prisoners to try to escape: "run, run!" When one of them futilely attempted to follow the order, Hamann shot him. After launching the cruel spectacle again, he shot the second. Both prisoners were now considered to be "shot on the run." Another time, some police officers amused themselves by shackling three Jews together and throwing them into the town's river, where they drowned. On another occasion Johann Bornholt, one of Hamann's henchmen, was annoyed by a barking dog. He identified the owner and shot him on the street. Jews and Poles were so afraid of Bornholt that, even in the ghetto, he faced empty streets—and beamed with pride. If any Jew dared to show his face, he was as good as dead. One such victim, a man named Chastell F., was suffering from swollen feet and failed to get away quick enough, so Bornholt shot him down. Jews of either sex who hesitated to give their belongings and savings to Hamann's men were also often killed on the spot.[24]

The Germans' power exploded when, in fall 1941, the Kraków-based Commander of SiPo and SD, the regional head of the SS and the police (KdS), ordered that the Jews were to be killed in situ. From then on, the Germans murdered Jews systematically throughout their territories, including Nowy Sącz. Once or twice a week German officers brought Jewish prisoners to the Jewish cemetery and shot them there. It was up to the Jewish community to bury them. Brought to court twenty years later in West Germany, one of the officers stated, "The executions were considered business as usual. Nobody made a lot of fuss about it."[25]

There seemed to be no rule for when the police would shoot Jews, even those who deliberately remained in their homes. Yet there were rules—the grammar of genocidal ethics. The perpetrators drew their internal hierarchies not only from their military rank (certainly not from their previous status as civilians) but also from their ability to be merciless. In fact, one was the precondition of the other. The officers of the Border Police in Nowy Sącz knew well that their chief, Hamann, would give the most brutal torturers precedence when it came time for promotion. When he was under investigation in 1961, Johann Bornholt painted a clear picture of the culture of brutality in Nowy Sącz. His former comrades, he said, "Böhning, Brock, Rouenhoff, Wegener, Siehling, Denk, Domanski, these and other men were always in on it." They did not just "reluctantly" participate in mass murder. "Everyone wanted to be the best. Everyone wanted to stand out with killing Jews. . . . Brock shot his Jews, and Rouenhoff shot his Jews. Both were eager to perform best."[26]

One of the most striking examples of these German occupiers was SS man Joachim Hamann (no relation to Heinrich Hamann). Leading a unit of Einsatzkommando 3 in Lithuania, he boasted of having "bumped off" seventy-seven thousand Jews. Hamann's chief, SS Colonel Karl Jäger, commander of Einsatzkommando 3, submitted a unique document on the Holocaust: the "Complete List of Executions Carried Out in the EK 3 Area up to 1 December 1941," listing for every day and every place the number of Jews killed, starting with 4 July 1941—"Total 137,346." The first thing a junior officer learned when joining Jäger's troop late in fall 1941 was the pecking order. At the top stood the "old guard," who were the "old men" who had "established the facts." He who was new had to learn, "once and for all," as Jäger would tell him, to shut up when it came to executions.

In the Warsaw ghetto, shooting Jews became a routine for Police Battalion 61 soon after its arrival in January 1942. Some policemen kept a list of their totals by leaving notches on the door of their favorite pub—one line per killed Jew. They also decorated the pub's interior with paintings of their deeds. One showed a comrade beating an animal with the head of a Jew. The competitions for mercilessness demanded documentation. Trophies were collected and treasured. The SS men took photos to document their sangfroid. August Mertens, SS man with Karl Jäger's Einsatzkommando 3, kept an entire stack of photos "as a souvenir for his son." Back home in Germany, he proudly presented them to police comrades.[27]

"Kicking Up a Fuss"

A spectacular "action" took place in Nowy Sącz on 28 April 1942. Police officers there rounded up about three hundred supposedly Communist (but who in fact were social democratic and apolitical) Jews for shooting in the Jewish cemetery. None of the police officers involved had sufficient experience with such numbers, however. Chaotically, they started shooting at their victims, who were forced to stand at the edge of the large hole that had been excavated to serve as a mass grave for the murdered. Many did not die immediately. Screams of lethal pain echoed over the large cemetery. The ground became slippery from the rivers of blood. More and more police officers joined the shooting, some of them likewise having no experience with such massacres. Shooting at close range, they sometimes hit the aortas of their victims, resulting in their blood pouring forth over the hands and weapons of their killers. Further, the hole that had been dug proved to be too small, so the executioners were compelled to interrupt their "job" to order the dozens of Jews who were still to be murdered to enlarge the hole. It was late in the day before the police officers got the execution under control.[28]

When they finished, the executioners marched back to the police station, singing the Horst Wessel song, the Nazi anthem, which glorified a martyr of the Nazi cause, killed by political enemies in 1930. The final stanza runs:

> Flag high, ranks closed
> The S.A. marches with silent solid steps.
> Comrades shot by the Red Front and by reaction
> March in spirit with us in our ranks.

The song conjured up cohesion and strength of the Nazi fighters. Closing the ranks means to fulfill a sacred order the martyr had assigned the Nazi movement. The martyr marches "in spirit with us." He calls for revenge.[29] Revenge for what? According to the Nazi propaganda, Horst Wessel had sacrificed his life not only for the Nazi movement but for Germany, just as any of the millions of soldiers had done on the battlefields of World War I. The martyr represented the German nation, which, according to Nazi propaganda, had been defeated and humiliated in 1918 by the treason of Communists and Jews.

Coming from the lower middle class, most of the German police officers in Nowy Sącz had joined the Nazi movement before 1933 and were dedicated Nazis.[30] Hamann, born in 1908, had entered the NSDAP in 1931 to pursue a career as an SS and SD officer instead of running his parents' retail store. Born in 1912, Günther Labitzke was the son of a mayor in Silesia. He became a member of the Nazi Party in 1931 and then served with the police and the SD as a driver. Josef Bornholt, born into a farm family in 1904, had found a home as an SA thug in 1930; later he became a concentration camp guard in Sachsenhausen. The son of a postal secretary, Josef Rouenhoff was born in 1911 and had a strong Catholic background that kept him from joining the NSDAP until 1933. Nonetheless, the paramilitary group Stahlhelm had attracted him. In 1941 he came to the SS and was transferred to Nowy Sącz. Paul Denk, a chemist's son born in 1908, entered the Nazi Party and the SS to support his career as a car technician and test driver with Porsche in his hometown of Stuttgart.[31] All of these men were typical of the killers at Nowy Sącz.

When brought to court in West Germany twenty years later, some of them frankly admitted that they had embraced anti-Semitism as a "revelation." Rouenhoff said that he had "really believed that the Jews would be Germany's ruin" and that they were planning to "exterminate us." So he understood why they were to be annihilated without any legal basis. Hamann stated "that going to Galicia had revealed to him the basic truth of the Nazi ideology." To him, "the only thing that counted was to decimate the Jews. . . . Who would have cared for a Jewish life?" As so often in Nazi Germany, hate blended with greed. Bornholt stated, "The hatred of Jews was great, it was about revenge—and people were looking for gold and money. Let's not kid ourselves; there was a lot to be got out of the Jews." Like terror, plunder was considered "business as usual." "The basement of the Gestapo station had a depot of fabrics, of which many clothing stores would be proud today," revealed a witness at the 1963 investigation. "All the stuff came from Jewish shops." When the Germans pulled out, Hamann brought with him back to Germany four large boxes of valuables formerly belonging to Jews, as well as a railcar full of Jewish furniture.[32]

But there was more than hate and greed. There was also joy, the joy of togetherness. The police in Nowy Sącz ran a casino where its members and other Germans serving in the regular police, the civil administration, or the military would meet regularly. In the evening they got together for boozy follow-ups of their murderous daily routine. The casino was the place for boasting, joking, and carrying on. War stories about the pleasure of humiliations and tortures—for instance, setting the beards of old Jews on fire—would be told with relish. Once, Josef Rouenhoff assured his comrades that he just had shot a Jew named Lustig "on the run," although he had not wished to hit him, as he said with an ironic undertone. The German word "lustig" translates as "funny." "Isn't it funny," joked one of Rouenhoff's comrades, "that this was just about 'Lustig.'" His comrades gladly congratulated Rouenhoff on his "lucky shot."[33]

A special kind of murderous celebration took place on the evening of 28 April 1942, the day when Hamann's men had killed three hundred Jews. These actions required alcohol to fight physical exhaustion and to wash away mental distress. Official SS guidelines suggested making "special accommodations for the spiritual care" of men participating in mass executions. "The impressions of the day are to be blotted out through the holding of social events in the evenings."[34] These events did not cool down the perpetrators; rather, they stimulated further violence. That night Hamann gathered his circle and other German officials, about twenty men, for an evening of drinking. Such sudsy gatherings were always about boasting. Who was best able to hold his drink? Who could drink the most without passing out? Without getting sick? Who was the toughest? Who was the best marksman? To prove his own toughness, Hamann loved to bite a piece out of a glass, pull a safety pin through his cheek, or challenge his comrades to a wrestling match.[35] Not all officers liked the atmosphere of such male bonding. Paul Denk, one of the police drivers, was more fascinated with cars than with torture, and he tried to hide at home—and met the displeasure of his comrades. Hamann's deputy Köster, who despised his boss, came to this get-together because he knew staying away would damage his reputation among his peers.

For a while the crowd members enjoyed themselves by shooting at a row of glasses on the bar. But by around midnight, such masculine pleasures no longer sufficed. Hamann suggested "kicking up a fuss." He wanted to check on his "lambs" in the ghetto, as he put it. Would they behave well or were they about to moan about what had happened that afternoon? No excuses: everybody had to come with him. In the ghetto, the group stormed houses, forced their way into apartments by kicking in doors and windows, and shot down whoever dared to show their face. Those who sought to hide were not much better off. Police officers entered bedrooms randomly and shot at Jewish couples in bed. Hamann's "little check-up" in the ghetto ended in an orgy of brutality. At least fifty Jews died that night.

On this occasion not only Jews were killed. One bullet hit a German, Hamann's deputy Köster; the shooter was his chief. As Hamann was storming the second floor of a building, he shone his flashlight on a Jew hiding in a corner and at the same time at another person who appeared to be escaping through a door. Shouting, "Son of a bitch, you want to run off?" Hamann shot the exiting figure. Only later did he and his comrades realize that the victim was Köster, who had worn a civilian coat over his uniform. Hamann's supervisor, the Chief Commander of the Security Police at Kraków, launched a superficial investigation. The punishment was a farce. "The king of Nowy Sącz," as the locals called him, was suspended for a week, and then he went right back to his job. Hamann's defense was compelling: he had mistaken Köster for a Jew, and killing a Jew was not a crime. Not even Hamann's drunkenness counted against him, and the fact that Köster and Hamann disliked each other did not prompt further investigation.[36] It was not the physical life of an individual that counted but the social life of perpetrators—the bonds of their community.

"I Felt at Home in Nowy Sącz"

In late August 1942, the decisive step of the Final Solution was enacted in Nowy Sącz. By then, most Jews were already concentrated in the ghettos.

Following an order from the KdS in Kraków, the police selected some one hundred Jews for forced labor detachments. At the same time, however, more than fifteen thousand Jews were made to walk to the next train station, where they would be sent to the Bełżec death camp. Asked what would happen to them, Hamann answered: "You all will be shortly with St. Peter."[37] A third group of more than three thousand Jews were deemed too weak to walk. Over the next couple of days, Hamann's unit killed all of them at four different villages, leaving each a site of barbaric cruelty.

The largest of these actions took place in Mszana-Dolna. Hamann decided that its entire Jewish population, about nine hundred persons, was not able to walk in the summer heat and thus should be shot on the spot. The Jews were led outside of the village to a large hole that had been dug to serve as a mass grave. The local mayor Gelb, a *Volksdeutscher* (an ethnic German who had lived in Poland before 1939), felt particularly responsible for the well-being of the German police officers and bizarrely provided them with a picnic of alcoholic beverages and sandwiches. When the executions started, one Jew, selected for a labor command and who thus would survive this "action," witnessed a police officer whipping his wife, who was carrying their baby in her arms. Eyeing the baby, the officer shouted: "Throw it away, that shit!" Chaos ruled the entire "action." At one point, SD officer Labitzke felt the urge to reproach his comrades for their "inhuman butchery." He was met with laughter all around.[38] Frustrated with the slow pace, one of the officers started shooting indiscriminately into the crowd of hundreds of Jews awaiting their deaths. Often victims who were shot but only wounded were thrown into the hole while still alive. Slowly the grave, ten to thirteen feet deep, filled up with the victims.

When the job was finished, only some ten inches were left for covering. The perpetrators could relax. Following an invitation by Mayor Gelb, they joined a feast at the local restaurant. An orchestra played dance music. At the entrance a large poster decorated with flowers invited people to join the "Day of Mszana-Dolna's Liberation from the Jews." On the evening of 28 August Hamann could declare his district to be "cleansed of Jews."[39] Some Jews managed to survive for a while as members of labor commands, hidden in the woods, or helped by friends, though the Germans ultimately found and killed most of them. Hamann left Nowy Sącz in August 1943 to work with the KdS in Kraków on the conclusion of the Final Solution in other parts of Western Galicia.

What happened in Nowy Sącz occurred in innumerable other places in Nazi-occupied Europe as well. "Absolute power" ruled the district, as a witness later said, anticipating the term the sociologist Wolfgang Sofsky used to analyze the routine and dynamic of terror in the concentration camps.[40] In 1966 Hamann was sentenced to life imprisonment seventy-seven times—one term for each of the seventy-seven cases of murder for which he could be clearly and personally convicted. His former underlings got off more lightly, although the judge considered them as having acted from "base motives," understood as a combination of sadism and hatred of Jews. Hamann's subordinates had tried to gain some leniency for the qualms they had expressed about their misdeeds in Nowy Sącz. "Nobody really wanted to go," said one at the trial about Hamann's spontaneous idea of "kicking up a fuss" on the night of 28 April 1942. "Hamann explained that we had to go. Eventually, nobody really was able to resist him. I guess, at that point we were all afraid of Hamann." Günther Labitzke claimed that he had asked for another assignment in the summer of 1940 when Hamann assigned him to a squad that was to shoot three or four supposed Polish thieves. Hamann had turned him down, referring to an order from above: "Orders are orders." By placing the blame on Hamann and his rigid and brutal personality, the perpetrators attempted to portray themselves as victims.[41] The judge knew better. No police officer, no SS man, no soldier in Nazi Germany ever suffered serious punishment for refusing to participate in the murder of Jews or other civilians.[42] And, as it turned out, none of the Nowy Sącz perpetrators had heard of a colleague being shot for refusing an order to kill civilians either.

Although some of the policemen claimed during their trial in the early 1960s to have wished to get away from Nowy Sącz, none of them provided any proof of ever having seriously applied for a transfer because of the murder of the Jews. Wilhelm Gaschnitz, an officer with the gendarmerie at Nowy Sącz and as such not formally a subordinate of Hamann, once suggested to Hamann that he "might go too far." Hamann told Gaschnitz that he "should not get sentimental." Gaschnitz never mentioned it again. Neither did other local police officers. Nobody wished to upset Hamann or any of the comrades. The police officers might worry about what would happen if Germany lost the war, but they would not reveal such thoughts to Hamann. As the policeman Rouenhoff said, "After all, we weren't complicated figures." If they had been, they would have confused rather than enhanced group cohesion. Bornholt, one of the most brutal of Hamann's accomplices, plainly admitted that he had been aware of committing a wrong. "However, as an SS man I was obliged to join in," he explained. They all had internalized the rules of shame culture. Though a burden, these rules also provided relief and security. During the trial interrogations Gaschnitz explained what made him stay on at the site of mass murder. "Life in Nowy Sącz wasn't too bad. I felt at home in Nowy Sącz."[43] In Nowy Sącz Hamann and his men found, at least temporarily, what they also wanted: a sense of belonging.

And it was not only Nowy Sącz that provided such a home. "The special situation at Auschwitz led to friendships of which I'm still saying today I like to look back on with joy," said former SS man Oskar Groening even sixty years after he had served as a guard and staff in the death camp. Groening often looked at the ramps but he did not "stand" at the ramp nor was he in charge of killing Jews or deciding life and death. He did what many Germans did in various ways—he helped keep the machinery running. And he found his place. "Auschwitz main camp was like a small town. . . . There was a canteen, a cinema, a theater. . . . There were dances—all fun and entertainment." When he left the camp in 1944 he lost a place where he had felt at home, just as Heinrich Hamann's mob did in Nowy Sącz. "I'd left a circle of friends whom I'd got familiar with, I'd got fond of," said Groening.[44]

"They Took It as a Party"

Terror in the East often served as entertainment. In Zhitomir, soldiers could attend special performances of revenge. SS Einsatzkommando 4a was in charge of mass shootings in the area. Jews were to be publicly hanged. It was said they had ill-treated the Ukrainians during the Russian occupation. "The execution was arranged as a form of popular entertainment" and was announced in advance all over town by a Wehrmacht vehicle loudspeaker. "There were soldiers sitting on rooftops and platforms watching the show."[45]

Photos taken at such events do not reveal ashamed spectators but amused ones. They celebrated their splendid community. The "Us" had triumphed over the "other." Kept like trophies, photos of atrocities also illustrated, and were intended to illustrate, the dichotomous social reality of genocide. On the one hand, we see the triumphant group of perpetrators, enjoying themselves committing or watching cruelty. They stick together, they act together, and they feel together. They experience belonging, the epitome of "humanity"—a special notion of "humanity," to be sure. On the other hand, there are the isolated, humiliated, naked victims—frightened and freezing, robbed of the signs of their personal identity, all looking alike, no longer retaining their humanity. Cynically, members of the Einsatzgruppen referred to the manner they piled hundreds of corpses in graves as "sardine procedure." First isolated and then thrown together, they were no longer social beings in the eyes of the perpetrators. "Dissociation" of the victims enhanced "association" of the perpetrators.[46]

The Holocaust did not consist solely of the act of killing the Jews. Before the perpetrators murdered, they felt compelled to humiliate these victims. They mocked them, and they made them stage grotesque ceremonies. This was not just about sadistic pleasure. In the Holocaust, humiliation was arranged as theater. Degradation carries meaning. It is constructive. According to the sociologist Harold Garfinkel, it binds the perpetrators to a collectivity and reinforces their solidarity. By destroying the symbols, the bonds, and the identities of their victims, the perpetrators strengthened their ethics of hardness and thus their own social identity.[47]

Jewish religious symbols and rituals were a favorite target of ridicule. Invading southwest Europe in the summer of 1941, some members of Einsatzkommando 11a suffered from boredom when operations stopped for a time. What could they do? Some Jews were always around to provide "fun." An idle unit in Romania assembled a group of Jews who were made to carry water from a well 150 feet away—but the Jews were told they had to run with the buckets. The Germans formed a line along this path and whipped any Jew who did not run fast enough. Another group of Jews were made to pull heavy carriages and tortured in the same way whenever they did not perform well enough to suit the Germans. A special "Jews Police" was established and equipped with sticks as "weapons." They had to drill and parade in front of the Germans. Above all they were forced to "police" and torture their fellow Jews, thus enacting the disintegration of their own society. Finally, the Jews had to kneel on the ground and stage religious ceremonies and thus mock their own values.[48]

A prelude to the Final Solution appears to have occurred in Białystok only a few days after the German invasion of the Soviet Union. The Wehrmacht entered the city early in the morning of 27 June 1941 practically without a fight. Police Battalion 309 was in charge of cleansing the city of potential resistance. Without any order or plan to kill or even round up the Jews, police officers combed the Jewish sections of city and plundered houses and shops. Jews who looked anything like anti-Semitic stereotypes were favored targets of humiliation. The policemen set their beards on fire, made them dance, or just shot them down. Soon, the police units had worked themselves into an orgy of blood. In the afternoon they drove more and more Jews— men, women, and children—into the main synagogue, shut the doors, and shot whoever tried to escape. Some petrol canisters were fetched and poured inside. It took only a few shells before the building went up in flames. Some seven hundred people suffered an agonizing death. The fire spread to the wooden buildings nearby and destroyed major parts of downtown Bialystok. Approximately two thousand Jews died during this one-day action.[49] They, and at the same time their culture, as represented by the synagogue, were destroyed. The perpetrators survived, their social bonds and their ethics of community intact.

Before, during, and after killing the Jews, the Nazi perpetrators aimed at "Jewishness"—Jewish culture, social life, and solidarity. Rahel Auerbach, a survivor of the Warsaw ghetto, made this point when she testified in the Jerusalem Eichmann trial in 1961. Before the Nazis came, she said, "There was a complete Jewish state there"—vital and intense Jewish life. The "enemy," though, "wanted to destroy us also from the spiritual point of view; this was also a prelude to physical destruction, to humiliate us and to convince their own people and the world at large that this was a nation of parasites who were not fit to live in the world." Auerbach was right. In fact, the Nazis' tactic to demolish Jewish social structures went even further than her testimony revealed. In the ghettos, the Nazis at first actually conceded to allow the Jews to maintain some kind of social organization of their own—but only to make the Jews themselves dissolve it and thus to annihilate the solidarity of the victims even more efficiently. As the German ghetto commissar of Warsaw wrote in a letter to his superiors, it "has turned out most advantageously . . . to allow the Jews maximum freedom to regulate their own affairs inside the district. The entire communal administration lies in their hands." The effect was, he proudly reported, that "when deficiencies occur, the Jews direct their resentment against the Jewish administrations and not against the German supervisors." To be sure, the Nazis did not succeed completely in destroying the bonds of their victims. What made the Nazis' genocidal utopia so monstrous was its consistency in making all kinds of people somehow complicit—even the victims.[50]

Germans were not alone in carrying out the Holocaust. Nor was it only Germans who combined physical, social, and cultural destruction. Throughout Eastern Europe, local populations participated. From the very beginning of the German occupation (and in some places even before), local people organized riots against Jews. In Kovno, Lithuanians murdered some 3,800 Jews in a period of five days in late June 1941, immediately after the invasion of the German army, while the Germans watched. After the war, one of them, the Wehrmacht colonel von Bischoffshaussen, gave a brief report on "probably the most frightful event that I had seen during the course of two world wars. On the concrete forecourt of the petrol station, a blond man of medium height, about twenty-five years old, stood leaning on a wooden club, resting. The club was as thick as his arm and came up to his chest. At his feet lay about fifteen to twenty dead or dying people. Water flowed continuously from a hose washing blood away into the drainage gully. Just a few steps behind this man some twenty men, guarded by armed civilians, stood waiting for their cruel execution in silent submission. In response to a cursory wave the next man stepped forward silently and was beaten to death with the wooden club in the most bestial manner, each blow accompanied by enthusiastic shouts from the audience." Another German witness, an army photographer, said that the killer needed about forty-five minutes to kill about forty-five people. "After the entire group had been beaten to death, the young man put the club to one side, fetched an accordion and went and stood on the mountain of corpses and played the Lithuanian national anthem." His countrymen "joined in singing and clapping. In the front row there were women with small children in their arms who stayed there right until the end of the whole proceeding."[51]

In Lithuania, as well as in other parts of Eastern Europe, most people felt relief when they saw the Soviets depart. Although only a few local Jews had held influential positions under Soviet rule, non-Jews widely believed that the Jews had supported and profited from it. Such perceptions were fueled by long traditions of anti-Semitism and the recent need for scapegoats that could be blamed for the economic misery, political turmoil, and brutal terror to which they had been subjected under the brief Communist occupation after World War I, and even more since Stalin's annexations after his pact with Hitler in 1939. In response, nationalist movements envisioned and planned the liberation of their countries from supposed Jewish Communism—with the help of Nazi Germany. Even before the German invasion, the Lithuanian Activists Front issued leaflets warning that the "crucial day of reckoning has come for the Jews at last." "Lithuania must be liberated," stated a leaflet, "not only from the Asiatic Bolshevik slavery but also from the long standing Jewish yoke."[52] Similar nationalist visions spread over most parts of Eastern Europe. Polish nationalist underground groups, for instance, envisioned that the "liquidation of the Jews in Poland will have a deep impact on our further development as it liberates us from a parasite with millions of heads."[53]

Such was the language of ethnic cleansing and integral nationalism. Its grammar posited the utopia of an ethnically and racially purified nation. All elements seen as alien, as not belonging and different from the Us, would be eliminated, deported, or killed. In pursuing such visions, Eastern European nationalists did not differ much from the Nazis, with whom they collaborated. The obsession with racial and ethnic homogeneity fueled mass violence throughout the twentieth century. Jewish Communists had polluted the community before the Germans arrived, according to these views.[54] Now there was a chance to purify the community, to restore its honor and moral integrity, and to set an intimidating example for the future. For that, massacres were staged as theater. By shaming, torturing, and executing the culprits, the proper order of the community would be reestablished. Thus the "death-dealer" of Kovno and his audience sang the Lithuanian anthem when the deadly cleansing ritual was finished.

Similarly, the Germans in Nowy Sącz concluded the murder of three hundred supposedly Communist Jews with the Horst-Wessel song. When interrogated in the early 1960s, the ex-SA thug Johann Bornholt did not speak of individual intentions or qualms. Rather, he referred to the communal and theatrical experience, which went far beyond instrumental killing. "The members of the Border Police Station," he recalled, "were always happy to join in the execution of Jews, with few exceptions. They took it as a party. . . . Nobody would have missed it."[55] The party united all of them. It granted community and togetherness par excellence.

Deadly terror often took the shape of orgies of destruction, reflecting and at the same time generating a sense of spontaneous community. However, neither in Nowy Sącz nor elsewhere was it just a furious mob that sought revenge and thus spontaneously carried out its part in the Holocaust. Although anti-Semitic pogroms were deeply rooted in the political traditions of Eastern Europe, it required the Nazi occupiers to stimulate and orchestrate local collaboration. Only the German occupiers could integrate indigenous pogroms into systematic genocide. As Walter Stahlecker, chief of the Einsatzgruppe A, reported to SS headquarters in Berlin, his units had initiated anti-Semitic pogroms immediately after the invasion. "The impression had to be created that the local population itself had taken the first steps of its own accord as a natural reaction to decades of oppression by the Jews and the more recent terror exerted by the Communists."[56]

All over Eastern Europe, the German invaders encountered, and could count on, deep resentments against Jews and Communists. Paramilitary or self-appointed police units were ready to join in the murder of the Jews, or they could easily be made to do so.[57] Like the German perpetrators, they were driven by a broad range of motives—revenge for supposed Jewish misdeeds, opportunist adjustment to the new occupiers, greed for Jewish fortunes, or just yearning for a Jewish apartment. Such personal motives were satisfied here and there. The local collaborators' grand vision of national revival, though, was never realized under Nazi rule. At no point did the Germans think of granting sovereignty to the collaborating nations in the East. Instead, these countries always remained mere instruments of Nazi rule. The specific achievement of the Nazi occupiers was their success in first orchestrating local cravings for ethnically homogenous nations, and then in subordinating them to their own vision of an Aryan Volksgemeinschaft ruling over all of them.

"I Don't Want to Bother My Comrades"

A sense of community generated by mass murder was never embraced unanimously. What endured was the integration of different individuals and social entities, of varying degrees of willingness to participate, into a genocidal society. Such a result was not guaranteed. As the perpetrators celebrated their massacres as a party, they momentarily overcame emotional, social, and ideological heterogeneities. But the ecstasy of the genocidal party could not last. Uncertainty and dissenting convictions seethed in the culture of cruelty. They might be hidden behind a mask, as Rudolf Höss put it. Nonetheless, they still existed. Thus, some "tolerance" toward weaklings was needed.

An ethical revolution fueled the Holocaust. Ethics do not change within just a couple of years, however. Pangs of conscience, that is, concessions to traditional ethics, needed to be suppressed with alcohol, stereotyping, and cynicism. In his Posen speech, Himmler did not praise the born killers or the sadists, but excused them as "exceptions due to human weaknesses." They had not overcome or controlled their emotions but rather were given free rein. Yet standards were flexible. Neither Heinrich Hamann nor any of his men was ever prosecuted by their organization. The same laxity governed other practices. At a meeting of high-ranking SS officers in 1943 several commanders expressed concerns about SS men increasingly disregarding the laws on racial defilement (*Rassenschande*); it was assumed that every other SS man serving in the East had "undesirable sexual intercourse with ethnically alien women." But no action was taken. Even Sepp Dietrich, commander of SS *Leibstandarte Adolf Hitler* and an old friend of Hitler, had stated that the orders forbidding intercourse with women of other races did not apply to his troops. Other officers reported that in fact no serious punishment was given for breaking that rule. In a formal opinion prepared for the Auschwitz trials in the 1960s, the historian Hans Buchheim understood these lax practices as " 'tendency toward moderation in practice' counteracting the worship of 'hardness.' . . . Towards others the most utmost cruelty was permissible, but within the fold the weaker brethren was protected. . . . In the name of *camaraderie* increasingly serious failings become acceptable, offences can be covered up; communal dereliction of duty can be concealed both from the authorities and the outside world."[58]

Buchheim's take on camaraderie zeroes in on Nazi ethics. Whatever served to bond people, whatever generated communal spirit, was good, as long as it concerned the right group; whatever challenged it was evil. Hans Frank, the governor-general for the occupied Polish territories, meant nothing else when in 1940 he supported "instructions to police authorities making it obligatory to take some account of the physical state of those charged with carrying out executions." As Frank explained, "every SS or police commander on whom is laid the cruel duty" of these executions "must be one hundred percent clear in his mind that he is acting in fulfillment of a judicial sentence passed by the German nation."[59] Those who demonstrated toughness in perpetrating genocide to save the German nation were eligible for exemption from the rigid rule of toughness. A bit of weakness did not weaken the order of toughness but made it sustainable. Above all, the "tendency toward moderation in practice" fueled the engine of community and spurred its claim for independence. We are different, we have our own rules, and the most important rule is that we can exempt ourselves from our rules. It is always the group interest that defines what, and in which situation, is legitimate or illegitimate.

Flexible rules applied also for those who refused to join in the murder of the Jews. Occasionally the SS leadership worried about mental damage their men might suffer from carrying out face-to-face mass murder. On 15 August 1941, Himmler visited an execution at Minsk together with SS General Erich von dem Bach-Zelewski. The longer the execution went on, the more Himmler's condition deteriorated. Von dem Bach said to him: "Look at the eyes of the men in this Kommando, how deeply shaken they are! These men are finished for the rest of their lives. What kind of followers are we training here? Either neurotics or savages!"[60] Episodes like these stimulated plans and experiments about more anonymous ways of mass killing; eventually they led to the gas vans and the gas chambers. Until then, however, some tolerance toward those who did not meet the bar of toughness was observed. Again, the Nazi ethics revolved around community and cohesion. Toughness came second. He who stuck to the group had a good chance of exemption from the rigidity of hardness.

SS Colonel Ernst Ehlers asked successfully for a discharge when confronted with his assignment as leader of Einsatzkommando 8. He then served on the staff of Einsatzgruppe B, still in Russia and in fact in charge not only of organizing mass murder but also of doing some of the killing. Max Thomas, leader of Einsatzgruppe C, which was responsible for the murder of at least twenty-six thousand Jews in 1941 alone, allowed SS men who were too weak to take part in shootings to be redeployed for other duties or to be sent back home. So did many high or lower rank commanders. Major Trapp, the commander of Police Reserve Battalion 101, fits into this category. When Trapp in July 1942 got the order to kill the Jews in Polish Józefów he informed his officers ahead of time. One of them, Lieutenant Buchmann, although a member of the Nazi Party, made it clear that as a Hamburg businessman he "would in no case participate in such an action in which defenseless women and children are shot." Asking for another assignment, Buchmann was detailed to escort selected "work Jews" to Lublin. When Trapp assembled his men to explain "the battalion's murderous assignment, he made his extraordinary offer: any of the older men who did not feel up to the task that lay before them could step out." At first, only one man stepped forward, provoking the anger of his direct superior. Trapp, however, "cut him off" and took the man under his protection. Then, "some ten or twelve other men stepped forward as well." Trapp himself suffered from qualms about the order; he even cried in front of his men. Eventually, he stayed away from the shooting, thus earning the ill will of his men who had to do the nasty job.[61]

Other Germans, SS men, police officers, and soldiers who refused to commit mass murder faced the same mild consequences as Ehlers and Buchmann. They got other assignments, and though some may have been barred from further promotion, none of them suffered serious damage. What, however, is serious damage? None were executed or jailed. Nevertheless, their reputation stood at risk—not a minor issue in a society that praises group honor rather than individual responsibility. Already before Major Trapp made his generous offer, a hard-liner among the sergeants had warned his men that he "didn't want to see any cowards." A coward was a man who did not perform as a man. He did not stick to the group. He would come under the gaze of those left to carry out the job; he might be shamed, ridiculed, ignored, harassed, isolated, or ostracized. Not even an officer was safe from such treatment. Lieutenant Wolfgang Hoffmann, company leader in RPB 101, often reported sick when it came to shooting assignments. Thus he ruined his authority. His men, who had to do the job, considered him a shirker, calling him a *Pimpf*, a cub—the lowest and youngest category in the Hitler Youth: Lieutenant Hoffmann, the kid.[62]

Martin Mundschütz, member of Einsatzkommando 12 and thus of Einsatzgruppe D, was better off. After having served in various executions by the autumn of 1941, he felt unable to cope with more killing and provided medical papers documenting mental issues. Otto Ohlendorf, the head of the Einsatzgruppe, relieved him from killing and assigned him to the food supply of the unit. Thus, he had to stay with his comrades—who did not leave him in peace but harassed him as an "Austrian wimp." Suffering from depression, Mundschütz finally asked Ohlendorf for a transfer back to his home country. In a letter to his chief he first apologized for not having "performed as a man." "My nerves have failed. That they have failed is only a result of my nervous breakdown three weeks ago which makes me suffer day and night from obsessions that drive me almost mad. Although it seems as if I now manage to handle these obsessions, I apparently still have lost completely the control over my nerves and am no longer able to manage my willpower. I can't suppress my tears. . . . Now I am supposed to drive around shopping. I am asking you to save me from this charge, because I don't want to bother my comrades nor other people with the unhappy performance of a crying soldier. . . . If you, sir, have a heart and understanding for one of your subordinates, who wishes nothing more than to sacrifice himself for Germany but does not want to stage the drama of a supposed wimp, please do remove me from here."[63]

Appealing to the softer side of comradeship, which the SS upheld as did other military and paramilitary troops, or just to "stage the insane," as Mundschütz later explained his strategy, proved to be a successful tactic.[64] His superior knew that Mundschütz's exemption would not undermine the unity of the group; Mundschütz's depression had not done so during a mass execution in Nikolayev, when his comrades had performed with perfect "hardness," humiliating the victims by hitting their genitals and enjoying tea time close to the grave. No executions of Jews had to be cancelled due to a lack of executioners. According to Christopher Browning's investigations and other documents, only a minority of those delegated with the task—less than 20 percent—dared to step aside and thus to be ridiculed and shamed. Asked in 1967 for rough percentages, a former member of the Security Police and SD in Warsaw estimated: "Absolute executors about 30 per cent, the anti-group about 20 per cent, and then a group between, which stuck to the methods of the hellraisers."[65] The majority conformed, and usually the proportion of those who "wanted to be the best" was significantly larger than the proportion of dissenters.

As isolated as the objectors might have felt, they supported the unity of the group. The killing group stuck together and fulfilled its duties, not despite but because of inner fractions, various skills, and different personalities. The objectors were "a 'built-in' out-group" (Albert Cohen) just as any outsiders were. But the objectors also served the group in another way. Although they declined to be directly involved in the killing, they confirmed its moral basis. The police officers of Battalion 101 who stood aside not only had to swallow being labeled "weaklings" or "kids" but had to assess themselves in the same light. In fact they did not claim to be "too good" to kill, but "too weak." They did not question the morality of the community, but instead interpreted their own psychological constitution as abnormal. In opting out, these individuals saw themselves as exceptions to the rule of the symbolic order of the male community on which they were still dependent. They kept a marginal position that alleviated their social isolation. In a culture of dominant "tough" masculinity, they represented the other, and thus helped to make the hegemonic virtues properly visible. Unity requires functional differentiation. Acting together by coming to terms with obstacles and confusion made the community.[66]

"The Mafia Has Always Practiced It"

Often men dropped out only after having participated in one or more executions. So it was with Mundschütz, who became depressed after he had carried out mass murder. Some higher-ranking SS men also asked to be discharged from killing commands only after they had participated for a while. Erwin Schulz, who as head of Einsatzkommando 5 led the execution of Jews in Lvov in July 1941, asked for a transfer as early as August, considering himself too weak for his job. In other cases police officers asked only for exemption from shooting women and children. Apparently commanders were rather tolerant with reliable executioners who suffered from temporary crises. Even Heinrich Hamann was sympathetic when Günther Labitzke, after the mass execution in Mszana-Dolna, felt close to a breakdown.[67] All of these men who suffered from "weakness" had previously proven their "toughness."

Not all commanders were as tolerant as Major Trapp or the Einsatzgruppen commanders Ohlendorf and Thomas, however. Ohlendorf, for instance, did not even observe consistent rules. Mostly, he put massive pressure on his men, in particular the officers, to join killing actions in order to make them "hard as steel so that they would be able to manage the tasks that were still waiting for them."[68] And some commanders were even more rigid. After refusing to execute Jews, Inspector Georg Ulrich was dressed down in front of his comrades by Einsatzgruppe A leader Stahlecker. "He shouted at me," testified Ulrich in 1964, "called me a coward and shirker" and said "that I would be out of place in today's Germany and that he would send me to the front line."[69] (He was not sent to the front line, nor did he suffer any other punishment.) Karl Jäger, head of Einsatzkommando 3, referred to orders "from above" to make all of his men participate in murder.[70] Such orders may never formally have been issued. But many commanders liked to refer to them anyway. Heinrich Hamann cited an order from Himmler according to which "everyone" had to carry out executions, and he made his men comply. In September 1942, when a new member of his police station named Lindert arrived, Hamann ordered him to imprison and then to shoot a Jew. To make sure that the novice would not shirk his duty, a police officer pointedly watched Lindert kill the Jew.[71] Bruno Müller, head of Einsatzkommando 11b and like Hamann known as a brutal and hard-drinking SS man, began a mass execution in early August 1941 by picking a two-year-old child from the gathered crowd of Jews and shooting it, then killing the mother. Having set a "good" example, he asked the other officers to follow. Everyone, he said, had to shoot at least one person.[72] To become one of Us, you had to kill at least once. Only through an "irreversible act" that burned "the bridges to respectable society" could you be trusted and "admitted into the community of violence."[73]

The military in many countries has long offered a model of making individuals accept killing as legal—execution by a firing squad. A group of soldiers is charged with carrying out capital punishment on a delinquent comrade who is convicted of cowardice, desertion or mutiny, or spying. To diffuse responsibility, and to stifle qualms, the executioners are required to shoot simultaneously so that none of them can tell whether he was the one who had fired the lethal bullet. The firing squad represents the epitome of a unit that constructs its bonds through killing and at the same time dispels worries about guilt. This is what Otto Ohlendorf referred to when he said, at the Nuremberg Trial, "In the Einsatzgruppe D the mass executions took place regularly in the form of shooting by details. The shooting by individuals was forbidden in Einsatzgruppe D, so that the men who were to perform the executions were not faced with the task of making personal decisions."[74]

In many ways, of course, the firing squad in a regular army does not have much in common with the modus operandi of Himmler's death squads. The first operates in an at least formally recognized moral and legal framework, even if the shooters might suffer qualms about violating the fundamental "Thou shalt not kill" precept. Himmler's squads, though, did not just kill. They murdered. Anti-Semitic propaganda and the skewed ethics of the Volksgemeinschaft offered ideological justification, but the aura of crime never left the perpetrators. Intoxicated at the party of mass killing, they might forget about responsibility for a while. But what followed were sleepless nights and talks with comrades about what would come after the war. They were never safe from overpowering revulsion in the face of—and of remembering—the piles of bloody mangled bodies, agonies of the dying, crying children, screaming mothers, and maybe even the incredible stoic bravery of many of the victims.

One has to wonder whether the authorities of the Nazi state actually wished to fully relieve the perpetrators of their qualms. In his Posen speech, Himmler did not suppress the aura of crime that surrounded his exclusive public. Rather he ran the gamut of its cohesion-building effects. Just before addressing the murder of the Jews, he reminded the SS elite of the Night of the Long Knives of June 1934, the brutal elimination of internal Nazi Party dissenters and other adversaries in the course of the so-called Röhm Putsch. "We can now very openly talk about this among ourselves," Himmler said, "and yet we will never discuss this publicly. Just as we did not hesitate on

30 June 1934 to do our duty as ordered and put comrades who had failed up against the wall and execute them, we also never spoke about it, nor will we ever speak about it."[75]

The emphasis on secrecy deserves attention. Although Himmler considered the Night of the Long Knives and the murder of the Jews as justified for the good of the Volksgemeinschaft, they were to be treated as secrets. For the murder of the Jews an entire language was invented to hide what actually happened; Final Solution is only one example.[76] Talking too openly about the Holocaust or even spreading rumors about the death machinery was a risky thing in Nazi Germany; people were penalized for doing so.[77] At the same time, the Holocaust was no secret. Neither was it really meant to be kept as such. It was an open secret. Elaborating on the mass shootings in fall 1941, Hitler found it "just fine that the horror of our exterminating the Jews hurries on ahead."[78] The Nazis constructed a cult of secrecy that radiated monstrous moral transgression. The secret, asserts the sociologist Georg Simmel, is "the sociological expression of moral badness." Employed as a "sociological technique," wrote Simmel, secrecy fosters inclusion and exclusion; it separates those who know and are included from those who do not and who are excluded.[79] Secrecy is the glue of conspiracy based on breaking the norm. Thus, fraternities and brotherhoods throughout history have embedded their cohesion in a cult of secret symbols and rituals. Initiation rituals force the novices to break normal taboos and sacrileges, to separate themselves from mainstream society and become members of countersocieties of sorts, and to keep the brotherhood's secrets forever.[80] In the Holocaust, the cult of secrecy worked accordingly. It enhanced the social cohesion of the perpetrators' network and underscored the difference between them and the rest of the world.

Asked to join an "action" against a camp of fifty Jewish women and children in late summer 1941, Police Commissar Harm Harms refused, but his colleague Böhme decided, "You have to join in too . . . you'll get a SS uniform and a formal order." Then, considering that Harms was the father of a family, Böhme relented, but he had an alternate scheme. One of Böhme's comrades took photos of the "action," showing an SS man grabbing a naked Jewish woman by her hair and shooting her in the neck. After the "action," the executioners confronted Harms with these photos because the taking (and showing) of photos of these "actions" were strictly forbidden.[81] But nobody cared. In truth, the prohibition was not strictly enforced, neither in this unit nor elsewhere. And there was some reasoning behind that contradiction. Banning photos and spreading them anyway fostered an aura of secrecy surrounding the murder of the Jews that made sure that the perpetrators would not forget what separated them from the rest of the world. Himmler's SS men and police officers knew they had abandoned the morality of the civilized world, and they should be aware of that fact. They should know that they belonged to a very different society, and leaving it was not an option. And so it was with Harms, who would still remember his complicity when he gave testimony during the Ulm Einsatzgruppen trial in 1956.[82]

Nothing serves better to unite people than committing crimes together. The aura of secrecy demands cohesion, forges the spirit of community, and creates a particular kind of belonging—the consciousness of a revolutionary and yet criminal gang. Erik H. Erikson has called Hitler a "gang leader, who kept the boys together by demanding their admiration, by creating terror, and by shrewdly involving them in crimes from which there was no way back."[83] Hitler indeed was well aware of the sociology of crime. In a speech in Munich in 1923, talking about radical political movements, he presented it as a political prescription. "There are two things which can unite men; common ideals and common criminality."[84] In 1934, the Night of the Long Knives indeed instituted community building by criminal means in Nazi Germany. Members of the SS and the Reichswehr jointly carried out the murders, thus driving the new and the old machinery of the Nazi state on a track with no way back. With the Holocaust the ultimate goal of uniting people by criminal means was reached. Applying Himmler's logic, committing genocide merged a huge variety of different perpetrators, collaborators, and accomplices into a single community from which it was not possible to resign.

Not all of them were equally eager. Nor could they be considered equally reliable. The problem with accomplices and collaborators was that if they had "betrayed once . . . they can betray again. It is not enough to relegate them to a marginal task; the best way to bind them is to burden them with guilt, cover them with blood, compromise them as much as possible, thus establishing a bond of complicity so that they can no longer turn back. This way of proceeding has been well known to criminal associations of all times and places. The Mafia has always practiced it."[85] This is how Primo Levi described the steps the Nazis took to make even Jewish victims—the Kapos in the concentration camps—fuel the machinery of death. Levi's observations, however, apply even more to the broad range of German perpetrators and local collaborators all over Europe. The "Mafia principle" united the hard-core group of fanatic, eliminationist anti-Semites and included murderers, occasional doubters, more serious dissenters, and unwilling yet submissive collaborators. They came from different social backgrounds, classes, denominations, age groups, and regions. They were involved at different levels. At the same time, they all worked on establishing the new murderous society.

Any society needs structure and thus hierarchies, based on the ownership of, or access to, various sorts of capital. In the capitalist society economic power is decisive, but networking (social capital) and education (symbolic capital) is important as well, as the French sociologist Pierre Bourdieu has shown.[86] The Nazi state introduced two new kinds of capital that promised to revolutionize the entire society completely—race and ethnic origin on the one hand and hardness and mercilessness on the other. Those who were considered lacking the physical capital of healthy blood were sent to death right away or placed at the lowest level of the society. Local collaborators in the East (and in the West) were granted the status of junior partners, without offering them any chance of sovereignty. The hierarchy within the "master race," however, relied on ideological commitment and the ability to overcome the old moral order of universal rights. The more mercilessly a man behaved in the grand annihilation of Jews, the greater his chance to climb the hierarchical ladder in Himmler's police and terror empire, which was to serve as the elite. Toughness and mercilessness against the perceived enemies served as the crucial symbolic capital to stratify the Volksgemeinschaft.

When Himmler praised the toughness of his elite troop in late 1943, the project of building the new society was still in its infancy. To that society the subjugated territories in the East served as a huge training camp and moral purgatory, thus following the model of the military and paramilitary camps within Germany. Like the inmates of these training camps, the German occupiers in the East were disconnected from their families, neighbors, social clubs, and all the civilian rules to which they had been accustomed. Those rules—the ethics of home—no longer counted. "At an official meeting last Saturday we have decided to behave, as officials, exactly the other way round than at home, that is, like bastards. We consider greeting a Pole as inappropriate. Of course, I go through the door first, if a Polish woman is there." This is how the German city governor of Lublin, Dr. Fritz Cuhorst, concluded a report in December 1939. As "the standards back home in Germany cannot be applied here," terror against Jews needed no further justification.[87]

Himmler's cult of secrecy, Cuhorst's commitment to loutishness, Felix Landau's inner monologue on mercilessness, Major Trapp's offer of choices, Heinrich Hamann's pressure on his men to join in murder—all this does not indicate a complete loss of the ethics of individual responsibility or of guilt. It illustrates rather the moral tensions caused by the perpetrators' actions. Occasionally these tensions may have blocked this or that perpetrator from joining in enthusiastically enough, but basically they forged the bonds of the genocidal society. Uniting people by collective crime works best if people are aware of their crime, thus of their separation from the rest of the world. This is what Himmler's, Cuhorst's, Landau's, and all the others' considerations and confessions were about. They all worked on constructing the SS, its respective organizations, and eventually the entire Volksgemeinschaft as outcasts—as pariahs, although as a special type of pariahs.[88]

In his 1923 speech Hitler had envisioned this Volksgemeinschaft. "Domestic cleansing" of the "traitors"—the Jews—would be the necessary precondition to any liberation of the nation, Hitler said. Fighting against Germany's continual humiliation since 1918 should be the only goal that counted, he declared. Which weapons would be used should not matter. "Be that weapon human or not! . . . If we look into the eyes of demanding German children, if we face millions of German comrades [*Volksgenossen*] suffering blamelessly from that terrible disaster, then we laugh at being cursed by the entire world, if this curse only comes with freedom for our race!"[89] Twenty years later, when the success of the Final Solution and Germany's military disaster became apparent, Goebbels agreed with Göring about "what would threaten us all were we to weaken in this war."

Both knew. "On the Jewish question in particular we are so committed that there is no escape for us at all. And," noted Goebbels in his diary in March 1943, "that is good. Experience shows that a movement and a *Volk* that have burned their bridges fight much more unconditionally than those who still have the chance of retreat."[90] Goebbels was right. Not only the Nazi movement nor even just the SS, but the entire German nation would adopt the pariah role Hitler had envisioned so long ago.

FOUR

Spreading Complicity

Pleasure and Qualms in the Cynical Army

In late June 1941 three million German soldiers invaded the Soviet Union on a front of almost one thousand miles and chalked up incredible gains. Within four weeks they destroyed thousands of Soviet tanks and aircraft and took more than five hundred thousand Soviet prisoners. By the end of July the Wehrmacht was poised to take Kiev, Leningrad, and Moscow. The grand vision of *Lebensraum* for the German Volksgemeinschaft seemed imminent. By 3 July, Franz Halder, chief of the *Oberkommando des Heeres* (General Staff of the Army, or OKH), declared, "The Russian campaign has been won in the space of two weeks." On 16 July, Hitler assured his entourage that Germany would never leave the vast territories in the East. Many ordinary soldiers were even more intoxicated with omnipotence and grandiosity. With the troops invading Lithuania, Private Albert Neuhaus, a Westphalian grocer, was sure that "the impetuous German advance cannot be stopped. Such an advance has never been seen in the world." Hitler's Volksgemeinschaft was at its peak. A soldier known only as Lieutenant Otto D. bragged, "What a divine people we are! Could the Führer's claim of German leadership in Europe be better justified?"[1]

Not all soldiers shared this enthusiasm, however. Fritz Farnbacher, a clerk from Nuremberg who was proud to be a lieutenant in the prestigious Fourth Tank Division, felt uneasy about the "strange war" in Russia, as he noted in his diary on 22 June, the day of the attack. It wasn't so much the "pictures of death" and the horribly mutilated bodies along the battlefields that worried him, for he had seen them before in Poland and France. And he wasn't any more afraid to die than anybody else, especially, because, as a believing Protestant, he knew that "I am not subject to a blind fate." What confused him first were the enemy civilians. They weren't as horrible looking as he had been led to expect. "Actually, they are not disagreeable," he wrote, and their behavior is "astonishingly decent." More worries were caused by his German comrades. Though "of course" the troops had to be "fed off the land," it bothered him a lot that "all manner of things are being 'pinched.'" His comrades did not waste time before they started "requisitioning," the units jealously competing with each other for the bigger and more valuable hauls. On 24 June, Farnbacher's division reached Kobrin in Belarus. Walking through the city, he saw the synagogue set afire by the Germans. "The fire spreads out as a cancerous ulcer," a perfect setting for plunder all around, he observed. "I enter a bank. As everywhere else, it is all ransacked here. . . . All useful stuff has been taken away, the division staff having 'collected' the last typewriter." He wonders if the local people around won't think it is even worse than with the Communists before: "Have they ever seen such destruction before?"[2]

"Something very unpleasant," which Farnbacher "had not thought possible," occurred in late July, three hundred miles closer to Moscow. His unit picked up a string of Russian deserters, among them a Jew whom they "somehow suspect to be a commissar or some such. . . . They decide to shoot the Jew because commissars are to be shot, according to a higher order. That is extended to Jews." First, though, the "very dashing" Major Hoffmann interrogated the suspect. By means of his "Jew comforter," a sturdy stick, the major tried to beat the whereabouts of other commissars out of the suspect. Farnbacher found it "terribly spine-chilling." After innumerable kinds of mistreatment the Jew was led off to be shot. Before Farnbacher heard how it ended, he had entered into his diary, "I don't know whether he actually is shot; I don't even want to know." However, "as I learn later on the Jew actually was bumped off."[3]

Farnbacher knew about international laws of war; he was aware of soldierly traditions of chivalry toward the defeated enemy soldier and of mercy to the enemy civilian. He realized that none of them mattered in this "strange war." The truth was that he too did not always care that much about them. Early in July, after having heard that some men of his unit had been brutally mutilated by the Russians—"the skulls smashed and pierced by bayonets"—he concluded that the German soldiers "should not be too lenient," and agreed with his comrades that they should take no more prisoners. So he felt no pity for the more than one hundred partisans shot by "our motorcycle soldiers." Indeed, partisans did not enjoy protection by the Geneva Convention or other war laws. But it was not clear what they had done. In fact, in the Soviet Union at that time no real partisan movement yet existed. But having seen their comrades mutilated, the German soldiers were thirsty for revenge and not about to waste time asking questions. Once the dynamic of brutality was launched, it did not stop; Major Hoffmann soon became known for his boast of setting Russian villages on fire every night. Farnbacher remained passive in face of plunder, murder, and torture. Passive was also the language he used to join in. Though shocked by the greed of his comrades—"You have to look into their eyes and at their hands, how they yaw and grasp"—he "willingly" kept a piece of soap that "is brought to me." Soon after, when the neighboring battery "received" a barrel of pickles, Farnbacher decided, "I accepted a couple of them and enjoyed them. We aren't really that bad off!"[4]

Farnbacher was among the approximately seventeen million German men who served in the Wehrmacht during World War II; most of them, approximately ten million, served at some point on the Eastern front.[5] They were from all levels of German society—middle class, working class, peasantry, and some from the aristocracy. They were Catholics, Protestants, or atheists (plus a very few "part Jews" who managed to hide in the Wehrmacht). They ranged from apolitical, including those who kept some distance from the Nazi regime based on religious, socialist, liberal, or even conservative backgrounds, to fanatic Nazis. Many embraced military service as the ultimate test of their maleness; others hated it as the epitome of the "rape of one's own life."[6] Some had volunteered; most had been drafted. On the Eastern front and also in other theaters, they carried out criminal and genocidal war whether, like Major Hoffmann, they were ready to murder without compunction or just lacked conviction like Lieutenant Farnbacher. Either way, soldiers knew about the mass crime committed by Germans. They thus became part of a huge brotherhood of crime and bad conscience. This chapter tracks the various ways soldiers acted to murder civilians, refused to do so, or just stood by. It explores how a mutual sense of belonging emerged out of the diversity in Hitler's army.

"We Must Forget the Concept of Comradeship Between Soldiers"

The *Oberkommando der Wehrmacht* (High Command of the Armed Forces, or OKW) issued the "higher order" on 6 June 1941 as "Instructions on the Treatment of Political Commissars." It was the second of two decrees laying the pseudo-legal ground for criminal warfare. It blamed the commissars of the Red Army, who actually were in charge of political indoctrination, as originators of "barbaric, Asiatic methods of warfare," so that to consider them "in accordance with international rules of war is wrong and endangers both our own security and the rapid pacification of conquered country." They were not to be "treated as soldiers. The protection afforded by international law to prisoners of war is not to be applied in their case. After they have been segregated they will be liquidated."[7] Pervasive anti-Semitism in the Wehrmacht meant that Jews were considered the same as commissars, so of course they, too, had to be shot.

Whereas the Commissar Order directed the murder of an at least vaguely defined and limited group of persons, Hitler's "Decree on the Conduct of Courts-martial in the District of 'Barbarossa' and for Special Measures of the Troops," issued on 13 May 1941, went much further.[8] According to international laws and conventions of warfare, the German army as the occupation regime was required to provide legal jurisdiction for enemy civilians. According to the Jurisdiction Decree, though, in the Soviet Union the German army was to defend itself "ruthlessly against any threat by the enemy civil population," and not waste time on handling judical issues of enemy civilians. There was no law whatsoever for the subjugated people. Moreover, it stated that in a country full of enemies attacking German soldiers from behind, "guerillas" were "to be killed ruthlessly by the troops in battle or during pursuit," or even after their capture, once they had become POWs. The decree went on to order "collective punitive measures by force to be carried out immediately" against villages from which the Wehrmacht was "insidiously and maliciously attacked." Ultimately, the decree allowed

German soldiers to do whatever they liked to enemy civilians by guaranteeing amnesty in advance. "For offenses committed by members of the Wehrmacht and its employees against enemy civilians, prosecution is not compulsory, not even if the offense is at the same time a military crime or violation." As Field Marshal Fedor von Bock noted after reading the Jurisdiction Decree in early June, it "virtually" gave "every soldier the right to shoot from in front or behind any Russian he takes to be—or claims that he takes to be—a guerilla." The two orders declared de facto open season on both prisoners of war and the civilian population of the occupied areas of the USSR.[9]

But the criminal orders were not promulgated to secure German soldiers a playground of sadism. Rather, the Soviet theater was designed to become a training field in Nazi ethics. Young German men were to be rid of soldierly universal ethics, the ideals of chivalry toward the defeated enemy soldier and of mercy for the enemy civilian. Already in a secret meeting on 30 March 1941, more than two months before the Russian campaign, Hitler announced to some 250 Wehrmacht generals: "We must forget the concept of comradeship between soldiers. A communist is no comrade before or after the battle," he said. The war on Russia would be the ultimate "clash of two ideologies," a "war of extermination." "Bolshevism," the epitome of "social criminality," had to be destroyed once and forever. "If we do not grasp this, we shall still beat the enemy, but thirty years later we shall again have to fight the communist foe."[10]

Such rhetoric cleverly incorporated some traditional military thinking such as the "either-you-or-me" alternative, familiar to any soldier fighting in battle. Killing the enemy soldier is legitimate, in particular if it is the only way to save one's own life. Hitler, though, radicalized such soldierly commonsense morals by demonizing the enemy: the Jew, the Communist, the Slav is so barbaric, the orders and Hitler said, that we cannot stick to the rules of humanity if we want to defend ourselves. "In the east, harshness today means leniency in the future. Commanders must make the sacrifice of overcoming their personal scruples."

Hitler's speech and the two criminal orders were in effect commands to act illegally and immorally. And those in command would get the message. Carrying the seal "top secret," they were to be passed to the lower ranks only orally and only a couple of hours before the 22 June attack began, thus sending the German soldiers into a moral no-man's-land with no way back.[11] Invading the Soviet Union, they would have to internalize merciless-ness and to share in a distinctive community from which traditional moral considerations had been eliminated. And the Jurisdiction Decree went even further. By conjuring Germany's humiliation in 1918, its suffering afterward, and the "numerous blood sacrifices" of the Nazi movement, all of which "were decidedly due to Bolshevist influence" and which "no German has forgotten," the decree stirred a climate of revenge. Blaming Bolshevism for "1918" justified any treatment of Russian civilians in 1941. Such thinking was a result of the Nazi community ethics, which denied personal responsibility in order to stress collective guilt. So, the message to the Wehrmacht soldiers in Russia was not just to do what you want with the enemies, but to know that the more you mistreat them the better for the German Volksgemeinschaft.

In fact, the German army had blurred the boundaries between regu-lar, antipartisan, and genocidal warfare long before 1941. Traumatized by their fear of guerilla fighters, dubbed "franc-tireurs" in the Franco-Prussian war of 1870–71, the military had developed a "realistic" theory of "military necessities" to annul conventions of humanity in war and international war laws. Dealing with existential emergencies in war required "terrorism" as a "necessary military principle," when it came to striking down any "popu-lar uprising." The infamous "Belgian atrocities," the massacre of civilians including women and children in 1914, showed how far the German mili-tary was willing to go when it came to "military necessity." In World War II, terrorizing civilians was to become the preemptive German response to fear of guerilla resistance, in particular when such fear was intensified by rumors of mutilated or tortured German soldiers.[12] Fear of guerillas was fear of one's own weakness—of the dissolution of troop unity. Such fears could be countered only by demonstrating absolute strength. Any kind of civilian resistance, real or imagined, should be taken as a provocation that automati-cally required violent counteraction to reestablish the honor and unity of the troops. "Military necessity" left no choices. All had to stick together to perform strength through brutality. "Military necessity" fueled groupthink and escalated violence; combined with eliminatory racism, it blended tradi-tional with genocidal warfare.

According to Nazi propaganda, Poles and Jews in particular were subhuman beings threatening everything Germans worshipped—German blood, German culture, and German civilization. When the attack on Poland began, propaganda hammered into the minds of Wehrmacht soldiers a derogatory image of the Poles as inferior but fanatically angry and capable of sabotage and other vicious attacks. The German soldiers, invading Poland, indeed encountered a reality that seemed to verify and even to trump the propaganda. Often, for the first time, they saw the unusual appearance of orthodox East European Jews—"countless oriental or oriental-seeming individuals with unusually long side-locks and bushy, unkempt beards."[13] The lesson to be drawn from encountering the "other" seemed clear. "In Bricza we understood the need of a radical solution to the Jewish question," explained a private. "There you could see these monsters in disguise. With their beards and caftans, with their grotesque faces they gave a horrible impression. Everyone who was not already a radical anti-Semite would necessarily become one there."[14] Minor or even alleged partisan attacks and a very few Polish atrocities stimulated fear and overreactions among the troops.[15] As one lieutenant observed on 2 September 1939, "Our men are still somewhat nervous. The guards smell a sniper behind every bush. Sometimes, a particularly nervous one shoots at his shadow." Another officer diagnosed even a "guerilla-psychosis" spreading through the troops.[16]

The occupiers could not accept resistance nor could they admit fear. Resistance cast doubt on their alleged racial superiority, and fear eroded their social cohesion. "Courteous treatment will be seen as weakness," the soldiers were advised.[17] Thus "military necessity" commanded brutal reaction, in order to guarantee unity and integrity—integrity no longer defined by chivalry and humanity but by group honor, the same code of honor that rules in societies and gangs that lack or despise law enforcement. There are no individual responsibilities, only collective ones. By that code, communal force has to be exerted against those who wrong members of your own group. The group establishes itself by taking revenge, even for acts anticipated in the future. It must execute retribution to secure its own identity.

Apotheosizing the cult of honor, German soldiers did not bother with prosecuting partisans individually but took revenge on randomly chosen members of their "clans," for instance, the inhabitants of a village or town.

On 3 September 1939, the Germans marched into the town of Wieruszów in Poland and "led twenty Jews into the marketplace and shot them," reported a survivor. "Liebe Lewi, the daughter of Israel Lewi, ran over to her father to bid him farewell. The German brutes ordered her to open her mouth for this imprudence, fired a bullet into it and she fell dead on the spot." The Germans forced the remaining Jews between the ages of seventeen and forty to run a gauntlet of abuse and then herded them into vans to be deported to internment and labor camps. The vans carried the inscription "They shot at Germans." Nobody knew who actually had shot at them, but the codes of collective responsibilities and group honor did not require details.[18]

The campaign in Poland in the fall of 1939 provided a training ground for mercilessness that hadn't existed in Germany. The aim of the war, Hitler announced to the military leaders in August 1939, would be the "elimination of living forces, not the arrival at a certain line."[19] Although the murder of Polish civilians was assigned to the SS, once in Poland, Wehrmacht soldiers often willingly joined in to rob, torture, or even kill civilians—Jews in particular. For the victims, there wasn't much difference between the SS and the Wehrmacht. In Poland, German soldiers could sow the wild oats they had never dared dream of sowing on the Rhine or the Mosel. Marcel Reich-Ranicki, deported as a young German Jew to Poland in 1938, remembered German soldiers robbing, humiliating, and murdering Jews— and having fun "hunting down the Jews. . . . Any German who wore a uniform and had a weapon could do whatever he wished with a Jew in Warsaw. He could compel him to sing or to dance or to shit in his trousers, or to go down on his knees and beg for his life. He could suddenly shoot him dead or kill him in a slower, more torturous manner. He could order a Jewish woman to undress, to clean the street with her underwear and then, in front of everybody, to urinate. There was no one to spoil the fun of those German troops, no one to stop them from maltreating Jews."[20] From 1 September 1939, no day passed without soldiers, SS men, or police officers shooting, beating, or stabbing Jews to death, hanging them or burning them alive. Non-Jewish Poles were fair game as well. By that December, Germans had slaughtered—outside of combat—about fifty thousand Poles, seven thousand of them Jews. The Wehrmacht did not stand aside. Already by early October, their squads had executed no fewer than sixteen thousand Poles, both Jewish and non-Jewish.[21]

Yet not all parts of the Wehrmacht supported the murder and torture of civilians. Numerous commanders despised what their troops and the SS were doing. They often court-martialed the Wehrmacht's rank and file for plundering, indiscriminately destroying houses, needlessly slaughtering livestock, and especially for rape. Wehrmacht officers risked open conflicts with SS leaders when they challenged them for rounding up and shooting civilians or for attacking Jews specifically. In some cases, Wehrmacht commanders even court-martialed SS men for crimes against civilians.[22] On 19 and 20 September 1939, Eduard Wagner, quartermaster general of the Wehrmacht, and Walther von Brauchitsch, commander-in-chief of the army, protested to Heydrich and Hitler against the actions of the SS in Poland. Such protests and actions taken against the brutal treatment of civilians were motivated not least by fears of losing disciplinary control over the troops. But senior officers also despised the moral grammar of genocidal warfare as it crystallized from September 1939 on. In February 1940 Colonel General Johannes Blaskowitz submitted a formal note to Brauchitsch to articulate widespread discontent within the officer corps about the murder of the Jews in Poland. Anticipating increasing Polish resistance as well as "dreadful damages to the body of the German people," he prophesized a "tremendous brutalization and moral profligacy that will spread like a pest in precious German manpower." What Blaskowitz criticized, though, was exactly what Nazi leaders wanted: a moral revolution through genocidal warfare to create the merciless Volksgemeinschaft. Already on 4 October 1939, Hitler had issued a secret blanket amnesty for crimes committed by Germans on Poles during the campaign—a clear signal to soldiers like Wagner and Brauchitsch.[23]

"The Troops Must Do Their Share"

During the Polish campaign—and also that occurring in France in May and June 1940[24]—the illusion could still be nourished that Wehrmacht atrocities were mere aberrations from the rule of chivalrous warfare. The war on Russia would change the rule itself. In spring 1941, orders from Hitler as well as OKW decrees stipulated again that the SS Einsatzgruppen would be in charge of those "special tasks" that arose from the "final struggle between two opposing political systems" in the Soviet Union. On their own responsibility, the Einsatzgruppen were to execute "measures with respect to the civilian population."[25] By now the Wehrmacht did not even intend to stand aside. On 6 May 1941, Franz Halder stated that the troops "must do their share in the ideological struggle of the Eastern Campaign."[26]

How they would do so was the subject of extensive planning long before the mid-1941 attack on the USSR. With Germany's World War I hunger crises and the strikes on the home front in mind, the OKW and leading Nazi officials decided that the army would not just live off the occupied land but would send huge amounts of foodstuff back home to Germany. What that meant for Russia was that "umpteen million people will starve to death, if we extract from them the least we need."[27] A similar disaster of unthinkable proportions was anticipated for Soviet prisoners of war. Germany had signed the 1929 Geneva Convention on the treatment of POWs, and an OKW order from 16 June 1941 claimed that they were observing it. The very same order contains, however, stipulations that constituted a massive flouting of the Convention. Not only would Soviet prisoners be sent to forced labor in Germany; they were also to work for the Wehrmacht and thus against their homelands. Or they were to be simply shut up in huge, overcrowded compounds where they would be without shelter and cut off from possible Red Cross aid. Finally, the crucial issue of how to feed them was supposedly postponed by that order, but further planning in spring 1941 left no doubt that the captured Soviet soldiers would receive only the poorest quality food and not even enough of that for survival.[28]

All this became brutal reality. The troops did "their share." Tens, possibly hundreds of thousands of Soviet POWs were "liquidated" immediately after capture, whether as alleged commissars or just because their captors did not want to bother with transport and custody. Often blatant racial superiority was reason enough. "If stupidity caused pain, these creatures would do nothing but cry. . . . Those who fall and can't get up during long POW marches are just shot in the neck, so that the rest do not lose the pace," reported a Wehrmacht soldier annoyed with the "Soviet paradise" in August 1941.[29] Many, many more perished later in prison camps. All in all, more than half of the 5.7 million Red Army soldiers captured by the Wehrmacht died wretchedly as a result of the "hunger plan" or from inadequate care and shelter, or because they were worked to death as slave laborers in the Reich's armament industry. Roughly 2.8 million civilians and POWs were forced into abusive labor service. Recruiting them was the job of German labor authorities, who relied on army and police support. Often acting like colonial slave hunters, Wehrmacht soldiers were responsible for the seizure of about half of them.[30]

Without the Wehrmacht's support, the Einsatzgruppen could not have killed more than a million Jews in just a few months. Wehrmacht headquarters registered the Jews of a region or city, forced them to wear visible identification, and concentrated them in ghettos. To carry out mass executions Wehrmacht soldiers rounded up the victims and herded them to the execution sites, which the soldiers then shielded from public view. Sometimes the victims were even made to dig the mass graves. Sonderkommando 4a of Einsatzgruppe C murdered more than thirty thousand Jews on 29 and 30 September in Babi Yar, near Kiev, after which it gladly reported to Berlin headquarters on the "excellent working climate with all Wehrmacht duty stations" they had developed.[31]

Individual soldiers and sometimes entire units joined in when the shootings started. Or a unit would initiate mass murder itself. The 707th Infantry Division did so in Belorussia. "We are now busy hunting . . . Jewish partisans," wrote a company commander to his brother in October 1941. "There are always some wild goings on here. . . . We're clearing out the whole lot—just your kind of thing." When that company went on patrol, the commander took along only volunteers, as a soldier testified during a trial after the war. Although these "actions" officially were directed against partisans, "it was generally known in the company that this meant Jews who were in no way partisans." In fact, these soldier volunteers murdered as cynically and cold-bloodedly as the SS, German police officers, and local collaborators did. "Our returning comrades-in-arms tell us that they . . . shot several Jewish families. . . . One of the company . . . said, in his exact words, 'Jew brain, that tastes good.' He said they had just shot Jews, and their brains had sprayed him right in the face."[32] Another soldier reported in July 1942 that in Belarusian Biaroza, "where I just had lunch," 1,300 Jews had been shot the day before: "They had been transferred to a hollow outside of the town; men, women and children had to strip to the buff and were shot in the neck. The clothes were disinfected to be reused. If the campaign continues much longer, they will have to make sausages of the Jews and offer them to the Russian POWs or the skilled Jewish laborers."[33]

The majority of Wehrmacht soldiers did not join in murdering the Jews. Nor did they all approve of such acts. But the private letters and diaries of many soldiers across all military ranks, social classes, and ideological backgrounds suggest widespread approval of German terror against Jews. Fighting in the north of Russia, Albert Neuhaus agreed that "here in former Lithuania" there is "too much Jewishness" (*ziemlich viel verjudet*) and found it OK that "there is given no quarter." Occupying Riga in July 1941, Helmut Wißmann, son of a left-wing working-class family, wondered in a letter to his "little cherub" whether it might be "possible to ever exterminate this pest?" He had just learned that "in Lithuania they had hanged all Jews with no exception." In early August 1941, Private Franz Wieschenberg, a Catholic craftsman, reported to his wife "how the Jews in a town we just conquered had to move out of their party offices and to march through the streets on their way to the stake, carrying photos of Stalin and Molotov in front of them—that was a sight for sore eyes. What fun!" Such sights seemed to validate popular anti-Semitism in Nazi Germany. "The Jews move away, they move through the Red Sea, the waves go back to normal, and the world is given peace," was a favorite song verse of anti-Semites. Wieschenberg's comrades loved to sing it.[34]

Like the soldiers in Poland, soldiers in Russia as well saw themselves as crusaders in defense of a superior culture and translated primitive living conditions as diabolic mentalities. "The conditions here are antediluvian. Our propaganda has certainly not exaggerated but rather understated things," claimed a corporal in late August 1941. "Hygiene is something totally foreign to these people. You folks back home in our beautiful Fatherland cannot imagine what it's like," tank commander Karl Fuchs wrote to his mother. "These people here live together with the animals, indeed they live like animals." In a letter to his wife, he praised an evening with comrades "under the Russian sky" singing German folk songs. "While we sang, our native Germany materialized in front of us. Our homeland seemed more magnificent and beautiful than ever before. . . . No matter where you look, there is nothing but dirty, filthy cabins. . . . We now realize what our great German Fatherland has given its children. There exists only one Germany in the entire world."[35]

In the East, Hitler's Volksgemeinschaft took its most glorious shape. But it was soaked with fear. "The German people have a great obligation to our Führer," wrote a corporal in mid-July 1941. "If these beasts who are our enemies here had come to Germany, murders would have occurred such as the world has never seen." "They all look emaciated and the wild, half-crazy look in their eyes makes them appear like imbeciles," said Karl Fuchs. "And these scoundrels, led by Jews and criminals, wanted to imprint their stamp on Europe." Fuchs was raised in a militarist middle-class Nazi family, but the experiences of soldiers with very different backgrounds confirmed the Nazi propaganda for them as well. Even students of Catholic theology, though keeping some distance from Nazism, could see themselves as "crusaders" against "godless powers." "The newsreels were just fantastic and horrifying," wrote Wißmann. "Hopefully, the beasts will soon be defeated." And a couple of months later: "The Führer is completely right. . . . Nobody can tell me a thing about communism. . . . All they have here is pests and rubbish, not culture and civilization as we know it." Everywhere there were "masses of Jews," observed Stefan Schmidhofer, a lower-class Bavarian. Well-versed in Nazi clichés about the insidious Jew, he was easily able to understand the "strange" fact that some of them spoke "a bit of German." It was just a trick, a pretext of familiarity, he explained in a letter to his girlfriend. "They're like a gang of Pharisees you will believe, worse than any cartoon in the *Stürmer*."[36]

Under Soviet rule from late 1939 on, a large number of civilians in the Baltic countries, Belarus, and the Ukraine had been imprisoned. When the Red Army withdrew from the German invasion in June 1941, the Soviet NKVD murdered thousands of them. When the Germans invaded the Ukraine in late June 1941, they revealed these massacres. Nazi propagandists took them as a gift and left no doubt that the Jews stood behind such Communist cruelty. SS units stood ready to guide Wehrmacht soldiers to piles of mutilated corpses of mostly Polish civilians. What made the news of NKVD atrocities so powerful, though, was that they paralleled rumors of Russian partisan attacks and cruel mutilations of the bodies of German soldiers. In summer 1941, such attacks were, in fact, rare but made real previously fabricated clichés of the "Bolshevik-Jewish" enemy in the East, intensifying ubiquitous fears of Them, and stimulating a climate of revenge. In short, they fed the soldiers' Us. Sergeant-major Christoph Banse reported to his wife in July 1941, "You get an idea of the chosen people. The Jews here also organized the cruelties against Ukrainians." Conflating large-scale NKVD massacres of Ukrainians with rare Russian partisan attacks in the war, Banse went on: "And German soldiers also have been victimized by the deviousness of these dirty bastards. Thus we Germans have no longer any reason to spare these creatures. Currently, they count less for us than a dog."[37]

Revenge in fact became the standard reaction to partisan attacks. Also in July 1941, Private Herbert Veigel had faced "seventeen comrades murdered in the cruelest way. When we arrived shortly after the attack, some of them were still alive. All of them were cruelly mutilated. They had cut out the heart of one of them and put it on his stomach; they had stripped the 'face and pulled off the skin of another. . . . As reprisal, some soldiers went and burned the entire village down, where the Russians came from." They didn't care whether any of the inhabitants had supported the partisans. Frustration with partisan attacks caused even previously reluctant soldiers to join in criminal warfare. Since 1939 Wehrmacht officer Udo von Alvensleben had been greatly concerned about the genocidal tendency of the war but, after seeing the corpses of 150 Wehrmacht soldiers murdered and mutilated by Russians in mid-August 1941, he gave in. In principle, he noted in his diary, "German soldiers are inclined to be good-natured to POWs, but now the desire for revenge is unlimited."[38]

Such was exactly how Hitler, the OKW, and the OKH wanted the army to feel and act. At a meeting with top Nazis and OKW chief General Keitel on 16 July 1941, Hitler already welcomed the first Russian partisan attacks, which were still minor: "This partisan war . . . has some advantage for us. It enables us to eradicate everyone who opposes us."[39] Hitler envisioned murderous exploitation under the guise of a seemingly defensive counterinsurgency war that allowed German perpetrators to see themselves as victims. In fall 1941, high-ranking Wehrmacht commanders further spurred on genocidal warfare by ordering soldiers to conduct the most brutal kind of retaliation. When Franz Böhme became Plenipotentiary Commanding General of Serbia in the fall of 1941, he inflamed his soldiers by declaring, "If we do not proceed with all means available and with maximum ruthlessness, our losses will rise to incalculable levels. You will be carrying out your mission in a strip of territory where, thanks to the treachery of the Serbs, both men and women, rivers of blood flowed in 1914. You are the avengers of those dead. We must deliver a warning that will make the greatest possible impression on the population. Anyone who shows compassion will be sinning against the lives of his comrades." Indeed the Wehrmacht organized the Holocaust in Serbia mostly on its own, without the SS. Böhme's appeal found fertile ground. "Wanna join me shooting Jews?" a Wehrmacht soldier asked his comrade who had just returned from a vacation in Belgrade. His company was about to take revenge for twenty-two German fatalities by executing twenty-two hundred Jews. Enough Wehrmacht volunteers stood ready to carry out the action.[40]

Condemning compassion for the enemy as a sin against one's own comrades was the essence of Nazi genocidal ethics. "Soldiers on the Eastern front are not only fighters according to the rules of war, they are also the bearers of an inexorable folk concept and the avengers of all the bestialities inflicted on the German nation and its kindred peoples. So soldiers must show understanding for the necessity of tough but just atonement to be extracted from the subhuman Jewish race," declared Field Marshal von Reichenau on 12 October 1941 in an even more influential order. Hitler was delighted with it and recommended it as a model to all parts of the army.[41] Precisely what "just atonement" would be, Chief of Staff Keitel laid down in a decree on 16 September 1941, the most decisive order to brutalize warfare in the East. Conjuring the "Jewish-Bolshevik" threat to Germans, he justified the most excessive reprisals. From now on, fifty to one hundred Communists were to be killed as "atonement for one German soldier's life," the order declared.[42] And Communists, in Nazi language, equaled Jews. That these proportions were regularly jacked up from five for one or ten for one or even one hundred for one was consistent with the politics of toughness and deterrence that regarded leniency as weakness. Consequently, every destructive act suffered was answered with ever greater destruction, in order to demonstrate the strength and the identity of the group.[43]

"These Shootings Are Not Acceptable for a Civilized People"

Justified by "military necessity," fueled by "guerilla psychosis," and embedded in an ethics of mercilessness, the code of revenge and retaliation made the German army complicit in genocide. Yet, there were choices. Human beings are "always better than their culture," the German-Jewish philosopher Theodor W. Adorno wrote after the war.[44] In fall 1941, Field Marshal Reichenau worried that this was too often true in the army. In his order, he blamed "many" troops for still sticking to an outdated "routine of soldiering" and of having only "vague ideas" of how to fight against "the Jewish-Bolshevistic system," which was his not very subtle criticism of those who opposed genocidal warfare. Already before 1933, Reichenau had been one of Hitler's closest followers in the military; in 1934 he had been complicit in preparing the Night of the Long Knives, the act that bound the Nazi Party and the German army together as the two major elements of the new state based on common crime.

Reichenau knew his troops. In late August 1941 Lieutenant Colonel Helmuth Groscurth, First General Staff Officer of the 295th Infantry Division that was part of Reichenau's Sixth Army, had angered his field marshal by trying to save ninety-one Jewish children in Beleya Tserkov in the Ukraine. Their parents had been massacred by Sonderkommando 4a a couple of days earlier with logistical support of the army; the children had been locked in a school with no food or water, only junk, rags, and old diapers, waiting for their execution. When enlisted men heard them crying, they complained indignantly to two military chaplains who turned to Groscurth for help. After arguing with the SS sergeant on duty at the school, Groscurth made his way up through several echelons of superior officers, none of whom would take action to save the children. Eventually he ended up with Reichenau, who ordered Sonderkommando 4a to "complete the action appropriately." The next day the children were executed and, in front of Wehrmacht and SS officers, Groscurth was rebuked for delaying a necessary operation. As one of the army officers said, the young people were "spawn" that had to be "eradicated." Groscurth, though, in his official report of 21 August, referred to his army training in soldierly decency, which forbade brutality toward defenseless civilians, and protested against "these measures that in no regard differ from the atrocities of our enemy, as they are continuously announced to the troops."[45]

Despite its massive Nazification, the Wehrmacht still had traditions of chivalry and compassion and so produced a much broader spectrum of attitudes toward blatant murder than Himmler's SS troops did. So Wehrmacht and SS officers were ordered to attend a course on "Fighting Partisans" in Mogilew in late September, at which the highest-ranking SS officers—the leader of Einsatzgruppe B, SS-Brigadeführer (Major General) Arthur Nebe, and SS-Gruppenführer (Lieutenant General) Erich von dem Bach-Zelewski—gave the major presentations. The essence was: everywhere partisans showed up there were the Jews, thus the Jews were the partisans. (There were, of course, Jews living in virtually every town, village, and hamlet.) The Mogilew course ended with all participants attending an antipartisan "action" especially arranged for their instruction. In a nearby village a police unit singled out "suspects" and killed the thirty-two Jewish men and women chosen. Indeed, before the course, the German antipartisan units had not been particularly successful in fighting partisans, for the very good reason that the local population was still kindly disposed toward the German occupiers. The Mogilew course, though, was to stir up fears of invisible enemies. Shortly after the course, the 1st battalion of Infantry Regiment 691 proudly reported the shooting of a Red Army officer and twenty-two Jews whom they had suspected of supporting partisans. Another nineteen Jews were shot to avenge a German soldier who was slightly wounded, "in all likelihood by a Jew," as the report said.[46]

But not all troops automatically joined in genocidal warfare. Early in October 1941 Captain Friedrich Nöll, leader of the 3rd company of the 1st battalion of Infantry Regiment 691, was given an assignment that caused him grave disquiet. In Krutscha, a village west of Smolensk, his battalion commander, Major Kommichau, ordered him to shoot the entire Jewish population—men, women, and children. The other two companies of the battalion received similar orders. But the three commanders reacted in different ways. The youngest of them, thirty-three-year-old Lieutenant Kuhls, carried out the order without hesitation. He was a member of the Nazi Party and the SS. The opposite reaction came from Lieutenant Sibille, a forty-seven-year-old teacher. Though also a Nazi Party member since

1933, he told Kommichau that he "could not expect decent German soldiers to soil their hands with such things" as the killing campaigns of the
Einsatzgruppen. He said that his company would shoot Jews only if they
were partisans, but that he had been unable to establish any connection
between the Jews and the partisans. The old men, women, and children
among the Jews were, he maintained, no danger to his men, so there was no
military necessity for such a measure. Asked by his superior when he would
finally get "tough," Sibille answered: "in such cases, never."[47]

The third company commander was Friedrich Nöll, a World War I veteran who was slightly younger than Sibille and also a schoolteacher. He, too,
was in no doubt that carrying out such shootings was murder and had no
part of the duties of the Wehrmacht, and that, according to paragraph 47 of
the German military penal code, he could and should reject an order that
he recognized to be criminal.[48] But Nöll was afraid of being considered soft
and of making himself unpopular with Kommichau. All the same, he did not
wish to burden his conscience with the deed. So he ordered his company
sergeant-major to carry out the executions. The sergeant-major was furious that Nöll had passed the buck and given the job to him, or so he told
comrades and subordinates, but he defused the indignation expressed by his
soldiers by reminding them that "orders are orders." Before evening, he had
organized the shooting of between one hundred and two hundred Jews.[49]

Just as Kommichau's three commanders responded in completely different ways to the order they received, the soldiers of Nöll's company
reacted differently. Some soldiers showed "enthusiasm for the executions,"
and many more had certainly bought into the Nazis' anti-Jewish propaganda. During the trial against Nöll in 1956, one of his former subordinates,
annoyed with all the interrogations, said bluntly: "The Jews were persecuted anyway; they were our enemies, weren't they?" Most of the soldiers
obeyed the order with reluctance yet regarded the matter as necessary in
view of the danger from partisans. Some of them, however, refused to pursue escaping Jews and grumbled later about the "dirty business" demanded
of them, especially since "pregnant women" had been among the victims.
And a few soldiers were "totally shocked and close to nervous breakdowns."
After the executions, a theology student told a comrade of his "spiritual
distress" over "being compelled as a theologian to have to take part in such

terrible measures." None of the soldiers refused to take part at all, other than some members of Police Battalion 101, when ordered to murder the Jews of Józefów in July 1942.[50] These men, however, were given the choice to stand aside, whereas such an option was not offered to Nöll's company.

Embedded in the Wehrmacht were two different value systems: the racist ideology of hardness and the universal virtues of mercy. Though the boundaries between them were blurred, they were not erased. Even the members of the especially brutal 707th Infantry Division did not commit genocide uniformly. Infantry Regiment 727, under Lieutenant Colonel Pausinger, developed outstanding success in "Jew-hunting" in fall 1941, but its "actions" stopped when Pausinger was promoted and replaced in January 1942 by Colonel von Louisenthal, who did not want his soldiers shooting women and children and forbade them from participating in massacres of Jews. Colonel Carl von Andrian, the commander of the parallel Infantry Regiment 747, had done the same earlier. Andrian, though, was by no means an anti-Nazi nor did he object to brutal reprisals in the Wehrmacht's war on the Soviet Union. A highly decorated World War I officer, he had been shocked by Germany's 1918 defeat and then already believed "that the Jewish race is an alien element within our people and thus needs to be exterminated." From the beginning of his summer 1941 service, he fancied himself sensing the "poison of Jewish subversion" everywhere. He had no qualms about brutal reprisals against Jews in a village where three of his men died during a partisan attack. But as strongly as he approved of what he considered justifiable reprisals, he rejected the indiscriminate massacres by SS and police units. "A terrible thing," he wrote of the murder perpetrated by the Einsatzgruppen, and of his comrades he noted in late November 1941, "We all . . . stick to the same view: We condemn these shootings, they are not acceptable for a civilized people [Kulturvolk] such as we wish to be."[51]

Captain Wilm Hosenfeld went a decisive step further than Adrian. His first job during the German occupation of Poland was establishing a camp for Polish POWs; later he was in charge of sport and training programs for German soldiers in Warsaw. Although an NSDAP and SA member, Hosenfeld was alienated from Nazism as he came to understand its politics of annihilation; what the Gestapo did to Poles and Jews was "not just about retaliation" but followed "a systematic order" of extermination, he realized in late 1939. Rereading Hitler's *Mein Kampf* in March 1941, he anticipated that "after Hitler, there will no longer be a single Jew in Europe," and by 1942 he knew that "millions of Jews" were about to be murdered. Like many Catholics, he had joined the Nazi Party because of his belief in nationalism. But now he understood that the Catholic virtues of mercy, compassion, and humanity were the important ones. As a devout Christian, he advocated exactly those universal ethics of human solidarity that the Nazis wanted to overcome. He was increasingly troubled by the "horrible blood guilt" that would now burden the entire German people, and he was concerned about the passivity he saw everywhere. "What cowards we are . . . that we let this all happen." But he determinedly tried to set counterexamples by acting as the "decent soldier that respects the captured enemy." He allowed Polish wives to visit their husbands in the POW camp he was responsible for, befriended persecuted Jewish and non-Jewish Poles, and saved some of them from the SS's death machine. During the last months of 1944, he helped the Jewish pianist Władysław Szpilman to hide and survive in the ruins of Warsaw. "I try to save each one I can," he said to his wife in August 1944 when he, unwillingly, was in charge of interrogating members of the Polish Armia Krajowa during the Warsaw uprising.[52]

"It Is Not Right Not to Be with Your Crowd"

Hosenfeld was not alone in opposing the murder of Jews, Poles, and other civilians. He repeatedly met soldiers and officers who were "fraught with compassion and embarrassment," who felt "ashamed of being a German," and who saw their "honor as a German officer" disgraced. "They offer their criticism openly," he said about his comrades in June 1943.[53] To be sure, criticizing Nazi anti-Jewish and anti-Polish politics was risky. Hosenfeld, though, relied on the protection of comradeship as an "anti-structure" (V. Turner). Other soldiers, too, appreciated a sense of freedom of speech among soldiers which no longer existed inside Germany. Wehrmacht soldier Helmut Schmidt, who became federal chancellor of West Germany from 1974 to 1982, put himself at great risk by railing at Göring and the Nazis. His superiors, though, knew how to protect him from court-martial.

They were, as Schmidt acknowledged, "good and elderly comrades." Even soldiers like Kurt Kreissler, a high-ranking leader in the Hitler Youth, set his Nazi ideals of conformity aside when comradely backing was required. He despised but did not denounce a notorious "defeatist" in his unit. In some cases, even men of Jewish descent, "half-Jews," according to the Nuremberg Laws, had a chance of being shielded.[54]

"Among comrades, different opinions are openly discussed," observed Private Jochen Klepper, a popular conservative Christian writer whose wife was Jewish. "It is precisely the uniform that allows diversity," he found. On one occasion he met a traveling soldier in need of accommodation who turned out to be an SA man. Klepper shared his bed with him, a symbolical gesture of comradeship that expressed the desire for tenderness, radiated the sacred ideals of charity, and initiated deep nightly talks. In the army, "German men" still got along, "apart from all partisanship issues," he noted, deeply touched. Ostracized by the Nazi Party, he still adored Prussian soldierly virtues and yearned to belong. He diligently took care of his comrades and volunteered for unpleasant duties to prove his belief in the existence of a male bond that was elevated above the refractions of the world outside—including the terror of the Nazi regime. Depressed and humiliated, he nonetheless found in the army what he badly sought: comradeship and that one great "experience: that I belong to [real] men. They have shared their best with me."[55]

But Klepper painfully sensed that in truth, in Hitler's army the male community of soldiers was no longer elevated above the rest of the world. "I can talk freely to anybody about everything. But not about the Jewish question. . . . All the talks with comrades do have such a beautiful human touch. However, always I see that propaganda has been almost completely successful. Nobody spends any more thought about it. 'The Jews have to go.' "[56] Though not Jewish, Klepper had to go as well. As he refused to divorce his Jewish wife, the Wehrmacht discharged him "dishonorably" in fall 1941. Expelled from the army, banned from professional organizations, realizing that not even his daughter had a chance to emigrate, he committed suicide with his family in late 1942.[57]

Comradeship should not be mistaken for some military version of the enlightened ideal of tolerance. As the Wehrmacht's official training manual noted, comradeship was, next to discipline, "the inevitable glue to make the troops stick together. Without discipline, they would dissipate into a riotous crowd; without comradeship, soldiers' life would be unbearable."[58] Comradeship was not to overcome discipline but to make it flexible, by neutralizing the ideological gaps that were the remnants of civilian identities. Mutually backing each other, even in sensitive political issues, fueled a sense of conspiracy that strengthened cohesion.

But it wasn't this type of comradeship that the Nazis wanted. They ranked ideological uniformity higher than military effectiveness. A 1943 dictionary explained that comradeship had been redefined in the Third Reich as "the principle that unites Adolf Hitler's followers into a community bound by sacred oath [*verschworene Gemeinschaft*] and based on belief and obedience." So in the Nazi state, the traditional concept of soldierly comradeship came under pressure. Comradeship, decided the Supreme Court (*Volksgerichtshof*), could not be granted to "individuals who exclude themselves from that comradeship by subverting the Volksgemeinschaft." As of 1938, the Wartime Penal Code (*Kriegssonderstrafrechtsverordnung*) considered any expression of discontent with or doubt about the regime as subversion of Germany's fighting power (*Wehrkraftzersetzung*), that is, as a capital crime to be punished by death.[59]

Thus, relying on comradeship was risky, as the fate of submarine commander Oskar Kusch shows. He once assured a comrade that if a soldier denounced an anti-Nazi comrade his superior would throw the denunciation into the trash bin and bawl out the denunciator. Taking over the command of submarine U 154 in March 1943 he announced, "We don't do idolatry here," and removed the Führer photo from the wardroom. Hitler was "insane," he lectured his comrades, well aware that two of his subordinate officers were dedicated Nazis. Nothing happened to him, though. Comradely cohesion trumped ideological rivalries—or so he thought, until he refused to support the promotion of one of the Nazi officers, who felt deceived and denounced him. Kusch was court-martialed, sentenced to death, and executed.[60] In total, thirty to forty thousand people were convicted of Wehrkraftzersetzung, mostly after being denounced by comrades, neighbors, or even relatives.[61] "Abhorrent denunciation proliferates amidst and among us," found Hans Scholl in February 1942 as a member of a

Wehrmacht company of medical students in Munich. They had mocked a Nazi professor and were court-martialed right away. On that occasion Scholl got off lightly, but later he was arrested, convicted, and executed in 1943 for having distributed the famous "White Rose" flyers.[62]

Most soldiers were more cautious than Kusch and Scholl. Fear of denunciation helped propel conformity. In the Wehrmacht, comradeship provided only a little protection from political persecution. It still generated a sense of community, which German men rarely experienced outside of the military. But it did not challenge the principle of military obedience or that of totalitarian repression. Nor did comradely conspiracy undermine the soldiers' anti-Semitism. Though he occasionally met a comrade who felt equally alienated from the regime, Hosenfeld still felt "lonely," something that mattered especially when it came to taking action on behalf of Poles and Jews.[63] No solidarity existed in the Wehrmacht on behalf of any persecuted group. Comradeship did not block genocidal warfare. Rather, it fueled the culture of honor, revenge, and cruelty.

"Comradeship, this word may be written in bold letters; however, it will never be realized," proclaimed the recruit Stefan Schmidhofer after he had been in the barracks for a short while. "All that comradeship does not pay off," added the recruit Franz Wieschenberg. Although never "alone" in the army, Willy Peter Reese felt "a stranger among strangers." These men were like many other soldiers who had not been drafted right after being trained in the Labor Service or in the Hitler Youth but who were older, in their twenties or thirties, when they were about to pursue a stable career or marry and establish a family. Soldiering seemed a waste of time to them. They despised what contemporary pedagogy attributed to military service, that is, its ability to rid men of their private, individual identities and to make them submissive members of a larger community—that of true men and the Volksgemeinschaft. Those who sought to escape this conversion would be isolated and harassed; comrades would shun them, superiors would bully them. Not many soldiers were able to bear such a life, so most of them adopted the basic rule of military life: "Always join in!" Or they at least acted as if doing so. "As a comrade, I have to join in," Wißmann realized, and soon after he did just that. "The connection to my comrades is established," he proudly reported to his fiancée. Most other soldiers also became joiners. After a while, even Reese "felt at ease in my company, one of many who shared the same destiny" and drove away homesickness together with a "barrel of beer," sitting around a campfire and singing melancholic soldiers' songs. "Our shared privation and distance from home," he said on reflection, "made us comrades."[64]

Living together, acting together, and communicating with each other, the soldiers established common goals, values, habits, and ideologies. They understood that a man was someone who conformed and did what other men did. Such a role was no longer compatible with the role of the family father. In July 1941 Wieschenberg explained to his wife, who had long urged him to avoid heroic adventures, why he was about to volunteer for a front-line unit. "A real man cannot stay at home with his family when his fatherland is at war. . . . Had I remained in the rear I would have felt a coward and weakling for the rest of my life." One of his old friends had already proved his bravery. Standing back was not an option to Wieschenberg. "When this war is over, I will stand next to him proudly and in freedom."[65]

In the Wehrmacht's flush of victory in summer and fall 1941 the soldiers' inner conflicts between private "I" and military "We" seemed to finally evaporate. The myth of comradeship, as told in World War I novels and Nazi propaganda, seemed to become true. His comrades would always share whatever they had, wrote Wieschenberg, and he himself was filled with the need to take care of them: "This is how true comradeship has to be." And Wißmann was deeply impressed when a colonel and a general saluted his unit at the front line: "I have to say, here is comradeship at home." The soldiers knew where they belonged. Among comrades, including superiors, Albert Neuhaus felt like he was in a "large family and this is amazing." As a member of the Nazi Party, he could have opted for a safe position in the military administration "anywhere in the rear," as his wife suggested. But this was out of the question. Only "here at the front do I feel really needed with my entire person; behind the front, I would feel utterly ashamed." This war, he said, "needs men not stewards." When he felt homesick, Wieschenberg said, "I just have to look around to know that I am not alone. . . . Everybody needs to bear up at his post until called. That becomes your second nature as everyone knows how badly he is needed here." Wieschenberg was dead-on. Adopting the ethic of comradeship—"always join in"—meant to rid oneself of one's previous private identity and to internalize the controlling gaze of comrades and superiors. Forget about your I. It is solely the We that counts.[66]

Transforming the I into the We was nevertheless an everlasting challenge. The grand military advances and victories of summer and fall 1941 soon merged into tedious stalemate and "depressing" visions, as Farnbacher said.[67] "Bunker tantrum" spread over the German troops in the East. By August 1942 Neuhaus wrote that "dwelling all the time in bunkers and in the woods really ticks you off. . . . All that oomph and the resilience we had when the campaign started is gone. We are so badly craving for being back home." Threatened by an increasingly powerful enemy, grieving for innumerable fallen comrades, suffering from insufficient supplies, the soldiers were reminded of Napoleon's disastrous Russian campaign. Russia is a "cruel experience," groaned Wißmann as early as October 1941, also craving home. Suffering from psychosomatic skin issues for a while in 1942, he was hospitalized in Austria, haunted by nightmares of close combat, death, and mutilation. Even Kurt Kreissler, a high-ranking Hitler Youth leader concerned with proving his soldierly manliness, admitted that "you felt so lonely, so abandoned in the midst of that battlefield." Suffering from heart disease, he was sent home after only two weeks in a frontline unit in the summer of 1941, to be hospitalized for months; back at home, he pondered whether to apply for the safe occupation of continuing his career as Hitler Youth leader.[68]

But he did not. Nor did Wißmann look for a chance to stay home. Even in the hospital, both were afraid of being seen as cowards. In his "entire life" he "would not get over" that, said Kreissler, even after the disaster of the Sixth Army in Stalingrad in January 1943. Finally back to a frontline unit in June 1943, he observed that "everybody" felt as he did—just throw yourself into the battle. Wißmann was less dedicated to soldierly virtues. But the experience of comradeship had not left him untouched either. Once, on a hopeless suicide mission, Wißmann's closest comrade Flattmann, who, unlike Wißmann, was a father, had refused to back out, although urged by Wißmann to do so. "He came along with me. If we have to, we'll fall together," Flattmann had said and so became Wißmann's model. Wißmann would never again hesitate returning to the front to stay with his comrades.

Wieschenberg had no doubt, either, that his "holy duty" as a man was to endure what "millions of other men" endured. Even Willy Reese, though full of disgust for the uniform, despised the coward, "who trembled for his life and sought to avoid ruin."[69]

All these soldiers had internalized the gazing public eye that in shame culture deters the one who is about to break ranks. In war, this controlling eye had a mystical dimension. Apart from the eyes of living comrades, those of the fallen comrades exerted pressure as well. "My fallen comrades," Wieschenberg said, "oblige me to hang on." They must not have died in vain. Soldiers like Wieschenberg may have yearned to return home or at least for a vacation. But once at home they decided sooner or later that "it is not right not to be with your crowd."[70] There was not just one meaning of comradeship, it was a set of concentric circles, pulling men in: small "primary groups," as sociologists have called them, that is, face-to-face communities and dyadic buddy relationships on the one hand; on the other hand, "secondary," large, anonymous, and imagined groups such as the entire army, the mystic community of fallen soldiers, and not least the Volksgemeinschaft.

"We Lived Like Gypsies and Vagabonds"

Once back with their units, the soldiers constructed "motherly," family-like comradeship to fight homesickness. "Just as with sugar mommy," the men said whenever a "household" decorated its simple dwellings with flowers and pictures, cultivated a small garden, and in spring prepared a whole field, close to the front line, for planting.[71] None of these comforts would last long; they had to be redone all the time. That exactly was the point. All these efforts were not about physical harvest, but about social yield. The social dynamic that generated community depended on the destruction of its physical resources. The soldierly comradeship, produced in the machines of destruction and deprivation, was quite different than family life at home, but then men would make it seem similar. "Just as at home," noted a soldier on Christmas Eve in Stalingrad 1942, "harmonica, fiddle, singing, happiness, and all is mutually done. . . . And what we felt. . . . Some got teary-eyed." "Comradely love" fought "tearfulness." The soldiers were ending the party with a bottle of champagne when a bomb hit the bunker. "One dead and four casualties." Those who survived moved even closer together. Death fed community.[72]

Christmassy idyll or melancholic singing easily merged into a bawling jag. You were not supposed to stay away when boozing was on the comrades' plate.[73] Lifting a glass together strengthened comradeship, just as did sharing food parcels, common singing, or storming into the battle. The booze made soldiers forget about frictions, frustrations, and catastrophes. "We just heard the news about the destruction of the Sixth Army at Stalingrad, the most severe blow we've got in this war so far," noted a soldier on 3 February 1943, and he went on: "rude partying at night as usual. . . . We kicked up our heels, danced on the table like mad. Half of our glasses and bottles are broken. Past midnight the stalwarts went on downstairs. My apricot brandy bit the dust. On duty from four to six am. Then continuation in high spirits as before till eight." Sometimes the affair got out of control. "Huge mess in the artillery position." A lieutenant, "more drunken than dry," had threatened his comrades, including the commander, and needed to be arrested.[74]

Such lapses did not undermine male bonding, though. On the contrary, they established events that would be narrated again and again. Official orders banned boozy excesses but usually a blind eye was turned even to serious crimes committed out of comradely drunkenness. Comradeship lived off of collectively breaching the norm. On the battlefield the soldiers created comradeship by invalidating the civilian ban on killing. Drinking bouts and little riots mediated a sense of elevation above the rules of military discipline and civilian decency. The male bond was stronger than external expectations and orders. Bad-mouthing women, cracking dirty jokes, and dwelling on obscene talk proved one's "true masculinity." Abusing women in the occupied areas was the ultimate performative masculinity, that is, an assertion of the sovereignty of the male bond. Shortly after the Germans had invaded her home town Pskov in early August 1941, Genia Demianova, a Russian teacher, was tortured and raped by a Wehrmacht sergeant. He did so not only for sexual gratification but also to position himself among comrades, as the victim's account reveals. Immediately afterward, he started boasting. "There is a roar of cheering, the clinking of many glasses. The sergeant is standing in the open doorway: 'The wild cat is tamed,' he is saying.

'Boys, she was a virgin. What do you say to that?' Another burst of cheering," and the sergeant closed the door, but Demianova was not left alone. "The others came in" and "flung themselves upon me, digging into my wounds while they defiled me. . . . Then everything passed. The Germans kept coming, spitting obscene words towards me, guffawing as they tortured me."[75]

Unlikely though it may seem, sexist bonding, even based on rape, and "motherly" comradeship did not exclude each other. By showing feminine qualities and staging family-like settings, exclusively male societies demonstrated their independence from real women and real families. The message was: being on our own, we men are able to generate a warm sense of family as well as cold brutality. "Today one of you moms should have been with us," wrote Fritz Farnbacher to the mother of a fallen comrade, "not to help us, oh no, but to watch us cooking . . . this is so amazing, watching these gorgeous men upon whom you can always rely, who always succeed, and with whom you are tied in a fighting community."[76] Fighting together or cooking together, either way these men demonstrated to themselves and to women the male bond's autonomy from exactly these women. Whether fueled by misogyny or motherliness, by brutality or charity, the "anti-structure" of comradeship relied on challenging the "structure" of the civilian world outside.

Inner frictions fermented anyway. As their letters and diaries show, the soldiers felt betwixt and between. Yearning for privacy and security, they craved to be back at home. Yet they wanted to belong to the community of men. Coping with these frictions, most of them resigned themselves to being a small cog in a machinery of orders and conformity. "Out there," said a soldier to his family before he returned to the Eastern front, "you don't think much about what all that murder is good for. You are with your comrades and you do your duty, that's it."[77] Abandoning oneself to the virtue of duty meant to plunge into a world with no individual responsibility, no individual decisions, and no individual visions. "You are no longer the master of yourself," observed Wieschenberg already in fall 1941. "You just run, willfully and mindlessly. Never mind. . . . I surrender to lethargy and just don't care." Resigned to his fate in the territories of terror, murder, and death, the soldier would no longer wonder about how to save the rest of humanity. "I couldn't care less," was a phrase that justified debauchery, wild togetherness, and terror inflicted on enemy civilians. "As soon as you pledge yourself completely to the couldn't-care-less attitude, there is no longer any-thing remarkable about this war," stated a reactivated World War I veteran in fall 1941, wondering about the genocidal war he was now fighting.[78]

Soldiers might fancy themselves double personalities and resort to the polar metaphor of the hard shell that carries a soft core. Cynicism and bru-tality were only masks that would not really harm their inner identity, they pretended. In the rivers of blood, though, doubling was about to be swept away. "Individuality went under in a vast ocean of apathy and never took shape," Willy Reese realized.[79] Eventually, it was not the masked self but rather the mask that managed the soldiers' actions, whether they laughed at sexist jokes or terrorized enemy civilians.

Beginning in fall 1941, the Soviet partisan movement grew and threat-ened German soldiers more than ever. In late November 1941, some civil-ians who were suspected of being commissars or partisans were brought in and "bumped off right away" by Farnbacher's comrades. Others were sent to the division's headquarters for further interrogation—"they will shoot them," commented Farnbacher to his comrades. "They really don't make any bones about it!" Farnbacher still tried to keep his inner distance from ongoing brutalization. "All these executions," he noted, "are really not my thing; I am glad that I am not in charge of that stuff." He also refrained from setting Russian villages afire when retreating. "Anischino is in flames; every house burns when the troops are gone. However, I don't set fire to the places we have been whatever other people do, and the commander doesn't like doing so either." Knowing that he had "not shot a single time nor slaugh-tered a chicken or a goose nor ever ordered executing a Russian or even attended an execution," provided some relief, as his diary shows.[80]

Yet his private diary reveals the moral and emotional roller coaster. Although concerned with saving the "I" from the morally stained "We," Farnbacher wanted to belong. So while he refrained from personally com-mitting crimes, he confirmed their ideological basis. "The Russians strip German prisoners to the butt, tie them on a sledge, pour water on them and let them freeze to death or push the entire sledge into a river," he learned in November 1941. "Beasts in human guise!" he wrote. "As a matter of course, such brutish murder of German comrades did provoke countermeasures. We did not take any prisoners." Neither did his comrades when transferring a group of thirty or so captives to a collection point. "They have bumped off all of them, as they tell us later; the assembly point was so far away. What I hear is an almost animal laughter," Farnbacher noted understandingly. Doubts surfaced only to be immediately suppressed. "What we've come to! Five months ago we wouldn't have even said that, let alone dared do it! And today it's a matter of course which, on reflection, every one of us approves. No mercy for these predators and beasts!"[81]

During the first three months of 1942, Farnbacher's unit was given a rest; only occasionally did some Russian partisans interrupt his boredom. A patrol fell into a trap and was carried off; a command in charge of requisitioning was attacked; a supply unit was slaughtered. Though the partisans were just resisting the exploitation and devastation of their homelands, the Germans "needed" to live and could not care for this "mean crowd of shit," as Farnbacher said. When an attempt to destroy a partisan base of a thousand men failed and his unit caught Russian civilians poisoning the food supply, Farnbacher no longer stood aside. For a long time, he had suffered from being treated as one of those "who are considered as good for nothing." A conforming believer, abstinent from alcohol and passionately working on his diary rather than joining alcohol-filled gatherings, he had been a prime target for mockery; often he felt "like an outcast" and did not know how to position himself or where to belong. Recent events gave him a chance to catch up. A daunting requisitioning foray in the locality was to be initiated under Farnbacher's leadership. Fifty soldiers formed an impressive force. It did not run into partisans and encountered sumptuous booty in one of the villages. Under the eyes of the frightened residents, potatoes, greens, fifty chickens, grain, three sucking pigs, "and above all a cow" were loaded onto thirty sledges. "Then I put myself at the head of my forces, once I have assured myself again that they're all present . . . and march off homewards. The evening is as beautiful as the morning before it. The wind is at our backs and we race along." The mood was one of elation, not least due to the ordinary soldiers' sense of humor: "On our expedition, when I asked whether the cow had been paid for, they just said 'Yessir!' To my question, how had they paid, came the answer 'With cigarette coupons!' "[82]

Whereas Farnbacher's beliefs were rooted deeply in Christian traditions, Lieutenant Werner Gross had joined the Nazis before they came into power. Even more than Farnbacher, he was intrigued by the ethos of male communities; he had been in the Hitler Youth and in labor camps before volunteering for the army. Following the model of Ernst Wurche, the hero of Walter Flex's most popular World War I novel, Lieutenant Gross saw himself as an example setter. "As officers, we are to precede our men" and "to sweep them along," he once explained to his parents, turning down their suggestion to seek a safe assignment. "I belong to my men," he said, whether on the battlefield facing death, in the bunker fighting lice, at a coffee party celebrating a birthday, or by venturous partisan actions that reminded him of trips with boys' leagues. With horses and carts, his troop roamed through occupied lands in the spring of 1943. They had, he proudly wrote, "searched villages, combed woods and cleared the area of gangs." To Gross, "gangs" was a synonym for partisans but it did not matter whether these people actually were partisans or just civilians whom they considered suspicious. Enemies were exchangeable. In fighting them, Gross's men discovered the emotional glue of Nazi virtues: collective joy and dense togetherness, based on the destruction of Them. "We lived like gypsies and vagabonds," Gross boasted.[83] The magic potion which enlivened these cleansing campaigns and plundering trips came from the conviction that they were above civilian society and indeed the rest of the world.

As a result of the battles of 1941 to 1943 and the German occupation, huge territories of the Soviet Union suffered from devastation, desertion, and depopulation. From spring 1942, millions of Russian civilians were forced into abusive labor service for Germans; Wehrmacht soldiers in the role of colonial slave hunters did their share in destroying families, societies, and lives all over the occupied countryside. Farnbacher's and Gross's actions were just two examples. In the retreat that began in 1943, the troops covered the rest of Eastern Europe with marauding, murder, and plunder. The policy of "scorched earth" concluded the destruction of half of a continent.[84] "Russia was turning into a depopulated, smoking, burning, wreckage-strewn desert," Willy Reese stated in early 1944, at the end of a distressed 140-page-long "Confession" of his own complicity. "On the way we torched all the villages we passed through and blew up the stoves. . . . The war had become insane, it was all murder, never mind whom it affected." Outbursts "of rage and hate, envy, fistfights, sarcasm, and mockery" replaced "whatever may have remained of comradeship," he wrote, sentimentalizing the warm side of soldierly togetherness. As the Germans were forced to retreat further and further, a new, very different collective identity emerged, based on "heroic nihilism" and pure cynicism. Yet already in 1942 Reese had depicted in a poem a gang of soldiers guzzling and whoring, boasting and lying, cursing and crowing. "As a bawling crowd," they had "marched to Russia, gagged people, butchered blood," and "murdered the Jews. . . . We wave the banners of the Aryan ancestors, they suit us well. . . . We rule as a band."[85] The band was the Wehrmacht, the spearhead of the Volksgemeinschaft, the German nation.

Approximately three million Soviet citizens lost their homes and all their belongings. An estimated three hundred thousand to five hundred thousand people were killed during the Wehrmacht's antipartisan war in the Soviet Union. The question of whether they were Jews, guerillas, or just different-looking civilians did not trouble their executioners. Taking a short break from the front in spring 1942, Albert Neuhaus and his comrades strolled through a Russian village where "our *Landsers* had hanged a woman who had agitated against German soldiers, on a tree. We are used to making no bones about these people," he explained to his wife. "Well, initially you might find it strange, but eventually you just laugh at it." So did Willy Peter Reese's comrades in 1943, when the visions of glory and victory evaporated. "Two hanged men swayed on a protruding branch. . . . Their faces were swollen and bluish, contorted to grimaces. . . . One soldier took their picture; another gave them a swing with the stick. We laughed and moved off."[86]

"I Had to Die Forlornly"

In Russia in March 1942, Private Erich Kuby bumped into a lance corporal who excitedly announced, "Tomorrow, it's a butcher's party." Joyfully he added, "The entire families!"[87] Everybody around understood what he meant. One hundred and eighty Jews were to be killed. Kuby felt "abysmally nauseated about those whom I need to call my people," who so "easily intertwined middle-class norms and barbarism. . . . They play the role of decent soldiers, and in fact they are criminal accomplices. . . . I would rather opt out than belong to them." Born in 1910, Kuby, who in civilian life was a left-wing journalist, accepted military service to explore the inhuman agreements of "my people" and to put its complicity in terror on record. But retaining a seat on the fence was not so easy. Like many other Germans, Kuby took part in plundering occupied France before being sent to Russia. "Shopping" in a wealthy private villa had made him wonder: does "ordered plunder need to be considered plunder? I have to say, nothing gnaws at my conscience. . . . I have picked a stove for the party. We get independent from needing supplies from the Reich," he cynically stated.[88] During the invasion of Russia in July 1941, he saw drunken German soldiers humiliating local peasants. The "uniform makes me an accomplice and prohibits me from intervening," he realized. When should he, or when would he, be able to "revoke" his complicity—and ignore personal consequences? In the army, "radical non-participation" was not an option. On one occasion in 1943 in Russia, his "party" requisitioned a pig to enjoy "the most opulent dinner ever in Russia." Oppressed Russian peasants had to prepare it. Kuby did not stand aside. "On each dish more meat than you get for your food ration cards in Germany in half a year," he boasted in a letter back home, though admitting, "Maybe never since 1939 I have sunk so deeply into war as now."[89]

Kuby still did not sink as deeply into the Nazis' war of extermination as other soldiers did. Yet by wearing a German uniform and following orders, he supported not only the institutional and social basis of this war, but also confirmed its moral framework. Shocked by the lance corporal who gleefully announced the butchering of Jews, Kuby frowned. It was noticed—only a frown but it was an expression that went too far. He was accused of sentimental humanitarianism, and he backed off. He would not object to the fate of the Jews, he assured the officer, but he was bothered by the Germans' attitude, which was inconsistent with the traits that qualified them to lead Europe.[90] Thus, he touched common ground with the basics of Nazi genocidal ideology. Not doubting German superiority, Kuby sang from the same hymn book as Himmler, who asked his troops to carry out mass murder with self-control and "decency" rather than with sadism. To be sure, Kuby's intentions had nothing to do with Himmler's genocidal ethics. But to save face among comrades he needed to confirm the language of "cool" murder.

Kuby strove to maintain individual responsibility as demanded by his conscience. Yet he was unable to resist the pressures and temptations of an ideology and social culture that encouraged men to join in oppression, terror, and murder. And he knew it. How to come to terms with such inner conflicts? Kuby stuck to the army, muddled through these conflicts, surrendered to the Americans in France in 1944, and became an icon of antimilitarist and antifascist movements in democratic West Germany, not least by publishing his war diaries and letters.

There were other choices. Private Stefan Hampel, born in 1918, took one of them. He deserted. After being incarcerated in a Gestapo prison in 1939 for criticizing Nazi racism, he was drafted into the Wehrmacht in 1940. In May 1942 he witnessed a mass execution of two thousand Jews—men, women and children—in Wasiliszki, forty miles from Grodno, his hometown, where he happened to have spent his vacation. He was shocked and even more appalled when, while wearing his uniform, he encountered two Jewish friends of a cousin. Dumbfounded, they stammered his name. In their eyes, the uniform he wore made him one of the executioners, or so Hampel, deeply ashamed, thought. He decided not to return to his unit but to join the Polish-Lithuanian underground movement, well aware of the deadly risk he would be taking. As an underground participant in 1943 in southwest Germany, he was caught by the police and sentenced to death. He was exceptionally lucky, though, as he survived the Nazi era in penitentiaries and lived until 1998.[91] Willy Reese, also utterly embarrassed by Germany's war of annihilation but feeling "partly responsible" for it as well, made a third choice. He stayed with the army to get killed in battle. "The armor of apathy with which I had covered myself against terror, horror, fear, and madness . . . snapped off the green shoots of hope. . . . I no longer dreamed of going home. . . . I had to die forlornly," he concluded in his memoir shortly before he was killed.[92]

After the Second World War, when former Wehrmacht soldiers asserted that they had not known of the systematic dimension of the murder of the Jews nor of the Wehrmacht's participation, they were either lying to or deceiving themselves. They may not have been aware of the dimensions of the Holocaust because knowledge of the death camps remained limited. But soldiers fighting in Eastern Europe could not close their eyes to the daily murder. If not actively supporting these actions, they had seen them, or at least heard of them. Hospitalized in Germany for some time, twenty-four-year-old Paul Riedel returned to his detail in Charkóv in May 1942 only to be shocked by his comrades' stories about German "deeds" during his absence. He put his abhorrence on record. "Thirty thousand Jews have been murdered in Charków. . . . The bullets splash through the heads of children, mothers are yelling and—fall silent. They are collapsing on hills of corpses, blood steams . . . and the murderers are wading through blood. . . . Now, there are no more Jews in Charków. In Kiev they have murdered seventy thousand; in all towns they have been exterminated. Maybe some people say, 'Oh, the Jews.' So I shall talk about other things. Twenty thousand Russian POWs had been in the prison of Charków. A few hundred are still alive."[93] Whereas Riedel, acting with a front unit, could gather knowledge of the Holocaust at just one spot, Wilm Hosenfeld, serving with the occupation regime in Poland during the entire war, acquired comprehensive knowledge. In spring 1942, he heard of the gas chambers in Auschwitz and found that, "notwithstanding all secrecy," in Poland such knowledge was no longer exceptional but rather was widespread. Two years later, he accepted "the extermination of a couple of millions of Jews" as a fact.[94]

"We Germans Are the Nation That Has Gone to This War Enthusiastically"

How did the soldiers respond? The deserter, Stefan Hampel, belonged to an evanescent minority. About thirty-five thousand deserters fell into the clutches of courts-martial or police, but many more were never caught. What made them desert, though, was not so much the sight of the terror inflicted on Jews, Russian POWs, and enemy civilians. They despised the military apparatus and the culture of obedience and conformity, and they desperately missed parents, wives, children, friends, and homes. Desertion became a mass phenomenon only at the end of the war when the risk of getting caught greatly diminished, not in 1941 and 1942, when mass executions of Jews were occurring on a daily basis.[95]

Whereas relatively few deserted, numerous soldiers acted like Colonel General Blaskowitz, Colonel Andrian, Captain Hosenfeld, Lieutenant

Riedel, or Privates Reese, Kuby, and Paul Kreissler. They *felt* embarrassed. And there they left it. They were loyal to the troops and fabricated excuses for their complicity. Blaskowitz and Andrian found comfort from commemorating old military virtues. Hosenfeld privately blamed the "current rulers" for betraying "the German people," contrasted SS "turpitudes" with the "honor" of Wehrmacht officers, or clung occasionally to the illusion that "we as Wehrmacht have nothing to do with that."[96] Riedel and Kuby nursed their self-image as critical chroniclers of the misdeeds of their comrades and their fellow citizens. Many of the rank and file resorted to blaming their victimization on the omnipotent military apparatus or on the eternal tragedy of warfare as an anonymous maelstrom of destruction. Paul Kreissler, observing Germans mistreating, abusing, and murdering Jews, "liquidating" emaciated Russian POWs, and expelling the civilians, railed about "those few potentates up there" and wondered about their "right to send people into such an insane war." He finally escaped into the "deep tragedy" of it all. "We keep still and stand by helplessly. . . . The bitter law of war wants it that way."

But all these excuses provided only minor relief. Kreissler still felt "ashamed of being a German soldier." So did Reese. Cursing Hitler, the "clown who had started this war" and who entrapped Germans into war and murder, he still knew that being German and wearing the German uniform made him complicit. Hosenfeld stated in late 1942 that "in the history of humanity there is no other example of a crime committed by a relatively few individuals but atoned for by an entire people just because this very people had been blind and too cowardly to defend themselves against the thugs. . . . And we idiots thought they would lead us into a better future. Anyone who has even slightly supported this system should feel ashamed."[97]

Shame, as articulated by these soldiers, was no longer shame in front of their comrades in the army or the German Volksgemeinschaft. It was shame in front of the watching world. "Will a German ever be able to face the world?" wondered Hosenfeld, shocked by "German blood-guilt." But such shame did not translate into action against the regime. "We all know," said Hosenfeld, even after the German disaster at Stalingrad in 1943, "that there is no other choice for us than fighting . . . to ban the horrible threat from the East." Though he opposed Nazi racist politics and used his position to give an example of German decency by rescuing Jews and Poles, Hosenfeld went along with Nazi anti-Semitic propaganda, believing in the deadly threat of Jews, Bolsheviks, Communists, and Asiatic "hordes." Supporting Nazism seemed to be "the lesser of two evils. The bigger one," he had decided already by 1942, "is to lose the war."[98]

After summer 1941, when the Final Solution had been launched and even more once the road to victory became jammed, leading Nazis amplified the consequences of a German defeat. Hermann Göring, chief of the Luftwaffe and designated successor of Hitler, said in October 1942 in the Berlin Sportpalast, "If we lose the war, you will be annihilated. . . . The Jew is behind everything, and it is he who has declared a fight to the death, and to ruin, against us." No German should fancy himself safe from Jewish revenge. The Jews, Göring insinuated, knew what not only the SS or the Nazi elite but what the entire German people had done to them. If Germany lost the war, no German should think he might say afterward: "I always have been a good democrat against these mean Nazis." The Jews will take revenge on all Germans, he went on. They "want to exterminate whatever is racially pure and German . . ., whether democrat, plutocrat, Social Democrat or communist doesn't matter."[99]

In public speeches, newspapers, and newsreels the regime spread the fear of a terrible Jewish revenge both among frontline soldiers and at home. The Nazi discovery of the NKVD murder of thousands of Polish officers in spring 1943 fueled this propaganda, just as the NKVD massacres in the Ukraine had done in 1941. "If the Jews win the war," threatened a Nazi newspaper in May 1943, "our entire people will be butchered just as well as the Polish officers in the woods of Katyn."[100] Distortions of the Old Testament were also used to support the cliché of the Jewish menace. Robert Ley, head of the German Labor Front, denounced the "God of the Jews" as "the God of revenge" in order to justify the systematic murder of the Jews. Göring in early 1943 tried to counter Germans' combat fatigue: "The Jew with his Old Testament hatred is what we are to expect if the Jew is enabled to take revenge on us."[101]

The soldiers got the message. "We have to win the war," stated a private, "otherwise we would be badly off. Foreign Jewry would take horrible revenge on our people, given the fact that here hundreds of thousands of Jews had been executed in order to establish calm and peace in the world." In fact,

the soldiers did not even need such propaganda. It simply enlivened dichotomous anti-Semitic and anti-Slav stereotypes they had already absorbed.
Unlike 1941, however, these clichés sank more and more beneath apocalyptic visions of Germany's fate. "One thing is for sure," elaborated an NCO in
May 1943, "Germany would no longer exist if we lose the war. . . . The only
thing we can do is to pray to the Lord to bless the *Führer* and our weapons.
It is just not thinkable that the Jew wins and rules." "Everyone around here
is filled with the idea that it would be a catastrophe for each individual if we
lost the war," noted the chronicler Kuby already in 1942, "and the government never stops efforts to strengthen this vision."[102] But when confronted
with the Wehrmacht's disaster at Stalingrad, pessimism infected "even those
comrades who had been so optimistic before," Helmut Wißmann wrote to
his wife. "Either we lose totally or we win. If these beasts savage Germany
and I can't be with you . . ., I am horrified at that very idea."[103] Such
visions charged fighting morale. From 1942 on, the allied air bombardments
of German cities and, in 1944, rumors about Ilya Ehrenburg's call for the
murder of German men and rape of German women by the Soviet Army
seemed to confirm the most horrible fantasies of impending revenge.[104]

The truth was that even those soldiers who despised the Nazi concept
of a racially pure Volksgemeinschaft and who were embarrassed about
German crimes against humanity supported the idea of the deadly threat
to their fatherland by the revenge of the Jews. The soldiers had to deal with
"things that make you feel ashamed of being a German. . . . This is not
just anti-Semitism, this is a kind of inhumanity you would never consider
possible in the twentieth century," noted a private in 1942 and wondered,
"What kind of atonement will we eventually have to face?" But he did not
know how to react except to join in: "What can we do? Shut up and keep
on serving."[105] A year later, another private wondered about his comrades'
frankness. "Among us comrades, now you can talk about anything. The
period of bigotry and intolerance toward opposing opinions is over," he said.
Nevertheless, "although the dreams of ruling the world are gone," there was
no reason to quit, he found, for "it is true, we have to win the war if we don't
want to put ourselves at the mercy of the Jews."[106] There was no belonging
outside of the perpetrator society. The German nation had shackled itself
to mass crime, and the soldiers knew it. As Private Franz Wieschenberg

wrote in August 1944 in a letter from the Eastern front, "We Germans are the nation that has gone to this war enthusiastically and will have to bear the consequences."[107]

Wieschenberg bore the consequences. He was killed in battle in spring 1945, when the Wehrmacht was thrown back to fight forlornly on old German territory, against the Red Army in Prussia and Silesia and against the Western allies on the Rhine. Wieschenberg was not alone. In summer 1944, millions of German soldiers could no longer ignore the fact that the future of the Volksgemeinschaft was not one of grandeur and mastery but of death and demolition. While the Wehrmacht in 1940 suffered from "merely" 83,000 dead or missing soldiers, the Russian campaign took a much higher death toll: 357,000 in 1941, 572,000 in 1942, and 812,000 in 1943. But even these numbers paled in comparison to the death toll in the single month of August 1944, when 277,000 German soldiers lost their lives across the Eastern front, and 349,000 in the entire army. In fact, during the last five months of the war, casualty figures increased exorbitantly, peaking in January 1945, when 451,000 died. During each of the following three months, almost 300,000 soldiers were killed.[108]

The darkest fears, as conjured by Nazi propaganda, became true. The soldiers realized that the war of annihilation no longer solely targeted Jews, Slavs, and other "subhumans" but the Germans too, both on the battlefront and at home. In addition to being deluged with accounts of the bombardments of their hometowns and of the mass rape of their wives, daughters, and mothers, the soldiers learned on a daily, or even hourly, basis that the mass death of their comrades meant that they themselves had little hope of surviving the war. Why did they continue fighting? What made them hold out? Why didn't they revolt against their leaders or just run away, as soldiers had done in 1918? To be sure, some did. Discipline and fighting in the Wehrmacht in early 1945 was no longer as strong as in 1941; up to five hundred thousand soldiers deserted, prolonged their vacations and hospital stays, or shirked their duties in other ways. Insofar as they performed their duties, most of them certainly did what they could to somehow survive. At the same time they kept fighting; no substantial mutiny was planned, let alone carried out. Why? To a certain degree, bunking would have been as lethal as fighting—especially on the Eastern front, where crossing over to the feared Soviets was not an option. And in the rear and at home the dreaded military police, the *Geheime Feldpolizei*, and other parts of the Nazi terror apparatus stood ready to catch and execute on the spot any wavering soldier or civilian.[109] Terror alone did not keep them at it, however. For a long time, at least through the winter of 1944–45, many soldiers were dedicated to a quasi-religious belief in Hitler, in the midst of all their hopelessness. "The entire situation is so knotty and strained that you just have no other option than blindly relying on the leadership," said Wieschenberg in summer 1944. Listening to Hitler speaking often affected the soldiers just as the Word of God touched true believers, and sometimes both merged together, feeding the hopeless hope that it could not be all in vain.[110]

But the rhetoric of blind and unlimited trust stood on an ambiguous emotional and cognitive basis. What did the leadership plan? Since the fall of Stalingrad at the latest, the regime had been drowning its own propaganda about final victory in somber visions of a monumental defeat. As State Secretary Ernst von Weizsäcker observed in May 1943, the mood in the Führer's headquarter was, "We will triumph. If not, we will be doomed honorably by fighting to the last." The military myth of the battle to the last, substantiated in the battle of Thermopylae and the Nibelungen Saga, not only fed die-hard slogans but stimulated an entire choreography of collective self-destruction aimed at transcending senseless bloodshed and preparing Germany's resurrection. It actuated fantasies of collective honor, eternal community, and the reputation of the group—the core values of shame culture. Forget about individual life, happiness, and conscience; the only thing that counts is how your group performs, what it looks like, how it sticks together. Whoever gave his individual, physical life in the battle to the last would be compensated by eternal glory and the rebirth of his nation: that is, by symbolic life. Physical death, the self-sacrifice of the people's community, would evoke immortal glory, and immortal glory would give birth to a new, even more splendid nation. "The more we have suffered," Hitler dictated to his secretary Bormann on 2 April 1945, "the more strikingly will the everlasting Reich rise again!" And the day before his suicide, on 29 April, he prophesized the "radiant rebirth of the National Socialist movement, and the realization of a true Volksgemeinschaft" out of the "sacrifice of our soldiers and out of my own close ties with them unto death."[111]

Such an apotheosis of national destruction and resurrection did not easily reverberate in the soldiers' own thoughts, feelings, hopes, and fears. As their private letters, diaries, and memoirs show, sacrificing themselves on the altar of the fatherland or on behalf of the Führer was not really what they desired. Suffering from bad conscience about the murder of the Jews and the devastation of Europe, fearing the revenge of their enemies, and facing mass death of their comrades and loved ones did not translate into yearning for self-destruction but into fantasies of victimhood, which indeed stimulated the spirit of comradeship and a sense of national belonging as wished by the Nazi regime. When soldiers like Wieschenberg thought about their nation's responsibility they did not doubt the legitimacy of the war. On the contrary, fear of the vengeance of the Jews or the "beasts" from the East only intensified fatalistic impressions about the nature of the war. "We could have done without the war," Wieschenberg went on, "but who would have wanted to answer to the coming generation for the consequences. . . . The truth was that Russia was an enemy country and a shit hole." A strong sense of the justice of their own cause was deeply rooted in the soldiers' ideological world. "You can honestly say, when a nation is deceived and faces a world of enemies [and] stands firm in spite of everything, that it is a chosen people. Should we still lose, then I don't know what you can call a just cause," stated Helmut Wißmann already in summer 1943, faced with Italy's "treachery."[112] Standing "firm in spite of everything," sticking together, even as a pariah nation, was the morality of shame culture. Nothing was more important to it than social cohesion. The good and morally right person was the one who, regardless of personal scruples, uncertainties, or anxieties, unswervingly did what the community did and kept "faith" with it. Those who broke ranks were morally reprehensible: "We have no time for traitors." Especially among small groups the rule was: "If you won't join in, you're a rogue."[113] Only those who joined in had a right to survive. Those who pulled out were outlaws.

Those who did join in and comply, though, even if only in the "outer regions" of their personality, as Frank Matzke had said in 1930, enjoyed the easy life of comradeship, which both exonerated them of guilt and gave them solace. For their dispensation from the requirement to show humanity toward their adversary was legitimized not only by the dehumanized image of the enemy but also by the humanity the group cultivated within its own confines. "Humanity," selflessness, mutual solicitude, security, even affection was not foreign to it. They just remained limited to one's own group. Physical destruction—mass death all around—did not demoralize social productivity. The soldiers knew in the final years of the war better than at the outset how to produce social cohesion in the small combat units, over and over again and with constant new personnel. When Corporal Kurt Kreissler returned to his company in January 1945 after convalescent leave, it was clear: "I shan't meet any more old comrades." The question "How few of us are left?" could not be suppressed. But it only made him redouble his efforts to ensure that "the men and their leaders get to know each other as soon as possible, so that they'll be warmed up ready for the battles to come and for difficult missions."[114] The *memory* of the great crimes committed together, kept alive through fear of the revenge of the adversary, promoted a sense of belonging to a pariah nation. At the same time, the *expectations* of the soldiers were narrowed to the radius of the action involving their own company and the sense of humanity this small in-group generated. "We chucked the Russkies out of some German villages. With barely 150 men we put over 1000 Russians to flight. . . . Everybody is in a brilliant mood. . . . In particular my small unit, the small section of the company that I lead, is of one heart and one soul. . . . The spirit in our unit has never been better than at this time. To stick together and to fight side by side and be wounded side by side, that's our wish." At the end of the war cohesion was no longer, as envisaged in the professional duties of the soldiers, the foundation of their fighting spirit. The battle itself, the destruction of physical life, formed the precondition for social experience.

FIVE

Watching Terror

Women in the Community of Crime

Although dedicated to the SS ideal of toughness, Felix Landau felt gloomy when reporting to an Einsatzkommando in the District of Radom in the Polish General Gouvernement in summer 1941. It was not the murder of the Jews that troubled him but rather his concubine, Gertrude. Having left his wife and two children in Vienna, Landau had begun an affair with Trude, a shorthand typist with the Gestapo, in Radom in August 1940 but broke it off when he realized that she was still seeing her fiancé. In June 1941 he transferred to Drohobycz, near Lvov, where the Einsatzkommando was remodeled into a local department of Himmler's Security Police and Security Service to organize Jewish labor commands. He felt pleased to be feared as a brutal and egomaniacal potentate. Spreading terror, though, did not cure his private misery. He missed Trude more than ever. No comrades, no boozy get-togethers, and no other women could alleviate his lovesickness. "My Trude is far too much on my mind. At the social evening I just could not get her out of my thoughts," he noted in his diary in mid-July 1941 and worried how to get her to Drohobycz. During the ongoing terror against Jews, he badly yearned for some "happy family life." On 6 August 1941 he wrote, "My comrades and I got the Jewish housemaid to roast some chickens for us. Everything was per-fect except for the empty places on my right and left. I looked at both chairs and said to my comrades that all that was missing was our sweethearts."[1]

Landau, though, was lucky. After he had struggled with superiors and with Trude's parents for half a year, she joined him in Drohobycz in late

1941. They enjoyed themselves in an aristocratic villa they had chosen as their home. On a Sunday in June 1942 they took a sunbath on the balcony of their villa. For a while they amused themselves with card games but eventually became bored, so Landau decided to give his girlfriend another lesson in shooting. They both used his light shotgun to aim at some birds and paid no attention to a group of "working Jews" constructing a garden across the street. Then Felix noticed a fifty-five-year-old Jew named Fliegner interrupting work while waiting for some companions who were scared by the shooting. To see a "working Jew" stop working was intolerable to the "General of the Jews," as Landau liked to be called. An example needed to be made, a demonstration of power to the Jews and to Trude. He grabbed the gun, took aim, and shot Fliegner in the heart as Trude watched. Both laughed and went back inside. For them, "happy family life" went on in the midst of the terror against Jews, occasionally enriched by revelries with SS comrades and Trude dancing on the table.[2]

On the balcony, watching her lover commit murder, Trude got a lesson not only in shooting but also in what politics in Nazi Germany were about. Not actively involved in the deeds of her boyfriend and thus not held responsible when the event was discussed in front of a West German court almost twenty years later, she, like many others in these days, was "only" a spectator. As such, Trude took part nevertheless. Her role was typical. In the Nazis' racist state, established traditions of female subordination to male-dominated politics were basically unchanged. Yet Aryan women's political status was somewhat elevated, not to promote women's emancipation but to weave them into the national community of crime.

"The Woman Has Her Own Battlefield"

In modern constitutional monarchies and democracies, citizens are asked to participate in politics by voting and by joining political parties and attending meetings. Politics is debating, negotiating, and compromising about different, even opposing, ideas and interests. The Nazi state, however, repressed political diversity. Politics no longer consisted of compromising but rather of eliminating perceived challenges to national unity. Political participation no longer meant deliberating and voting for or against different options but excluding and killing internal and external enemies. Execution sites, ghettos, and gas chambers replaced clubs, lobbies, and parliaments.

Since its creation in the late eighteenth century, politics had been negotiated in all-male institutions. According to its dichotomous biological assumptions of male strength, rationality, and sociability and of female weakness, emotionality, and selfishness, the bourgeois society in the nineteenth century had not allowed women basic political rights. Men were to run state politics and to manage the public sphere, whereas the family, the epitome of privacy, was the ancestral place of women. To be sure, there was no future for a nation unless women gave birth to children to become its citizens and soldiers. And women never completely stayed within the boundaries of domesticity. In various times of political turmoil, women stormed the barricades or marched against incapable governments, as they did in World War I. But most of them didn't question the principle of male politics. Even when women received political rights such as suffrage, the nation-state kept its gender bias. Only a small number of women ran for and won government offices, inevitably in the "motherly" departments and functions—charity, education, and welfare, and even then usually as auxiliaries to men.[3] Only slowly did the gender order come under pressure, when more and more women broke out of their corsets by requesting and assuming political rights, nonmotherly careers, and male clothes. After World War I, the bobbed "new woman," the unmarried female clerk, and the female politician indicated permanent changes. Not unexpectedly, many men were frightened by these "masculinized" women and became obsessed with the possibility of women taking over in politics and society.[4]

When the Nazis assumed power, they appealed to traditional gender stereotypes and took action to reverse women's emancipation, which they considered to be one of the innumerable errors of the liberal society. "Emancipation of women from the women's emancipation movement," proclaimed Nazi chief ideologist Alfred Rosenberg, "is the first demand to a generation of women which would like to save the Volk and the race . . . from decline and fall." Joseph Goebbels added, "The mission of the woman is to be beautiful and to bring children into the world," just as the "female bird pretties herself for her mate and hatches the eggs for him."[5] Consequently, the generous marriage loans introduced in 1933 were not paid to the wife but to the husband, provided that the woman gave up work and resigned herself to motherhood. The more proof she gave of her motherly dedication—that is, the more children she bore—the more the debt would be reduced. Symbolic incentives such as the Mother's Day and the Mother's Honor Cross honored the cult of motherhood in Nazi Germany.

The Nazis, however, did not simply roll back progress in gender relations, which would have protected the private sphere of female identity. The family had no rights of its own in the Third Reich. The personal and the private were to exist exclusively for the benefit of the racially defined Volksgemeinschaft. The Nazis praised motherhood and family as biological resources of the militarized Volksgemeinschaft rather than as a retreat from it. "The woman has her own battlefield. With every child she brings into the world, she fights her battle for the nation," explained Hitler.[6] At the same time, motherhood was subject to the racial exclusions of the Volksgemeinschaft. Only Aryan Germans were eligible for a marriage loan or the Mother's Cross; only her children were appreciated. Non-Aryan mothers and children were to be separated, removed, sterilized, and killed. The conventional signifiers of motherhood, altruism and empathy, came under scrutiny because they distracted women from understanding the "virtue" of racial exclusivity and recognizing themselves in what the racial state considered them to be—carriers of "racially pure stock." "Racial improvement" rather than childbearing was the highest good in Nazi Germany.[7] Finally, motherhood, family, and sexuality were robbed of their private shields and subordinated to the totalitarian, united, and uniformed Volksgemeinschaft that would not tolerate deviance. Female bodies, female health, and female appearance were to be standardized, controlled, and adjusted to the needs of the community. Neither the old-fashioned "Gretchen type" nor the woman "who can dance beautifully at five o'clock teas," nor the one who relies solely on "blond hair and blue eyes" was desired, but rather the one who was happy with "the simplest clothing, which is to be as uniform as possible," the one who was used to "early risings in the morning cold" to improve her health, and especially the one who possessed the Reich sports medal—the symbol of the nation's fitness.[8]

In the Third Reich the ideal woman "lived neither for herself nor just for that 'one' man; she lived . . . for her Volk."[9] She could do so by assuming different roles, though—for instance, as the mother giving the Führer children, or as the athlete with the perfect body, or as a district nurse, which made use of her position of trust in the local community to x-ray the Volksgenossen physically and ideologically. For the nurse was "appointed to a post where she faces, similar in a way to close combat, all the hazards that threaten the people's welfare," explained a brochure on NS-*Volkswohlfahrt*, the Nazis' social service organization. Reminding nurses of how easily people bare their souls and their physical problems to a caregiver, the brochure asked them to build up a "martial communal comradeship" to counteract "whatever threatens it: local diseases, entrenched bad habits, occupational diseases, infant mortality, superstition, ignorance."[10]

Nurses were not the only ones who served as watchdogs for the Volksgemeinschaft's ideological and racial purity. The *Heimtückegesetz*, or Malicious Practices Law, criminalized any subversive activity, including privately uttered criticism of the regime, and invited Germans to denounce their fellow citizens to the Gestapo or other authorities. To be sure, the Nazi state, afraid of eroding the Volksgemeinschaft, never made denunciation mandatory, yet it became a national sport. Men took the lead, but women joined in. They denounced husbands and neighbors to settle private conflicts and, at the same time, to validate themselves as full-fledged members of the Volksgemeinschaft. For example, in Berlin in November 1943, after a quarrel over the rent with her tenants, a woman named Frau Schulz reported to the local authorities that Herr J. had called Hitler a house painter (a common slur against the Führer). J. was arrested, sentenced to death, and executed in July 1944.[11]

The Nuremberg Laws prohibited sexual relationships between Aryans and members of an "inferior race." The laws thus inspired the Volksgenossen to make political use of their private issues. They denounced Jewish neighbors, bosses, and colleagues for race defilement or for just concealing their racial identity. Such denunciations offered women a chance to challenge patriarchal subordination and to regain dignity. Battered, divorced, and deserted wives denounced their husbands or former husbands not only as having agitated against the regime but also as having had sex with female foreign workers. In empowering themselves, these women entered the public sphere of the Volksgemeinschaft. While private motives were frequently the basis of denunciations, the denouncers had to raise their stories above the level of private chitchat by depicting themselves as genuinely concerned with the salvation of the fatherland and not driven by egoistic desires for revenge. By making their anger public, these women supported the Nazis' concept of an ideologically pure Volksgemeinschaft. Such female empowerment through cooperation with Nazi terror institutions was possible only by violating their own private sphere. Making private matters public allowed women to break out of the private.[12] Through destroying obsolete private patterns of belonging, the denouncers entered the national arena of belonging.

"We Felt Like Soldiers"

Denunciation, however, was only one of many ways Aryan women were able to transgress domestic boundaries. As with boys and men, girls and women were drawn into a tight net of organizations that trained them to renounce individual lifestyles and devote themselves to the needs of the nation. At age ten, the German girl was to enter the girls' section of Hitler Youth, the Young Girls (*Jungmädel*, or *JM*), and four years later she would join the German Girls' League (*Bund Deutscher Mädchen*, or BDM). At age seventeen or eighteen she would transfer to "Faith and Beauty" (*Glaube und Schönheit*). Then she would serve for half a year with the Labor Service (RAD), or she would do a "Year of Duty" working on a farm or in a household. Finally, at twenty-one, she was to join the National Socialist Women's League (*NS-Frauenschaft*) or the German Women's Organization (*Deutsches Frauenwerk*).

Not all women and girls were intrigued by the camp life, field trips, evening sessions, and household courses these organizations required. Joining in, forming up, and competing in sport matches were less than fun for girls who were raised in liberal families, hated sports, or despised the Nazis and their frenetic drive to organize people. A popular joke in Nazi Germany was, " 'My father is an SA member, my older brother is in the SS, my little brother is in the Hitler Youth, my mother is in the Nazi Women's League, and I am a member of the BDM.' 'But when do you see each other?' 'Oh, we meet every year at the Party Congress in Nuremberg.' "[13]

Before 1939, far fewer women—a small minority—than men joined one of the voluntary service schemes. The RAD, which became compulsory for men in 1935 but for women only in 1939, attracted even in the second half of 1939 only 36,219 young women while the Year of Duty mobilized over three hundred thousand girls. Things were about to change. Beginning in October 1941, further compulsion brought the numbers of females in the Labor Service alone above one hundred thousand. Whereas in 1933 roughly six hundred thousand girls aged ten to eighteen had joined the Jungmädel (JM) or the BDM, compared to 1.7 million boys in the Hitler Youth, in early 1939 the 3.4 million JM and BDM girls almost caught up with the 3.8 million Hitler Youth boys.[14]

To be sure, the Nazi regime exerted substantial force on girls to join in, whether through propaganda, social pressure, or formal compulsion. But there was more than pressure. Memoirs, testimonies, letters, and diaries leave no doubt that female youth organizations radiated a sense of adventure and departure that before 1933 had been limited to a relatively small youth movement. Now, it was state authority that backed girls who yearned to break out of stifling family life. "When I left home for the Year of Duty, I felt as if everything within me expanded," said a former RAD girl. "I felt liberated from home," where her acerbic father would not allow her to go out even early at night. Joining the RAD or the BDM was a rebellion. Establishing a counterauthority to patronizing parents, BDM and RAD offered departure not just from home but also from traditional gender clichés. Girls could measure up to boys. "What I liked," said a former BDM girl, "was that you were allowed to do lots of stuff that otherwise a girl was always forbidden. Like marching, climbing trees, stuff like that." Together with their comrades from Jungvolk, "our Jungmädel take up the fight against hunger and coldness," claimed BDM leader Jutta Rüdiger emphatically in 1939, explaining why Nazi propaganda advised girls to become even a little like men—not burly or earthy but still fierce, firm, and austere. Girls echoed even the male ritual of giving the "Holy Spirit" to the internal enemy of the group, such as covering one convicted of stealing from her comrades with shoe polish. But outsiders were only few, whereas insiders were many. And these girls came to enjoy that sense of belonging beyond family that had previously been the privilege of men. "The most beautiful thing in the Labor Service was the experience of comradeship," said Lore Walb, overwhelmed by RAD impressions in 1938.[15]

The desire of girls to share male experiences had not much to do with genuine sexuality. Girls did not want to become boys. But they wanted to share the power boys and men enjoyed or were promised. Political power in Nazi Germany was no longer defined by individual political rights but by dedication to the Volksgemeinschaft. Power equaled belonging, and belonging radiated power. "In the BDM, I became someone," commented a former BDM girl on the "best time of my life."[16] The visible symbol of being someone was the uniform, the "dress of comradeship" for "all boys and girls of Germany," as Baldur von Schirach called it.[17] In militarized Nazi Germany, the uniform stood not so much for subordination as it did for recognition, prestige, and belonging. "If you saw us in our splendid uniforms, then you would easily understand what a great thing this is," boasted a young woman to her former high school classmates, whom she addressed as "lads."[18] Many girls and women felt that the new state appreciated them, too, not just boys and men. Wearing the uniform meant to be "in," to be considered a full-fledged member of the Volksgemeinschaft.

Nothing had ever fascinated her quite as much as the catchword of the Volksgemeinschaft, stated Melita Maschmann in the memoir she published in 1963 on her "Former Self" as a dedicated BDM leader. Echoing Nazi propaganda, she said, "I wanted to help create the National Community in which people would live together as in one big family." In summer 1938, a national rally of BDM leaders in Bamberg, an idyllic medieval town in Bavaria, confirmed "this feeling of happiness—to be allowed to belong to a community which embraced the whole youth of the nation, even that part of it which was forced to grow up outside the national frontiers," as she wrote about *volksdeutsche* (ethnic German) BDM leaders who took long trips from abroad to join the meeting. "What made us so happy . . . was . . . the feeling that no one was excluded from it any more . . . the feeling . . . of loving one another in all the variety of our characters." Ongoing harassment of Jewish neighbors and classmates did not have anything to do with that feeling of harmony, in Maschmann's perception. "Our camp community," she said about her RAD experience in 1939, "was a model in miniature of what I imagined the National Community to be. . . . Amongst us there were peasant girls, students, factory girls, hairdressers, schoolgirls, office workers and so on."[19]

The camp made true the promise of the Volksgemeinschaft. Complete harmony transcended social diversity. Or so was it perceived by most Aryan girls and women. As a professional BDM leader, Maschmann was intrigued by the number of opportunities the Nazi state seemed to offer to women, although she was aware that the Nazi state was "dominated by men" and that most of her male colleagues "held the view that women's activities should be strictly confined to the family." She did not care, however. "In agreement with many of my female comrades," she decided "under no circumstances to yield to this tendency." She wasn't alone. The Third Reich provided a plethora of public functions that allowed Aryan women to abandon the private sphere, at least temporarily, and to acquire professional experience and public recognition, even if only on a low level, as leaders of small units and on a voluntary rather than professional basis. Collecting for the Winter Aid program provided "joy." It "gratified me to be useful," said Lore Walb. In 1936 she wrote a euphoric school essay on the motto "I am nothing, my Volk is everything." In 1938, she had an "amazing time" in the Labor Service, as she noted in her diary. She and her (female) comrades had "obtained responsibility everywhere. . . . As senior roommates (*Stubenälteste*), we were responsible for the dormitory. We also served as training staff, and you could easily say that we . . . were the 'heads' of the camp." Although aware of her eventual responsibilities as a mother, she wanted a professional career first, to prolong the freedom from family at least for a while. So did the RAD leader Änne Mann, commanding a small detail to build up a new camp. "I really don't miss the happiness of a marriage or the blessing of children," she said. "I rather enjoy my thirty-six kids here and the splendid tasks I face."[20]

The more that Nazi Germany approached total war and then carried it out, the more that propaganda emphasized female professional careers rather than motherhood. "For the first time," announced the National Women's Leadership in 1939, "we are fully integrated into the grand martial community of the German Volk with whatever we as woman can achieve."[21] Well aware of the unpopularity of female employment in factories, the regime remained reluctant to use coercion when it came to mobilizing women for war. Instead it used and abused forced labor drawn from the occupied countries to deal with labor shortages in munitions plants and other types of heavy and nasty industries. But the regime never stopped publicly envisioning the "possibilities of using women" as professionals; in July 1939 the *Völkischer Beobachter* announced that "the future will teach us completely new terms of female employment" and doubted that any professions necessarily required males; no longer should women only temporarily take over professional responsibility or be paid less than men doing the same job.[22] In the same way, Martha Moers, a psychology professor, questioned common views of biological or psychological "limitations on female employments" and took up the cudgel for training girls in technical professions rather than merely in so-called typically female professions, such as nurse, doctor, or schoolteacher.[23] Female heroes like Hanna Reitsch and Melitta Schenk Countess Stauffenberg, both prominent aviatrixes in Nazi Germany and highly decorated in World War II, exemplified how far the "new terms of female employment" reached. To be sure, both represented rare careers. Yet, they were not hidden. Even more than female actors or athletes, they disrupted gender clichés. They promised variety in women's lives within the totalitarian society and radiated gender equality within the state of men.[24]

It was total war, genocide, and ethnic cleansing that brought Aryan women these unparalleled opportunities to seize professional careers, participate in state politics, and win recognition as comrades in the Volksgemeinschaft. Melita Maschmann's career as a BDM leader and her communal euphoria were in fact rooted in extermination and expulsion of the "other." When, shortly after the celebration of community in Bamberg 1938 the German "national soul boiled over," as a policeman said to her on Kristallnacht, she easily bought into propaganda clichés of "World Jewry" that "has resolved to hinder Germany's 'new steps toward greatness.' " The Jews, she understood, were to destroy exactly that kind of belonging that made "the basis of my existence."[25] In fall 1939, she joined the *Osteinsatz* program to "Germanize" occupied Poland and to promote her career as a press officer for the Hitler Youth. She was one of some eighteen thousand young German women who embraced the role of missionaries of Germandom. During summer vacations or even for longer periods, they helped ethnic Germans resettle from their homelands in the Soviet Union to the Wartheland, the Nazi *Reichsgau* annexed from Poland in 1939. Carrying out the SS's program to "racially reshuffle" East Europe, the young German women were assigned to tidy up houses and farms of Poles who often had been forced to leave their homes only hours before the new settlers arrived. Above all, these women were to set up German schools and kindergartens for the new members of the Volksgemeinschaft. Not all women were involved to the same extent in the seizure and redistribution of Polish and Jewish property. They all, however, complied with the regime's policies of appropriation, discrimination, and destruction.[26]

Performing "a kind of 'colonization work' in 'advanced posts' " was not just "a great adventure . . . to satisfy our own desire for excitement," claimed Maschmann. She and her comrades instead felt they were fulfilling "our duty towards the 'Reich' " by restoring Germany's "honor" that had been destroyed through the Versailles Treaty and the loss of the eastern territories. Cleaning out dirty houses of Poles the morning after they had been expelled was not a prestigious assignment. But dirt "could not daunt them." It only confirmed them in their "arrogance." "Filthy" Polish houses proved the superiority of the German "master race." In a broader sense, it proved the genocidal ideology that legitimized ethnic cleansing as a disinfection measure to save Germandom. When the Osteinsatz girls had done their job and a Volhynian-German family could move into the "disinfected" home, they also became advisers to the new male family head on household issues. But climbing the ladder of gender hierarchy did not end there. Maschmann and her female comrades took over even more decisively "man's work." When an SS officer could not find enough men to "clear" a Polish village, he asked the BDM girls to jump in. They were uncomfortable with the idea of joining in the nasty part of the Nazis' Germanization program and also knew they could refuse the SS man's request and would be backed by their superiors. Yet none of the girls "hesitated for a moment." What made them comply was both their dedication to "Germany's mission" and their desire to catch up with male contributions to a nation "that was to conquer world empires. . . . We felt like soldiers on the home front." And they had learned one of the most crucial lessons the Nazis taught: battling against compassion—"sentimentality," in the Nazi jargon—ridding oneself of "a particularly humane concept of justice," of "spontaneous sympathy" for the sufferings of "foreign" people and of Jews in particular. Maschmann had won this battle long before, in 1940, after a volksdeutsch comrade "had criticized my 'thoughtless sympathy.' " Complying with the genocidal ethic, the heart of the Nazis' Volksgemeinschaft ideology, allowed the Osteinsatz girls a particular "arrogance towards the 'stay at homes,' " which included men as well as women. In other words, their "existence in the 'front line' " elevated female colonizers even above Aryan men at home.[27]

Some women drifted even closer to terror and murder. Whereas the mass shootings in the East were executed by all-male squads, roughly 10 percent of the concentration camp guards were women; most of them served in women's camps at Ravensbrück and Auschwitz-Birkenau. Usually they came from lower classes and had worked in factories or as farmers, hairdressers, clerks, or other less respectable jobs, or they had not worked at all, before the Nazi's terror machine offered them a chance to rise. As KZ guards, they had careers in the prestigious and secure public service. The desire for upward mobility, in terms of both class and gender, motivated them to apply for such jobs. Once installed, female camp guards sometimes imitated and exceeded men in their brutality, as female camp survivors have attested. As Hilde Zimmermann put it: They "flirted with acting like men" by torturing inmates, wishing to demonstrate what kind of tough guys they were.[28]

Blatant female sadism as that performed by the infamous Irma Grese was exceptional, however. The real novelty of Nazi genocidal politics was not sadism inflicted by pathological perpetrators of either sex but the manifold strategies of making ordinary people complicit by merging diversity into social unity and by awarding compliance with belonging. The regime had totalitarian aspirations, but German men and women had grown up in diverse social and ideological settings; they had different personalities and different aims in life, and most of them hoped for a better life after years of misery. The Nazi regime promised to realize their hopes, whether in terms of wealth, happiness, or prestige, so long as they complied with the needs of the Volksgemeinschaft as defined by the regime, which meant to approve the genocide of the Jews and the murder and torture of many other people. It was possible for Germans to do this in manifold ways and on many different levels—as perpetrators, followers, or bystanders, or just by agreeing.

Through 1945, the SS accepted about three thousand female members as SS auxiliaries. Unlike the camp guards, who were not members of the

SS, the auxiliaries had to pass rigorous racial and aptitude tests before being accepted. Most of them were daughters, wives, or widows of SS men. Unlike the female camp guards, they served as technically skilled and professionally trained staff in the camp system or in the SS administration, including the *Reichssicherheitshauptamt* and the *Einsatzgruppen*. There they witnessed and supported the Holocaust, most without dirtying their hands. So did thousands of other women employed by the SS and Gestapo as telephone operators, stenographers, and typists. None of them tortured people personally; instead they typed lists of expropriated Jewish properties and of train schedules to send Jews to death camps, took care of the deadly daily schedules of their male superiors, and forwarded orders to oil the Nazi death machine. And they made decisions. Irene C., stenotypist assigned to the Security Police and Security Service in Warsaw in 1939, testified in 1966 on how fifty, sometimes a hundred imprisoned Poles were selected to be killed in reprisals for one or two German soldiers killed by insurgents. "In the hallway, there was then a bunch of files, say a hundred files or so, and when then only fifty were to be shot it was in the women's sole discretion to choose the files. Sometimes the head of the division would say, 'This or that person must go, get rid of that piece of shit.' " Usually, though, "it was up to the receptionists to decide about who would be shot. Sometimes one of the women would ask her colleague, 'How about this one? Yes or no?' "[29]

"My Göth Was the King, and I Was the Queen"

Rather than seeing the SS as an ephemeral "male bond," Himmler envisioned it as an aristocratic "order," to which women would "belong just as men." Modeled along mythical ideas about the medieval *Ordensstaat*, the state of the Teutonic Knights in East Prussia, the SS would comprise many *Sippengemeinschaften*, kinship and family-like communities tied together by blood bonds. The emphasis on blood was crucial. In the SS Sippengemeinschaft, women were to be racially screened just as men were. "It would be useless," said Himmler, "to put together valuable blood from all over Germany" in an all-male fraternity and then waste it on racially impure women and families. Thus, "any SS man, who intends to get married," Himmler already ordered in 1931, had "to apply for a marriage

approval by the Reichsführer-SS"—meaning himself. Only "the future of
the Volk" should matter when it came to selecting a partner, rather than
sexual desire, individual love, or economic calculations, the SS journal
Das Schwarze Korps reminded its readers. The SS bureaucracy, and often
Himmler himself, spent an enormous amount of time thoroughly checking
the biological as well as emotional and ideological qualities of prospective
SS wives. The applicant and his fiancée had to provide 186 documents
to complete the SS family tree if they wanted to be chosen for the new
aristocracy of the Nazi state.[30]

Like all communities in the Nazi utopia, the SS as a new aristocracy
of men and women would not rely solely on pure blood but would also
demand ideological exclusivity. It wasn't just about filling out forms and
providing documents. Being worthy of membership in this aristocracy
had to be demonstrated continuously. Once married, or even before, the
spouse of an SS man would face the entire range of female roles offered
by the Nazi state to women. All of them, however, included compliance
with the genocidal Volksgemeinschaft. Those SS wives close to the sites
of mass murder worked diligently to provide a "normal" family life that
not only enhanced the biological reproduction of the Volksgemeinschaft
but also presented their husbands with an island of emotional relief and
recreation. Felix Landau wasn't alone in needing female comfort, love, and
sex to perform male terror, hate, and murder. Like other concentration
camp guards, Stutthoff's protective custody leader Theodor Traugott Meyer
"enjoyed a simple but utterly happy family life," as he said later. "We were
happy to own a small home, and all we cared for was the future of our
son." To Rudolf Höss, commandant of Auschwitz, his wife and his family represented an idyllic island of humanity amid the site of inhumanity.
"The children could live a free and untrammeled life. My wife's garden
was a paradise of flowers." Such idyllic happiness was in no way disconnected from terror. It was the inmates who provided the commandant's
family happiness. "Every wish that my wife or children expressed was granted
them. . . . The prisoners never missed an opportunity for doing some little act
of kindness to my wife or children." As household help, camp inmates were
somewhat safer than other inmates. At the same time, their lives depended
completely on the moods of the camp commandants' loved ones. By no

means were they all kind. Ilse Koch, the "witch of Buchenwald," marks the extreme of sadism performed by spouses of KZ commandants. And as Marian Rogowski, survivor of forced labor camp Janovska, testified in 1961, Elisabeth Willhaus, wife of Janovska's commandant Gustav Willhaus, took some pleasure in doing herself what Felix Landau's mistress only watched: shooting slave laborers. She did so in fall 1942 from the balcony of her villa—not with her husband but with her six-year-old daughter beside her.[31]

Höss's praise of his wife and family nevertheless revealed the principle of social ordering in Nazi Germany. Racial hierarchy prevailed over gender hierarchy. Making race the decisive category of difference was the crucial part of the Nazis' social revolution. Whereas in previous central European societies gender mattered most, even more than class, when it came to defining social hierarchies, in Nazi Germany any Aryan women stood above any Jew, any Pole, and any Slav, whether man or women, rich or poor. SS women, then, were at the top of the female Aryan world. They carried the most thoroughly scrutinized blood, and, whether as actual perpetrators or as wives of perpetrators, they had privileged opportunities to enjoy the new hierarchy. When interviewed by the historian Tom Segev in 1975, Ruth Kalder-Göth, the widow of KZ Płaszów commander Amon Leopold Göth, said, "It was a beautiful time. . . . We enjoyed being together. My Göth was the king, and I was the queen. Who wouldn't have traded places with us?"[32]

"Do Not Look at It"

Yet SS wives did not reach the very top of the new hierarchy. They did not rank above SS men nor, usually, even above other male members of the Aryan Volksgemeinschaft. In the hierarchy of concentration camp guards, female guards could not give orders to male guards. Patriarchal restraints remained obvious in the SS, the BDM, and the RAD, and even more so in the army. During the war, the Wehrmacht recruited some 450,000 to 500,000 female auxiliaries, who served in various jobs, mostly remote from the front. Almost as many women served as Red Cross nurses.[33] One of the Wehrmacht auxiliaries was Ilse Schmidt, born in 1919 into a lower-class family in rural Brandenburg. Frustrated by being barred from professional career plans at home and fascinated by uniforms and military marches, she volunteered for the Wehrmacht, serving first in Bordeaux and then in Belgrade, the Ukraine, and finally in Italy. Consequently, she saw the big, wide world through the lens of the Nazi Volksgemeinschaft and was flattered by officers and intrigued by soldiers. She climbed up on the social ladder, breathed the smell of liberation, and enjoyed life—mostly. In Belgrade in summer 1941, photos of shot partisans shocked her and then she stumbled into real partisans publicly hanged on lampposts. Transferring to the Ukraine in 1942, she strolled along a ghetto and became aware of nearby mass shootings of Jews. She sensed that she was complicit, somehow. But she found reasons to excuse herself. She was "only" a woman, an "auxiliary," just one of the female "gofers" in a "men's war."

Men kept their inner circle closed, sometimes ostentatiously. In August 1941 Ilse was present in a casino at which the Wehrmacht's victory at Smolensk was celebrated. At one point, Major L., her married superior, shouted over the crowd: "By the way, gentlemen, already heard of the new officers' brothel? Madam is supposed to be a real lady! Top class! . . . How about checking out this establishment?" Ilse was embarrassed by such intentional crudeness. The male bond needed to demonstrate its elevation over women, whether absent or present. Crudeness was only a part of it. Offering protection and advice to women was the other part. Although Ilse saw the results of atrocities and genocide, the soldiers asked her to look the other way. "Do not look at it," said a comrade in Belgrade when they came upon the hanged partisans, implying that, as a woman, she should not get too deeply involved. Ilse watched the atrocities anyway. She wanted to behave like a man, a member of the Volksgemeinschaft. She also supported the cult of silence and secrecy that enclosed criminal warfare and strengthened the bonds of the perpetrator society.[34] So did millions of German women, whether in the Frauenschaft or in the Frauenwerk, in the BDM or in the RAD, as SS wives or SS auxiliaries, as Wehrmacht auxiliaries, or as Red Cross nurses. They vacillated between traditional female patterns of passive support and hyperactive efforts to belong to the male corona of the Volksgemeinschaft.

Aside from a few exceptional and pathological cases, women were confined, or confined themselves, to the role of junior partners of men in the racial, ideological, and military wars the Volksgemeinschaft fought.

Whether men appeared in glamorous uniforms at home or performed with superhuman endurance on the Eastern front, their soldierly masculinity was sure of female admiration. In fact, such admiration was fueled by women's "male" experiences. In late 1942 Wehrmacht private Michael Sager's girlfriend Dorle reported emphatically on her activities as a nurse in a Munich military hospital at Christmas and fancied herself "serving anywhere in Russia. . . . This whole experience brought me so much closer to your and your comrades' experience." It was just a fantasy, though. Female comradeship would never measure up with male comradeship, as many women realized. "It is just a pity that girls are never able to achieve the same beautiful comradeship among themselves" as men did, lamented a girl to a soldier on the Eastern front, looking on her own Catholic youth group. Female comradeship never undermined male dominance. Rather it confirmed it, making a male vision come true, as articulated by SA man Gerhard Modersen in 1936, when his fiancée volunteered for female Labor Service in 1936. He was delighted. In the RAD, women would learn quite a lot, he expected, above all comradeship, and so they would "become better comrades in marriage." This is why pedagogues even before 1933 had recommended instructing girls in comradeship. They would no longer "bother men with desires for love" but "respect male patterns of comradeship." And they would understand that "men needed to elude femaleness and to bond among men" when "the people's destiny" was at stake.[35]

Overall, it was still a minority of women—though a strong minority—who tried to catch up with men by wearing uniforms, conquering Europe, colonizing the East, denouncing Jews, and torturing KZ inmates. Neither were most German women eager to take over male jobs nor did they want to be organized or uniformed; they stayed at home while their husbands, fiancés, sons, and fathers made politics in Nazi terms, fought domestic or foreign enemies, died in battle, or murdered civilians. Staying at home, though, did not mean to stay apart. Styled as "comrades," all women in Nazi Germany, whether BDM girls, professionals, or housewives, were asked to ignore private wishes and to support their men in fighting for the Volksgemeinschaft, which was not always easy, as private correspondences between soldiers and their wives reveal. Women weren't always ready to be stoically heroic when their men were drawn into battle, perhaps never to return home. But sooner or later they adopted their roles as "brave soldiers' wives," made themselves ready for sacrifices, and suppressed private worries. "Finally, you are a German soldier rather than a Jew," wrote Edith to her fiancé Helmut Wißmann, giving up her resistance to his plan to volunteer for a unit at the front.[36] And often women reacted less fearfully than Edith. Marie von N., over eighty years old, with a Christian background, maintained intensive letter communication with her grandsons, who served as soldiers in the East. Knowing about their involvement in atrocities against Russian civilians and their occasional qualms, she urged them to keep fighting at their utmost and by no means to develop any mercy for "these mean partisans. . . . Shall what has been done so far all be in vain again?" she asked in 1942, alluding to Germany's defeat in 1918. "This cannot be and may not be, you won't tolerate it, you beloved and brave boys! Don't forget the blood that has been spilled so far: it cries to the heavens."[37] A much younger woman, Liselotte Orgel, encouraged her husband, officer with the Wehrmacht, as late as 1944, "Shield your weak heart by extreme hardness, . . . harming the enemy whenever you can, that is your task, not making it easy for him to fight you."[38]

"There You Could See Piles of Corpses"

Though none of these women was a member of the Nazi Party, they all shared Germany's widespread anti-Semitism. During the *Blitzkrieg* period until early 1941, the Volksgemeinschaft celebrated German victories all over Europe; what discontent there was centered on the euthanasia action—the killing of seventy thousand people considered incurably sick by Nazi doctors—and thus on the murder of loved ones of "Aryan" Germans but not of the Jews. The "home front" was not ignorant of German cruelties in Poland. The Wehrmacht auxiliary Ilse Schmidt was confused in late 1939 when a Wehrmacht soldier friend wrote to her how he had cut off the beard of an old Jew. Schmidt's feelings stopped at confusion, though. More radical Germans, on hearing news about minor Wehrmacht casualties in Poland in September 1939, called for "putting the Jews up against the wall, ten per fallen German." And when in November 1939 plans for mass resettlement of Polish Jews in the Lublin district were "avidly discussed" within the

Reich, many Germans suggested that "also those Jews who were still living in Germany should get ready to march into that area," as the SS observed.³⁹

When in 1941 the deportations of German Jews actually started, they attracted public attention all over the country. In the picturesque university town of Göttingen, the NSDAP district officials moaned about being drowned in applications for the apartments of Jews, "as soon as people heard of the plans to deport the Göttingen Jews in the near future." Usually, marketplaces served as staging areas for the Jews being deported. The local commuter trains passed one such staging area in Hamburg and people opened their windows to see. Others gathered on the nearby streets to watch; a clapping crowd chased Jews into trucks; a group of hooting school kids accompanied the Jews as they moved out of the "workhouses." Such scenes became common in Germany in 1942 when deportations were launched all over the country. Snapshots taken by ordinary Germans clearly show that not only adults but also children united to celebrate the expulsion of the Jews. Something unusual had happened. Children no longer had to respect all adults. They had already seen how their Jewish classmates had been excluded, and many had seen or heard about the mistreatment of Jewish neighbors. Now they were allowed to watch their actual expulsion. These events were unmistakable signs of a fundamental change of ethics, and they also provided an arena where Aryans, young and old and thus in principle the whole family, could convene to demonstrate the purification of the Volksgemeinschaft—just as they had done before at the Nuremberg party rallies. Victor Klemperer, a former professor of romance who as a Jew living in Dresden in a mixed marriage was always afraid of deportation, once grievously realized how far the children's racism went. On his way home one day in August 1943, he was deeply hurt by a "well-dressed, intelligent-looking boy of perhaps eleven or twelve years of age," who shouted at him, " 'Kill him!—Old Jew, old Jew!' " Klemperer understood that the boy "must have parents who reinforce what he is taught in school and in the boys' organization."⁴⁰

Before deportation, Aryan couples sometimes enthusiastically denounced Jews, in particular those who lived in mixed marriages or who had managed otherwise to escape persecution. Such couples made true what the Führer was dreaming of: the Volksgemeinschaft's united racial struggle against the "community aliens." And while they did not necessarily go hand in hand to the Gestapo, wife and husband cooperated according to the military principle "March separately, strike united." Women stood ready to expose Jews in their neighborhoods, while men denounced their Jewish colleagues in the workplace.[41]

To be sure, not all Germans denounced Jews, lusted for their apartments, or plunged into rubbernecking and applauding the convoys of often old and fragile Jews. The regime occasionally articulated its indignation about "a certain wave of compassion to the Jews." The left liberal journalist Ursula von Kardorff observed in March 1943 a worker who offered his seat in the streetcar to a Jew and provoked the protest of a Nazi Party member. But the worker said to him: " 'It is me alone who decides where to put my ass.' "[42] The Germans did not unanimously support the Holocaust. But as a whole, society acted in conformance with the Nazi vision of the racist Volksgemeinschaft. Individuals may have felt pity with what happened to the Jews but no solidarity developed on their behalf, as Kardorff noted. The famous Rosenstrasse protest in Berlin in 1943 was a rare exception: Aryan women protested against the arrest and the possible deportation of their Jewish men until they were released. Usually, Germans who despised deportations and denunciations remained passive. On the home front as well as in the military a "spiral of silence" abetted a public climate of racism that neutralized individual deviation: those who viewed themselves as the minority shut up and left public communication to those whom they considered the dominating majority, whether wrongly or rightly.[43] Inwardly, many Germans may have opposed the anti-Jewish policy, but outwardly— through their actions and nonactions—they confirmed it.

From the beginning of Operation Barbarossa in the summer of 1941, Germans at home learned about the murder of the Jews in the Soviet Union through soldiers' letters, oral accounts, gossip, and rumor. In August 1941, a police officer serving in Lithuania wrote home, "Here all Jews are executed . . . men, women, children, all whacked. The Jews are to be exterminated completely." He added, "And don't tell R. a thing about it now; maybe later at some point."[44] When soldiers, SS men, and police officers wrote about "our Jewish war," they fostered the cult of secrecy that radiated monstrosity, caused uneasiness, and evoked curiosity. In spring 1942 Hilde

Wieschenberg's friends in Düsseldorf passed around photos from Russia. "There you could see piles of corpses. I was horrified," she wrote to her husband in Russia, wondering if he were involved in these actions which had nothing to do with regular fighting. He refused to provide further information on the photos. "Such things should not be sent home. Only rear units are doing this," he wrote. Wieschenberg, however, had informed his wife before about the murder of the Jews in Russia and hadn't left much doubt about his approval. And whether or not Wieschenberg provided further knowledge about the genocide, people in Germany had plenty of other ways to acquire it. In December 1941 a woman in a bakery in Rhenish Emmerich spoke compassionately about the Jews in Russia whom, as she had heard, the Germans had driven into the woods to gun them down. She did so in front of various patrons, one of whom reported her to the Gestapo.[45]

To many Germans, sensation trumped qualms. So it was with a seventeen-year-old Düsseldorf student who revealed to the Gestapo, also in December 1941, that a Wehrmacht officer had described to his son, a Hitler Youth comrade of the student, how German soldiers killed the Jews in Estonia and Latvia, using four to five bullets to kill the kids but only one or two for the adults. The student admitted that he had also related this story to his teachers. During a January 1942 vacation in Austria, a staff judge from Berlin mentioned to a waitress in a coffee shop that the Jews in Germany would be notified of their deportation and would then be shipped to Poland, where their graves were already prepared. Asked not to talk about such things, he said, "This is an open secret, any intelligent person knows about it, only the fools don't."[46]

It is impossible to estimate reasonably how many Germans, either men or women, either at the battlefront or on the home front, knew about the Holocaust, and what exactly they knew. Few Germans knew about the entire monstrous dimensions of the death machinery of Auschwitz or Majdanek. However, more recent research into Gestapo reports, private letters, diaries, and memoirs has left little doubt that Germans who wanted to know were able to acquire at least rough knowledge of the ongoing mass murder. The Nazis "organized" guilt, even the "consciousness of guilt," as Hannah Arendt understood in early 1945, looking to Germany from her American exile. "Organized guilt" fueled the cohesion of the Volksgemeinschaft. The regime kept a cult of secrecy around its crimes but only to transmit, or to allow the transmittance of, the knowledge of those crimes even more perfidiously, by whispering campaigns and indirect confessions in the mass media, so that Germans bore the "onus of complicity and awareness of what was going on."[47]

Karl Dürkefälden was such a German. A draftsman at a machine factory in Celle in Lower Saxony, he was an average German worker except that he kept an extensive diary. What he learned in 1942 can be taken as representative of those Germans who did not deliberately shut their eyes and ears. In February 1942 he read in the regional newspaper that Hitler, in his address to the annual party rally, had repeated his earlier "prophecy" that "it would not be the Aryan race but the Jew that would be exterminated in this war." The article was titled: "The Jew Will Be Exterminated." During a train ride only a few days earlier, a soldier had told Dürkefälden about the cruel fate of Soviet POWs and mentioned that such mass exterminations had not occurred in World War I. In June 1942 Dürkefälden's brother-in-law, who had worked as a foreman in the Ukraine, told him about witnessing mass executions carried out by German police officers. "There are no more Jews in the Ukraine; whoever didn't escape was shot," chronicled Dürkefälden. Only few days later, he learned from traveling soldiers about the murder of the Jews in Poland "in their thousands." Shortly after, his boss told him what he had heard from his son, who, deployed in Białystok, had seen entire villages being exterminated, including all the women and children. Dürkefälden's mother-in-law, who took care of wounded soldiers in local hospitals, told him that one of them had confessed to her: "We have whacked ten thousand Jews in Russia." Like many other Germans, Dürkefälden listened illegally to the German-language news broadcasts from England's BBC radio network and heard about the deportation of Jews from France and how Jews were thrown "on freight wagons, shut, driven into an open territory and then gassed, saying heartbreaking prayers." From the BBC he also learned that the Germans left only five thousand Jews in Serbia, where seventy-five thousand or eighty-five thousand had once lived. Some Germans knew even more. Wehrmacht soldier Wilm Hosenfeld, clearly aware that millions of Jews had been butchered, was one of them; Victor Klemperer was another. On 24 October 1944 he noted in his diary that "six to seven million Jews . . . have been slaughtered (more exactly: shot and gassed)." It is worth noting to whom the Jew Klemperer owed his knowledge. It was the "reports of Aryans," as he repeatedly stated.[48]

"A Volksgemeinschaft Bound Together by Suffering and by Joy"

On 30 September 1942, Hitler gave a major public speech in the Berlin Sportpalast to open a new wave of War Winter Aid (*Kriegswinterhilfswerk*). He stated that "1918," the trauma of national dissolution and defeat, had been overcome. Class differences were dissolved; men and women thought, felt, and acted uniformly; home front and battlefront were united. Hitler celebrated that "what we National Socialists envisioned when we came out of the First World War" had come to fruition: "the great Reich of a Volksgemeinschaft bound together by suffering and by joy. For there is a great, bright aspect to this war: namely a great comradeship." It was true. In late 1942 the Volksgemeinschaft was no longer bound together solely by joy but also, and increasingly, by suffering. As Hitler put it, the "constituent act" of the "true Volksgemeinschaft" was "signed with the blood of all." What he wanted to address was not so much the murder of the Jews, although he addressed their "extermination" also in this speech, by reminding his listeners of his 1939 Reichstag prophesy. What needed to be evoked now was the shedding of Aryan blood—the sacrifice of the "Aryan people of Europe."[49]

Aryan Germans suffered and sacrificed. By the war's end in May 1945, allied bombs turned German cities into mountains of rubble, killed over four hundred thousand Germans, separated two million children from their families, and left more than seven million Germans with no home. The Red Army raped innumerable German women in the east, as many as two million, according to some estimates. Twelve million Germans fled from or were expelled by the Soviets, the Poles, the Czechs, and others. More than five million German soldiers never returned home but would be buried on battlefields all over Europe; millions would return only after months or years in Allied POW camps. The concentration of violence within Germany—and no longer only outside of it—allowed Germans to see themselves as passive objects of an inscrutable destiny and thus as victims of the war they had begun in 1939—that is, victims like the six million murdered Jews, the twenty-five million dead Soviet citizens, and many others.[50]

But their own victimhood at the end of the war could not make Germans forget what they had perpetrated. Although the Nazi regime prosecuted Germans who talked about it in public, it indirectly admitted the Holocaust. It did so in vague terms, without revealing the details of how it was organized, who was in charge of it, and how many Jews were victimized. But by 1942 the regime needed to spread the open secret of the murder of the Jews in order to fight war exhaustion, as Allied bombers started to raze German cities, and to disseminate it still further after the fall of Stalingrad in early 1943, and when the rumors of the rape of German women by Red Army soldiers spread in 1944. No longer was the vision of a grand national future in superiority and exploitation invoked to make Germans fight, conform, and sacrifice; now it was the apocalyptic vision of complete destruction, enslavement, and abuse of the country. And it worked. Even fourteen-year-old BDM girl Edelgard B. understood why Goebbels's call for "total war" was "absolutely right"—"because we must win, of course. Better we give what we can now than ending up in Siberia."[51]

That was exactly what the regime wanted the Volksgemeinschaft to believe. It wanted Germans to realize that they were locked into a national community of crime and guilt. Göring's October 1942 insinuation that the Jews would take revenge on all Germans and "exterminate whatever is racially pure and German," whether "democrat, plutocrat, Social Democrat or Communist," had set the tone. Nazi leaders didn't tire from repeating it: the bridges had been burned, announced the Nazis' chief ideologist Alfred Rosenberg to local party leaders, but they knew it anyway. Germans understood: the only choice left was to fight on, into the abyss. It was the knowledge of the nation's responsibility for the murder of the Jews that fueled the sense of belonging to a community of fate (Schicksalsgemeinschaft) that left no other options. The fear of revenge united home front and battlefront, just as the rumors of the murder of the Jews had done since 1941, and even before. "If we should lose the war," said the Wehrmacht soldier Walter Kassler to his brother-in-law Karl Dürkefälden while on leave, "they will do to us what we have done to them." In a Mosel restaurant a customer in November 1943 raised the question "Do you actually know why they bomb our cities?" and had the answer down pat: "Because we have killed the Jews." It was just such street and tavern talk that Wurttemberg's Protestant bishop Wurm echoed three weeks later in a memorandum stating that "our *Volk* sees the air raids of the enemies as a retribution for what has been done to the Jews."[52]

The language is telling. Germans, when talking secretly about the murder of the Jews, acted exactly as Göring had advised them in October 1942. They did not blame "these mean Nazis" but the entire "Volk." The responsibility for the Holocaust was communicated in the language of Us, the German people, and Them, the Jews. Even during the horrors of spring 1945, workers in Berlin knew "that we have only ourselves to blame for this war because we treated the Jews so badly." The Nazi spy who reported this exchange noted that "similar observations now were often heard."[53]

There is no reason to disavow the massive and manifold inner frictions that shaped the German society at the end of the war. Social isolation in the rubble, loss of faith in Hitler, and collapse of war morale spread throughout Germany.[54] What united soldiers and civilians, men and women, young and old, war enthusiasts and war resisters, Nazis and anti-Nazis, the hangmen of the Gestapo and the few hidden or open opponents of the regime, was a new sense of national belonging, the knowledge of being part of a grand community of crime.

CONCLUSION

After capitulating to the Allies in May 1945, the Germans were taught lessons on the meaning of shame and guilt. The occupiers exposed Germans to what they—as a nation—had done. Most Germans had at least some vague idea, but now they could no longer evade knowing the complete truth. Horrifying photos, taken by American soldiers when they liberated concentration camps like those in Dachau or Buchenwald, showing masses of dead, naked, and emaciated bodies, were displayed on posters on public walls, columns, and offices, and in the newspapers, and they were unambiguous. "These Atrocities: Your Guilt!" read one headline. Or: "This Is Your Guilt—You Are Jointly Responsible for These Barbarous Crimes," read another. Naming camps, listing the numbers of the victims, and addressing the ways the murders had been carried out, the posters explained why Germans were found guilty: "You stood by and didn't care."[1]

The accusation presumed German "collective guilt" (*Kollektivschuld*) that had become widely believed in the Anglophone countries during the war. The news of the mass murder of the Jews and Germany's criminal warfare in the East had engendered stereotypes of a barbarian and power-obsessed German national character, culminating in Nazi Germany's anti-Semitism and master-race ideology. In Germany, such generalizations were met with denial and incomprehension. So was the reeducation and denazification program that the Allies launched in the western zones, although it was mainly concerned with identifying different degrees and types of support of the Nazi regime. Already in the Nuremberg Trial the defendants were convicted on the basis of individual guilt, whereas the notion of "collective guilt" and the assumption that all Germans or the majority of them had committed crimes against humanity was explicitly dismissed. But just because the Nuremberg judgments held only top-ranking Nazis responsible for the crimes, average Germans felt exonerated and opposed any further exploration of what they had done, thought, or felt during the Nazi era, and only a few were willing to examine their own consciences or question those of their fellow citizens. So the Nuremberg decisions helped the Germans to develop a strong solidarity of collective exculpation that shaped their "coping with the past" through the 1990s. It was the Nazis, the Nazi leaders, the Führer, the SS, some criminals, some sadists who were responsible for the crimes of the Third Reich—but not ordinary Germans.

And because the transfer of responsibility and guilt to a limited number of individuals did not entirely suffice, Germans escaped into a discourse of victimization that allowed them to eliminate questions of guilt and responsibility even more resolutely. This discourse revolved around arguments such as: we couldn't do anything; we had no choice; we were seduced by Hitler and terrorized by the Gestapo; we were at the mercy of a military machine; and finally, we lost our lives, our loved ones, our homes in a total war, not of our own accord but as a consequence of the Allied air raids and the Russian invasion. Perceiving themselves as victims allowed Germans to admit only collective responsibility, not collective guilt. As the historian Charles Maier has written, collective responsibility "means being willing to recognize the liabilities that emerge from group existence and membership," but—significantly—it "entails an effort at overcoming or repairing the consequences" *without* admitting guilt and without feeling morally contaminated. But no matter how desperately the idea of "collective guilt" is rejected, guilt is always individual, and if a collective is found guilty, then it is still the combination of individual membership, individual support, and individual action or passivity on which the judgment is based.[2]

When Germans after 1945 tried to rid themselves of an assumed "collective guilt," they were driven by paradoxical memories. On the one hand, they knew about their complicity—that the murder of the Jews was a German crime, not only a Nazi crime. From 1933 on, most Germans had been aware of the activities—the harassment, the exclusion, and, starting in 1939, the murder of the Jews—that were carried out on behalf of the German nation. On the other hand, most Germans, as individuals, insisted on not having done any wrong. Most of them had not personally committed murder; they had not pulled the trigger, nor had they opened gas chambers, and even the number of those who had been closer to such crimes—soldiers who rounded up Jews in the East, housewives who applauded the deportation of Jews from Germany, men and women who stole or bought the possessions of their former Jewish neighbors—did not represent the entire nation.

Precisely the relationship between different attitudes among Germans and the national unity that was nevertheless generated has been explored in this book. The conclusion is inescapable: the Nazi regime not only propagated a racially defined national community, the Volksgemeinschaft, but established it as a political, social, and psychological reality, not so much by providing Germans with economic benefits or by resolving their class conflicts but by making Germans complicit in mass crime. Such complicity was based on a variety of roles and allowed different degrees of commitment. Rather than breeding dissolution, differentiation enabled cohesion. How was that possible?

"Genocide . . . is an exercise in community building," Philip Gourevitch has noted in the context of Rwanda, reminding us that the techniques of social engineering deployed by the Nazis were not unique.[3] The Nazi genocide was certainly paradigmatic. However, it drew both its destructive and constitutive dynamic from radicalizing older thoughts about community-building by means of collective violence. In 1807 the German philosopher Georg Friedrich Wilhelm Hegel had written about what made the modern state. In his view, the state, the "whole," as he put it, embodied the engine of all human progress. Yet individuals, Hegel lamented, go "adrift from the whole, striving into inviolable self-existence and personal security." Families and other private communities are inclined to "break up the whole into fragments and let the common spirit evaporate," thus sinking back "into merely natural existence." To fight these centripetal and regressive forces, Hegel believed that from time to time government has "to shake them to the very center by war." In war, the individual feels "the power of their lord and master, death"—the life-threatening enemy. To fight the enemy, individuals reestablish what they had neglected: solidarity, or "common spirit."[4]

In the age of nation-states, Hegel's war wisdom would never lose its appeal. In war, the various societies within a nation stick together. The more they feel threatened by a mutual enemy, the more likely they are to ignore their internal conflicts. Though this idea was by no means limited to Germany, German politicians and thinkers were particularly fascinated with it when it came to building the German nation. "It is only through war that a nation becomes a real nation," Heinrich von Treitschke, an influential historian of Prussia's German mission, taught his students and fellow citizens in the 1890s. "Only acting together makes a people really stick together."[5] In summer 1914 the vision seemed to become true. But the attempt to conclude German nation-building by means of war led to disaster in 1918. Decomposition rather than national unity was the consequence of the First World War.

To be sure, there was no single lesson Germans took from the crucible of 1914–18. No one-way road led from 1918 to 1939 or 1941, or from the 1919 Versailles Treaty, which many Germans perceived as but an unbearable national humiliation, to the 1942 Wannsee Conference, which sealed the fate of European Jewry. After World War I, many Germans marched, voted, and spoke against warmongers who promoted another war as the way to regain Germany's lost power and prestige. By the mid-1920s it was not yet clear who would decide Germany's future—the leftists, pacifists, and democrats, or the rightists, militarists, and fascists. Germany's history was open, not least because the boundaries between these two camps were porous. In some regions of Germany, Jews suffered anti-Semitic violence, but in many places, particularly the big cities, they also felt welcome and at home. *Contingencies* did matter, and so did *continuities*. It was the unexpected economic crisis of 1929 that facilitated the rise of the Nazis, but the age-old desire for community did so as well—the utopia of a national community that would overcome all internal conflicts and cause that community to feel like a family, a group of friends, or a peaceful neighborhood. How could this utopia be realized in a modern society that necessarily created different and often conflicting interests, classes, ideals, and lifestyles? Precisely the ambiguities of this utopia allowed different and opposing political camps to subscribe to it—or to parts of it. Nationalist and rightist Germans were the most eager to promote the utopia of a Volksgemeinschaft, but Catholics and socialists found it attractive as well.

Though diverging about how the Volksgemeinschaft should appear, Germans developed some consensus about its nucleus—the kernel that was supposed to create the nation-community. According to the myth, soldierly comradeship in the trenches of 1914–18 had anticipated the Volksgemeinschaft. Small groups of comrades, thrown together by fate, had fought and suffered together, come what may. The good comrades had taken care of each other, shared each other's food, each other's worries, and their common mortality. Civilian differences and conflicts had evaporated. Trench comradeship had saved humanity in the inhuman midst of war. Why not transfer this mythical model to the entire society? The veterans' and the youth movement in the Weimar Republic sought to do precisely that. Feverishly, they spread the idea of comradeship.

But they did not succeed, at least not in the Weimar Republic. To be sure, war novels narrating comradeship sold very well around 1930. Youth associations, which practiced comradeship in social life, attracted more and more adherents. At the bottom of society, the changes were irrefutable. Germans felt uneasy or were even angry about divisions in their society and rendered homage to a morality that rejected the idea of individual responsibility but had group conformity as the highest value. Shame culture was about to replace guilt culture. However, parties, parliaments, and administrations remained divided along age-old lines of conflict and failed to stop the dissolution of the Weimar Republic. Only the Nazis put into practice what had been envisioned before: to build a nation along the model of trench comradeship. The Nazis did not invent the myth of comradeship or the vision of a Volksgemeinschaft. But they radicalized these and other preexisting ideas. They tied inclusion to exclusion; they replaced voluntariness with pressure; and they wove the myth of community into a revolutionary, racist, dichotomous morality.

When Germans in the Weimar period talked, wrote, and read about comradeship, or when they thought about the Volksgemeinschaft, they sensed fellowship, connectedness, harmony, security. Inclusion rather than exclusion shaped the ideas of community in Weimar Germany. Nazi Germany, though, brought to the warm and inclusive side of community its cold and dark brother: exclusion. There was no Us without Them. While the nation in pre-1933 Germany had been defined in terms of culture, language, or citizenship, the Nazis allowed only one understanding: the nation was to be racially and also ideologically exclusive. If Germans wanted to be included, they had to engage eagerly in excluding others—above all the Jews, but also a broad range of groups deemed to be "alien" to the community. To guarantee that "good" Germans would never forget the brutal side of social harmony, they were asked to spy on their colleagues, neighbors, and even family members to identify and denounce any kind of deviation or defiance.

To conclude their radicalization of the community discourse, the Nazis revolutionized the moral foundation of the society. Germans were to replace the Judeo-Christian tradition of universal humanity and individual responsibility with a dichotomous morality that revolved solely around the needs of the Us. This morality conceded material and immaterial benefits—gratitude, security, pity, mercy, tenderness—only to the Aryan Volksgemeinschaft, the combat unit, and the camp comrades. He who displayed pity or compassion for Them—Jews, other non-Aryans, "subhumans," "asocials," dissenters, enemies—revealed weakness and lack of community spirit. He would be either excluded from the Us altogether or downgraded to the bottom of social hierarchy. That hierarchy no longer relied on economic status, birthright, or academic credentials; it relied on the ability to perpetrate brutality against Them.

Putting this new morality into practice was not easy. The Nazis encouraged Germans to harass, boycott, and isolate Jews beginning in the spring of 1933. But many Germans remained reluctant and uncertain. They avoided contact or severed relations with Jewish neighbors, friends, and colleagues, but only a minority joined in violent anti-Semitic politics. Some even cultivated contacts with Jews. Although solidarity with the Jews was rare and barely eased the Jews' terror and fear, the regime wasn't satisfied with Aryan Germans' anti-Semitic performance, even after Kristallnacht. The regime's racist ideology did not suffice to make enough Germans act according to the new morals. It needed the training camps and the barracks—the military and paramilitary service—where they learned the basic lesson on how to "purify" their fatherland from its supposed "enemies" and from "aliens." The lesson was about comradeship. Comradeship radiated belonging, togetherness, and security, but only the one who conformed, joined in, and was ready to trade his individual identity for a collective identity gained the benefits of comradeship. Comradeship meant searching for, identifying, and excluding the Other. The moral grammar of comradeship obeyed one rule: anything was allowed that intensified the group's social life and secured its cohesion. The best way to unite people was to make them commit crimes together, as Hitler knew well. Youth in Nazi training camps and young soldiers in barracks usually did not commit real crimes. What they did learn was to break the norm; it didn't matter which one. Whether transgressing civilian norms of decency and politeness or violating the military norms of obedience through little conspiracies against the drill sergeant, it all served the same goal—to endow the group with a sense of social sovereignty, of independence from and elevation above the rest of the world.

Such bonding was not unique to Nazi Germany. Many of its features could be observed in Boy Scout camps and college fraternities in America, or in youth gangs and criminal associations there and elsewhere. Before and after the Third Reich, anthropologists studying tribal cultures have found patterns of male bonding, initiation rites, and liminality. What distinguished the Nazi version of male bonding from tribal cultures or modern gangs was not its internal grammar, but rather its social and political context. Modern gangs, fraternities, and camps as well as tribal liminality constitute an anti-structure, in the words of Victor Turner. They constitute exceptions to the rule, whether they are welcomed, tolerated, ignored, or criminalized. In Nazi Germany, though, liminal groups no longer embodied an anti-structure; they acted as paradigmatic for the structure. The Volksgemeinschaft was to be structured like a huge training camp.

Although the Nazis actively persecuted the Jews between 1933 and 1939, essentially the program of getting rid of them came to fruition outside of Germany—by occupation, exploitation, and terrorization of most parts of Europe beginning in September 1939. Overwhelmingly the worst was in East Europe, where millions of German men and tens of thousands of women engaged in a gigantic project of conquest. Its seductive magnitude derived in part from the size of the occupied territories, the amount of expropriated goods, and the number of subjugated people, but even more from the permission to do with them whatever the occupiers wanted. Conquering the East, Germans got a sense of the grandiosity of the Nazi utopia. In the East they realized what the Nazi revolution was all about: infinite possibilities, unlimited expansion, exceeding all the limits set by tradition, civilization, and conventions. In the East, the Volksgemeinschaft—the racially cleansed nation of the Aryan "master race"—came into being by suppressing, terror-izing, and killing all who did not belong.

According to the influential work of Benedict Anderson, a nation is "an imagined community." Whereas belonging in, say, a "primordial village" or a modern sports team is based on face-to-face interaction, the "members of even the smallest nation will never know most of their fellow-members, meet them, or even hear of them, yet in the minds of each lives the image of their communion." National belonging is based on shared ideas of similar interests and affinities. In modern nations, these ideas derive from collec-tive memory of glorious or disastrous events in the past, and from com-mon visions, fears, and hopes. Mass media often play an important role in spreading these ideas throughout the entire nation. Their suggestive and often destructive power originates from the way this kind of belonging is perceived—"as a deep, horizontal comradeship," regardless of "the actual inequality and exploitation that may prevail" in it.[6]

The basis for the "deep, horizontal comradeship" of the Volksgemeinschaft went well beyond ideas of national citizenship. State-organized face-to-face communities propelled national belonging as well. Small communities like the Border Police Station in Nowy Sacz, Police Battalion 101, the Auschwitz camp guards, Einsatzkommandos like that of SS officer Karl Jäger, Lieutenant Farnbacher's requisitioning corps, the brawling and murdering crowd of rank-and-file Willy Reese—all these communities provided evidence that the Volksgemeinschaft really existed on a daily basis. In these communi-ties, men and sometimes also women experienced togetherness as they had rehearsed it in barracks and training camps—by terrorizing others and by transgressing moral conventions on behalf of the Volksgemeinschaft.

But the joy of belonging in the Third Reich was permeated by pressure and compulsion. Although the Nazi dictatorship was not able to suppress freedom of action completely, taking advantage of the remnants of freedom was risky. You could refuse to participate in acts of brutality, but you would pay for it by being ridiculed, humiliated, and ostracized by your comrades and superiors. Only a few were able to withstand such pressure. And the same was true for the pressure to participate in murder at least once, after which you knew you could no longer turn back. In fact, the consequences of refusing to participate were limited. You would not be completely excluded, let alone shot or jailed. Instead you would be disgraced and subordinated. The hierarchic fabric of the group needed the "shirker" as an in-built outsider just as it needed the bully. The sociology of inclusion was perfidious. The gang did not leave the apostates alone but made them do the preliminary work such as rounding up the victims, or they made them at least witness the crime, thus evoking in them too a sense of complicity. Indeed, merely wearing the same uniform as the actual perpetrators sufficed to instill that sense of complicity.

And it did not even need the uniform. Simply being German—and knowing what was going on—was enough to establish a grand "imagined" community of crime that encompassed millions of ordinary soldiers serving all over Europe as well as Germans at home, including women, youth, and even younger children. What bound them together and made them feel as a nation was not only the pleasure of terror, which didn't last long, but even more a bad conscience, which persisted. Even in the core groups of the perpetrators only a minority was enthusiastic about terror and murder. The rest joined in, maybe even enthusiastically in a moment of ecstasy, but only to suffer soon after from qualms about what they had done. Qualms also haunted the millions of German soldiers who saw the initial steps toward the Final Solution in summer 1941 in the East and then adjusted to genocidal warfare, to murdering, plundering, and torturing. They oscillated between the collective joys and mushrooming pangs, always ready to escape into rampant cynicism. As chaotic as these sentiments were, there was one that ordered them: the sense of representing the German nation.

Even under the Nazi dictatorship, Germans had choices. Embarrassed about their regime, they could have left their country. By doing so they would have deprived the regime of its mass support. But only very few Germans did emigrate. Sebastian Haffner, not a Jew, was one of them. Most Germans instead made their peace with the Nazi regime, if they didn't actually revere it. Numerous Germans joined in anti-Jewish ostracism, approved terror against them, and applauded their deportation and extermination during the war. These Germans constituted a minority, though a large minority. A much smaller minority performed symbolic gestures on behalf of the Jews; but they did so only occasionally, and seldom in public. Most Germans were ambivalent and their actions ambiguous. They broke off with their Jewish friends and neighbors, not in a mood of grandiosity but in one of indifference. They looked the other way when Jews were publicly humiliated, or they stared blankly as the deportations began. And when they heard the rumors about the mass shootings in the East or about the gas chambers, many Germans probably were uneasy. But they knew how to reassure themselves: it was only the Jews.

The heinous acts of Hitler's soldiers may be compared to the actions of other soldiers perpetrating mass atrocities in war, for instance a small minority of American soldiers in Vietnam. These atrocities, however, never grew into genocide. American soldiers always knew that, if they survived, they would return to an intact civil society. This cannot be overemphasized; it applies to other wars of industrial societies in the twentieth century. Whatever the outcome of the war, Hitler's soldiers could not expect to return to a civilian society. An extremely militarized society, which eventually became a genocidal one, had burned all bridges to the rest of the civilized world. The gender bias, typical of all modern societies, prevailed in Nazi Germany as well. Women did not engage in genocide in the same way as men. Yet the gender gap lost its significance when the racial gap between Aryans and non-Aryans took precedence. The new society excluded Jews of both sexes, placed various groups of slaves on the bottom, and positioned Aryans of both sexes at the top. It was this seductive social advancement, experienced as progressive, that made women complicit in the genocidal morality.

Morality cannot be changed within a few years. Justifying and even demanding mass murder, Nazi morals certainly fueled and facilitated mass support for genocide. Shame culture undermined guilt culture. But it did not annul it. Germans, perpetrating or supporting mass murder, were still aware of how immensely they and their country violated the most basic values of their civilization. The terror of seeing their fatherland threatened by the Jews or overrun by Slavic hordes supported Germans' ability to compartmentalize crimes and cohesion, but it did not erase Germans' sense of guilt about what had been done to the Jews. The Nazi genocide was thus doubly paradigmatic: it developed the logistics necessary to spread mass murder over an entire continent, and—as this book has argued—it made an entire, civilized nation *feel* complicit in that mass crime. It was the knowledge of having perpetrated or supported the Holocaust that launched a completely new kind of nation-building. Its outcome was the national brotherhood of mass murder—Hitler's community.

ACKNOWLEDGMENTS

Written over the past few years, this book is embedded in earlier projects which I pursued in the 1990s in Germany. Whereas these projects resulted in a German book, published in 2006, on comradeship as a social practice in Hitler's army and as a war myth throughout the twentieth century, the book at hand takes a rather different view in analyzing the entire Third Reich society before and during the Holocaust. Nevertheless, both books refer to each other; the new one could not have been written without the support I have received from many friends, colleagues, and institutions when I wrote the first one. I am still grateful to the German Research Council, the Volkswagen Foundation, the University of Konstanz, and the University of Bielefeld for laying ground for my research in Germany. I am also grateful to Omer Bartov, Ute Frevert, Michael Geyer, Dirk Heinrichs, Alf Lüdtke, Dieter Langewiesche, Cornelia Rauh, Hans-Ulrich Wehler, and Benjamin Ziemann for their comments on my studies at that time.

Since 2003, I have profited from the exciting academic culture in America, from the encouragement of colleagues at Clark University and at the Strassler Center for Holocaust and Genocide Studies, from the material and immaterial benefits of an endowed chair, for which I am deeply indebted to David Strassler, and not least from a research grant from the Higgins School of the Humanities at Clark University. In my classes on Nazi Germany and the Holocaust Perpetrators, graduate and undergraduate students have been engaged in critical discussions of the project; their feedback was meaningful. The staff of Clark's Goddard Library worked diligently to provide me with innumerable books, even from remote places.

My archival research has been facilitated far away from Clark by the staff of the Bundesarchiv in Ludwigsburg, the Staatsarchiv in Munich, the Bibliothek für Zeitgeschichte in Stuttgart, the Archive at Yad Vashem, and, earlier, among others, the Bundesarchiv in Aachen, the Bundesarchiv-Militärarchiv in Freiburg, the Landeshauptarchiv in Koblenz, the Historisches Archiv des Erzbistums in Cologne, Walter Kempowski's private archive in Nartum, and the University of Chicago Library.

Presentations at numerous institutions and conferences have generated constructive criticism that has encouraged me to reconsider, sharpen, or revise my arguments. I am grateful to the following institutions for inviting me: Institute for Advanced Study in Princeton; Princeton University; Ohio State University; National Humanities Center; Harvard University; Yale University; Jewish Foundation for the Righteous; University of California at San Diego; College of the Holy Cross; Keene State College; Humboldt State University; University of Sheffield; University of London; Danish Institute for International Studies; Humboldt University in Berlin; University of Mainz; University of Saarbrücken; Ben-Gurion University; Hebrew University; Bar-Ilan University; and Yad Vashem.

At these institutions and elsewhere, many colleagues and friends have provided much more support, encouragement, and fruitful critique than I could have expected. Dan Bar-on, Volker Berghahn, Dirk Bonker, Timothy Brown, Christopher Browning, David Ciarlo, Déborah Dwork, Daniel Goldhagen, Karen Hagemann, Claudia Koonz, Robert Melson, Dan McMillan, Dan Michman, Geoffrey Parker, Uta Poiger, Raz Segal, Edward Westermann, and Benjamin Ziemann commented on basic arguments or early drafts of the book. Toward the final stages, Donald Bloxham, James Retallack, Helmut Walser Smith, Eric D. Weitz, and particularly Margaret Lavinia Anderson read the entire manuscript, suggested crucial clarifications and revisions, and provided invaluable assistance in improving its language. I am thankful to each of them.

Writing a book in a second language is exciting but also challenging. I would not have managed it without Diana Bartley, who worked with me on the manuscript from the beginning, urged me to make it readable, and spent endless time making it readable. For editing first drafts, I also wish to thank Ellen Gilbert and Nina Kushner. At Yale University Press I thank Jonathan Brent, Sarah A. Miller, Laura Davulis, and Jeffrey Schier for reliable advice and superior editing.

This book is written by a German, a child not of perpetrators but of the perpetrator society, and it is about the perpetrators and the perpetrator society. It explores only one side of the Holocaust. For teaching me the Holocaust from the victims' perspective, I am grateful to Déborah Dwork and to Na'ama Shik, who did so in their own, rather different ways.

NOTES

════════

Introduction

Epigraph: Interview with Christina Del Sesto, "Champion of Human Survival Tries to Awaken Academics to a Nuclear Menace," *New York Times*, 18 Nov 2000.

1. "The United Nations Convention on the Prevention and Punishment of the Crime of Genocide" (9 Dec 1948), in Samuel Totten and Paul R. Batrop (eds.), *The Genocide Studies Reader* (New York, 2009), 31 (Article 2); Martin Shaw, *What Is Genocide?* (Cambridge, 2007).

2. Andrej Angrick, *Besatzungspolitik und Massenmord. Die Einsatzgruppe D in der südlichen Sowjetunion 1941–1943* (Hamburg, 2003); Edward B. Westermann, *Hitler's Police Battalions. Enforcing Racial War in the East* (Lawrence, 2005); Robert Jay Lifton, *Nazi Doctors: Medical Killing and the Psychology of Genocide* (New York, 2000); Götz Aly and Susanne Heim, *Architects of Annihilation: Auschwitz and the Logic of Destruction* (Princeton, 2002); Michael Wildt, *Generation des Unbedingten. Das Führungskorps des Reichssicherheitshauptamtes* (Hamburg, 2002); Wendy Lower, *Nazi Empire-Building and the Holocaust in the Ukraine* (Chapel Hill, 2005).

3. Ian Kershaw, *The Nazi Dictatorship. Problems and Perspectives of Interpretation* (4th ed., London, 2000); Richard Bessel, "Functionalists Versus Intentionalists: The Debate Twenty Years On, Or Whatever Happened to Functionalism and Intentionalism?" *German Studies Review* 26 (2003), 15–20; Mark Roseman, "Beyond Conviction. Perpetrators, Ideas, and Action in the Holocaust in Historiographical Perspective," in *Conflict, Catastrophe and Continuity. Essays on Modern History*, ed. Frank Biess, Mark Roseman, and Hannah Schissler (New York, 2007), 83–103.

4. Thomas Kühne, "Der nationalsozialistische Vernichtungskrieg und die 'ganz normalen' Deutschen. Forschungsprobleme und Forschungstendenzen der Gesellschaftsgeschichte des Zweiten Weltkriegs. Erster Teil," *Archiv für*

Sozialgeschichte 39 (1999), 580–662; Yehuda Bauer, *Rethinking the Holocaust* (New Haven, 2001), 68–118; Dan Stone, ed., *The Historiography of the Holocaust* (New York, 2004).

5. Hans Mommsen, "Forschungskontroversen zum Nationalsozialismus," *Aus Politik und Zeitgeschichte*, no. 14–15 (2 Apr 2007), 14; Omer Bartov, *Hitler's Army. Soldiers, Nazis, and War in the Third Reich* (New York, 1991) established the benchmark. Cf. Konrad H. Jarausch and Michael Geyer, *Shattered Past. Reconstructing German Histories* (Princeton, 2003), 111–172.

6. Norman Naimark, *Fires of Hatred. Ethnic Cleansing in Twentieth-Century Europe* (Cambridge, Mass., 2001); Eric D. Weitz, *A Century of Genocide. Utopias of Race and Nation* (Princeton, 2003); Jacques Semelin, *Purify and Destroy. The Political Uses of Massacre and Genocide* (New York, 2007); Jörg Baberowski and Anselm Doering-Manteuffel, "The Quest for Order and the Pursuit of Terror. National Socialist Germany and the Stalinist Soviet Union as Multiethnic Empires," in *Beyond Totalitarianism. Stalinism and Nazism Compared*, ed. Michael Geyer and Sheila Fitzpatrick (Cambridge, 2009), 180–227.

7. Daniel Jonah Goldhagen, *Hitler's Willing Executioners. Ordinary Germans and the Holocaust* (New York, 1996); cf. Robert R. Shandley, ed., *Unwilling Germans? The Goldhagen Debate* (Minneapolis, 1998); Omer Bartov, *Germany's War and the Holocaust. Disputed Histories* (Ithaca, 2003); Saul Friedländer, *Nazi Germany and the Jews. The Years of Persecution, 1933–1939* (New York, 1997), 73–112; idem, *The Years of Extermination. Nazi Germany and the Jews, 1939–1945* (New York, 2007); Michael Wildt, *Volksgemeinschaft al Selbstermächtigung. Gewalt gegen Juden in der deutschen Provinz, 1919–1939* (Hamburg, 2007); Christopher Browning and Lewis H. Siegelbaum, "Frameworks for Social Engeneering. Stalinist Schema of Identification and the Nazi Volksgemeinschaft," in Geyer and Fitzpatrick, eds., *Beyond Totalitarianism*, 231–265.

8. Cf., as a sociological approach, Wolfgang Sofsky, *The Order of Terror. The Concentration Camp* (Princeton, 1997), but see Bartov, *Germany's War and the Holocaust*, 99–121.

9. To be sure, these views were never unchallenged; see, e.g., Robert Gellately, *Backing Hitler. Consent and Coercion in Nazi Germany* (Oxford, 2001); a concise account is also Norbert Frei, "People's Community and War. Hitler's Popular Support," in Hans Mommsen, *The Third Reich Between Vision and Reality* (Oxford, 2001), 59–77.

10. Claudia Koonz, *The Nazi Conscience* (Cambridge, Mass., 2003), 1–6. See also Harald Welzer, "Mass Murder and Moral Code: Some Thoughts on an Easily Misunderstood Project," *History of the Human Sciences* 17 (2004), 15–32.

11. Chapter One as well as some paragraphs of the fourth chapter follow elaborations in Thomas Kühne, *Kameradschaft. Die Soldaten des nationalsozialistischen Krieges und das 20. Jahrhundert* (Göttingen, 2006).

1 Craving Community

1. Erich Maria Remarque, *All Quiet on the Western Front* (New York, 1982), 216–225 (original Engl. New York, 1929.); (movie) *All Quiet on the Western Front*, directed by Lewis Milestone (USA, 1930).

2. Franz Faßbender, "Jugend und Dichtung," *Zeitschrift für deutsche Bildung* 7 (1931), 18–26; see also *New York Times*, 18 Jan 1930, 5, "Remarque tops list in German colleges." Modris Eksteins, *Rites of Spring. The Great War and the Birth of the Modern Age* (Boston, 1989), 275–99; Thomas Schneider, "Die Meute hinter Remarque. Zur Rezeption von *Im Westen nichts Neues* 1928–1930," *Jahrbuch zur Literatur der Weimarer Republik* 1 (1995), 143–170; Bärbel Schrader, ed., *Der Fall Remarque: Im Westen nichts Neues. Eine Dokumentation* (Leipzig, 1992).

3. Karl Hugo Sclutius, "Pazifistische Kriegspropaganda," *Die Weltbühne*, 2 Apr 1929, 517–522; idem, "Nochmals: Pazifistische Kriegspropaganda," in ibid., 28 May 1929, 826–827.

4. Remarque, *All Quiet on the Western Front*, 216–225.

5. Ibid., 26f; this translation uses "esprit de corps" instead of "belonging." "Esprit de corps," however, does not equal the German word "Zusammengehörigkeitsgefühl"; Remarque, *Im Westen nichts Neues. Roman* (Cologne, 1987), 28.

6. Remarque, *All Quiet on the Western Front*, 113, 211f, 201.

7. Ibid., 225–229.

8. New English translation: Ferdinand Tönnies, *Community and Civil Society* (Cambridge, 2001), 52, 32–34, 36, 66. Zygmunt Baumann, *Community. Seeking Safety in an Insecure World* (Cambridge, 2001), 9f, 12f.

9. Charles Horton Cooley, *Social Organization: A Study of the Larger Mind* (New York, 1909), 25ff; Emile Durkheim, *The Division of Labor in Society* (New York, 1997, French original 1893), 149ff.

10. Thomas Kühne, "Political Culture and Democratization," in *Imperial Germany 1871–1918. The Short Oxford History of Germany*, ed. James Retallack (Oxford, 2008), 174–195.

11. Gunther Mai, "*Verteidigung* und *Volksgemeinschaft*. Staatliche Selbstbehauptung, nationale Solidarität und soziale Befreiung in Deutschland in der Zeit des Ersten Weltkrieges (1900–1925)," in *Der Erste Weltkrieg. Wirkung, Wahrnehmung, Analyse*, ed. Wolfgang Michalka (Munich, 1994), 583–602.

12. Jeffrey Verhey, *The Spirit of 1914: Militarism, Myth and Mobilization in Germany* (New York, 2000).

13. Benjamin Ziemann, *War Experiences in Rural Germany, 1914–1923* (Oxford, 2007); Roger Chickering, *Imperial Germany and the Great War, 1914–1918* (2d ed., Cambridge, 2004).

14. Boris Barth, *Dolchstosslegenden und politische Desintegration: Das Trauma der deutschen Niederlage im Ersten Weltkrieg, 1914–1933* (Düsseldorf, 2003).

15. Walter Flex, *Wanderer zwischen beiden Welten*, new edition (Kiel, 1986).

16. Franz Schauwecker, *The Furnace* (London, 1930), 196f (English translation of
    Aufbruch der Nation, 1930). See Hermann Pongs, "Krieg als Volksschicksal im
    deutschen Schrifttum I," *Dichtung und Volkstum* 35 (1934), 61; Günther Lutz,
    "Das Gemeinschaftserlebnis in der Kriegsliteratur" (PhD diss., University of
    Greifswald, 1936), 82; Michael Gollbach, *Die Wiederkehr des Weltkrieges in der
    Literatur. Zu den Frontromanen der späten Zwanziger Jahre* (Kronberg, 1978),
    154–159. The motif has been omnipresent in war literature since the 1920s; see for
    instance Werner Beumelburg, *Die Gruppe Bosemüller* (Oldenburg, 1930), 261.
17. Johann Wilhelm Mannhardt, *Schützengrabenmenschen* (Hamburg, 1919).
18. Siegfried von Wegeleben, *Das Felderlebnis. Eine Untersuchung seiner
    Entwicklung, seines Wesens und seiner Bedeutung für die Gegenwart* (Berlin, 1921),
    25f, 35f, 105ff.
19. J[osef] Schneider, *Lebensweisheit für Deutsche, besonders Reichswehr und Polizei*
    (Berlin-Charlottenburg, 1926), 130.
20. Theodor Bartram, *Der Frontsoldat. Ein deutsches Kultur- und Lebensideal*
    (2d ed., Berlin, 1934), 18. Compare Eric J. Leed, *No Man's Land. Combat and
    Identity in World War I* (Cambridge, 1979), 80–90.
21. Uli Otto and Eginhard König, *"Ich hatt einen Kameraden . . ." Militär und Kriege
    in den historisch-politischen Liedern in den Jahren von 1740 bis 1914* (Regensburg,
    1999).
22. Victor W. Turner, "Myth and Symbol," in *International Encyclopedia of the
    Social Sciences*, vol. 10, ed. David L. Sills (New York, 1968), 576–581; Robert Alan
    Segal, ed., *The Myth and Ritual Theory. An Anthology* (Malden, Mass., 1998);
    general, on memory, Maurice Halbwachs, *On Collective Memory*, ed. Lewis
    A. Coser (Chicago, 1992); James Fentress and Chris Wickham, *Social Memory*
    (Oxford, 1992).
23. Schneider, *Lebensweisheit für Deutsche*, 31f.
24. Special pages in *Konstanzer Zeitung* and *Deutsche Bodensee-Zeitung* on "the day
    of the 114th," both 31 Aug 1925.
25. See Volker G. Probst, *Bilder vom Tode. Eine Studie zum deutschen Kriegerdenkmal
    in der Weimarer Republik am Beispiel des Pieta-Motivs und seiner profanierten
    Varianten* (Hamburg, 1986), 46ff; Christel Beilmann, *Eine katholische Jugend in
    Gottes und dem Dritten Reich. Briefe, Gedrucktes 1930–1945, Kommentare 1988/89*
    (Wuppertal, 1989), 220; Schrader, *Der Fall Remarque*, 24, 28ff (on reception of
    Remarque's novel).
26. *Mitteilungen des Reichsbundes der Kriegsbeschädigten und ehem. Kriegsteilnehmer*,
    6 Dec 1918. See also *Reichsbanner* 1 Apr 1926, and ibid., 26 Sept 1931.
27. The colors of the flag of the Weimar Republic stood in contrast to the black-white-
    red flag of the previous monarchy. See Karl Rohe, *Das Reichsbanner Schwarz
    Rot Gold. Ein Beitrag zur Geschichte und Struktur der politischen Kampfverbände
    zur Zeit der Weimarer Republik* (Düsseldorf, 1966); Benjamin Ziemann,
    "Republikanische Kriegserinnerung in einer polarisierten Öffentlichkeit. Das

Reichsbanner Schwarz-Rot-Gold als Veteranenverband der sozialistischen Arbeiterschaft," *Historische Zeitschrift* 267 (1998), 357–398.

28. *Reichsbanner*, 12 Sept 1931, *Mitteilungen des Reichsbundes*, 6 Dec 1918; Adam Scharrer, *Vaterlandslose Gesellen. Das erste Kriegsbuch eines Arbeiters* (Vienna, 1930), 93ff; Martin Hobohm, "Soziale Heeresmißstände als Teilursache des deutschen Zusammenbruchs von 1918," in: *Das Werk des Untersuchungsausschusses der Verfassunggebenden Deutschen Nationalversammlung und des Deutschen Reichstages 1919–1930, part 4, Die Ursachen des Deutschen Zusammenbruchs im Jahre 1918*, vol. II-11/1 (Berlin, 1929); *Konstanzer Zeitung*, 8 Dec 1927.

29. Ernst Johannsen, *Vier von der Infanterie. Ihre letzten Tage an der Westfront 1918* (Hamburg-Bergedorf, 1929), 11, 13f, 48f.

30. Remarque, *All Quiet on the Western Front*, 223; Schrader, *Der Fall Remarque*, 28ff; *Reichsbund. Organ des Reichsbundes der Kriegsbeschädigten*, 15 Nov 1925 and 10 May 1932; Bernhard Diebold, ed., *Das Buch der guten Werke 1914–1918* (Frankfurt, 1932). See Holger Klein, "Comrades? The Enemy as Individual in First World War Poetry," in *Intimate Enemies. English and German Literary Reactions to the Great War 1914–1918*, ed. Franz Karl Stanzel and Martin Löschnigg (Heidelberg, 1993), 181–199. On the rare reality of such fraternization during the First World War, see Jay Winter and Blaine Baggett, *The Great War and the Shaping of the 20th Century* (New York, 1996), 96–99, 235–38.

31. *Reichsbund. Organ des Reichsbundes der Kriegsbeschädigten*, 20 June 1932. On related politics, see Rohe, *Reichsbanner Schwarz-Rot-Gold*, 152f.

32. Dave Grossman, *On Killing. The Psychological Cost of Learning to Kill in War and Society* (Boston, 1995); George L. Mosse, *Fallen Soldiers. Reshaping the Memory of the World Wars* (New York, 1990).

33. Kurt Tucholsky, "Der bewachte Kriegsschauplatz," *Die Weltbühne*, 4 Aug 1931. See Michael Hepp and Viktor Otto, eds., *"Soldaten sind Mörder." Dokumentation einer Debatte, 1931–1996* (Berlin, 1996).

34. Benjamin Ziemann, *Front und Heimat. Ländliche Kriegserfahrungen im südlichen Bayern 1914–1923* (Essen, 1997), 185 fn 728 (quotation from a soldier's letter, 12 Apr 1917); idem, *War Experiences in Rural Germany*, 93f; Philip Witkop, ed., *German Students' War Letters* (Philadelphia, 2002); Raymund Dreiling, *Das religiöse und sittliche Leben der Armee unter dem Einfluß des Weltkrieges* (Paderborn, 1922), 39, 43f, 50; Leed, *No Man's Land*, 194f.

35. Ernst Jünger, *Der Kampf als inneres Erlebnis* (Berlin, 1922), 32, 55, 74; Werner Elert, *Zur Geschichte des kriegerischen Ethos* (Leipzig, 1928), 139 (despise of comradeship); Werner Picht, *Der Frontsoldat* (Berlin, 1937), 31–39 (soldier and civilian).

36. *Stahlhelm*, 15 Dec 1921, 345; *Kyffhäuser*, 5 May 1929, 337f.

37. *Deutsche Bodensee-Zeitung*, 31 Aug 1925, Festbeilage 114er Tag; *Konstanzer Zeitung*, 31 Aug 1925.

38. *Konstanzer Volksblatt*, 12 May 1921 and 2 Sept 1925; Lothar Burchardt et al., *Konstanz im 20. Jahrhundert. Die Jahre 1914–1945* (Konstanz, 1990), 167.

39. 'Brian E. Grim, " 'Was It All Just a Dream?' German-Jewish Veterans and the Confrontation with *völkisch* Nationalism During the Interwar Period," in *Sacrifice and National Belonging in Twentieth-Century Germany*, ed. Greg Eghigian and Matthew Paul Berg (Arlington, 2002), 64–89; Ulrich Dunker, *Der Reichsbund jüdischer Frontsoldaten, 1918–1938* (Düsseldorf, 1977).

40. Alois Klotzbücher, *Der politische Weg des Stahlhelm — Bund der Frontsoldaten in der Weimarer Republik* (Phil. Diss., Erlangen-Nürnberg, 1964), 43ff; Volker R. Berghahn, *Der Stahlhelm. Bund der Frontsoldaten 1918–1935* (Düsseldorf, 1966), 107.

41. *Stahlhelm*, 18 Jan 1925; see *Kyffhäuser*, 24 Apr 1927, 367f. On the making of the Volksgemeinschaft by Weimar nationalist associations, see Peter Fritzsche, *Rehearsals for Fascism. Populism and Political Mobilization in Weimar Germany* (New York, 1990); Frank Bösch, *Das konservative Milieu. Vereinskultur und lokale Sammlungspolitik in ost- und westdeutschen Regionen (1900–1960)* (Göttingen, 2002), 66ff; Helge Matthiesen, "Von der Massenbewegung zur Partei. Der Nationalismus in der deutschen Gesellschaft der Zwischenkriegszeit," *Geschichte in Wissenschaft und Unterricht* 48 (1997), 316–329; Claus-Christian W. Szejnmann, *Nazism in Central Germany. The Brownshirts in "Red" Saxony* (New York, 1999).

42. Rohe, *Das Reichsbanner Schwarz Rot Gold*, 110–147, 245–258; Jacob Toury, "Die Judenfrage in der Entstehungsphase des Reichsbanners Schwarz-Rot-Gold," in *Juden und deutsche Arbeiterbewegung bis 1933. Soziale Utopien und religiös-kulturelle Traditionen*, ed. Ludger Heid and Arnold Paucker (Tübingen, 1992), 215–235.

43. Burchardt et al., *Konstanz im 20. Jahrhundert*, 171–174; *Konstanzer Volksblatt*, 22 May 1926, 25 May 1926, 8 Dec 1927; *Deutsche Bodensee-Zeitung*, 26 May 1926; *Konstanzer Zeitung*, 8 Dec 1927.

44. Remarque, *All Quiet on the Western Front*, 211.

45. [Karl Ludwig] von Oertzen, *Deutsches Reichsheer-Handbuch (D.R.H.)* (Charlottenburg, 1923), 87 (my emphasis); see Erich Weniger, *Wehrmachtserziehung und Kriegserfahrung* (Berlin, 1938), 119.

46. Remarque, *All Quiet on the Western Front*, 131.

47. Hans Zöberlein, *Der Glaube an Deutschland. Ein Kriegserleben von Verdun bis zum Umsturz* (31st ed., Munich, 1939), 297f; Friedrich Altrichter, *Die seelischen Kräfte des Deutschen Heeres im Frieden und im Weltkriege* (Berlin, 1933), 18f (de-individualization); Till Kalkschmidt, "Kameradschaft und Führertum der Front," *Dichtung und Volkstum*, 39 (1938), 180–192, 181; E. Jäger, "Der Krieg wandelt den Menschen," *Deutsche Wehr*, 22 May 1931, 527 (the "I" is gone).

48. E. Jäger, "Der Krieg wandelt den Menschen," *Deutsche Wehr*, 22 May 1931, 527.

49. *Reichsbanner*, 7 Sept 1929.

50. Siegfried Kracauer, "Über die Freundschaft," in idem, *Schriften*, vol. 5/1 (Frankfurt, 1990), 29f, 33, 37f; idem, *Ginster von ihm selbst geschrieben* (Berlin, 1928); Leopold von Wiese, *Kindheit. Erinnerungen aus meinen Kadettenjahren* (Hannover, 1924), 77f; Helmut Plessner, *Grenzen der Gemeinschaft. Eine Kritik des sozialen Radikalismus* (Bonn, 1924).

51. Alfred Vierkandt, "Sittlichkeit," in idem, ed., *Handwörterbuch der Soziologie* (Stuttgart, 1931), 538.

52. Ruth Benedict, *The Chrysanthemum and the Sword. Patterns of Japanese Culture* (Boston, 1948), 222–224. Compare Millie R. Creighton, "Revisiting Shame and Guilt Cultures: A Forty-Year Pilgrimage," *Ethos* 18/3 (1990), 279–307.

53. Norbert Elias, *The Germans. Power Struggles and the Development of Habitus in the Nineteenth and Twentieth Centuries* (New York, 1996), 184; Ute Frevert, *Men of Honour. A Social and Cultural History of the Duel* (Cambridge, Mass., 1995).

54. Walter Z. Laqueur, *Young Germany. A History of the German Youth Movement* (London, 1962); Richard Braun, "Individualismus und Gemeinschaft in der deutschen Jugendbewegung" (PhD diss., University of Erlangen, 1929), 35, 42, 45, 52, 88; Matthias von Hellfeld, *Bündische Jugend und Hitlerjugend. Zur Geschichte von Anpassung und Widerstand 1930–1939* (Köln, 1987), 33f; Irmtraud Götz von Olenhusen, *Jugendreich, Gottesreich, Deutsches Reich. Junge Generation, Religion und Politik 1928–1933* (Cologne, 1983); Peter Dudek, *Erziehung durch Arbeit. Arbeitslagerbewegung und freiwilliger Arbeitsdienst 1920–1935* (Opladen, 1988).

55. *Das junge Deutschland*, 1930, 599. See Raabe, *Die bündische Jugend*, 56–58.

56. *Arbeiterjugend*, 1926, 108.

57. *Reichsbanner*, 17 Oct 1930, 336f; *Arbeiterjugend*, 1928, 174–176; *Das junge Deutschland*, 1931, 224, 303; Franz Strebin, "Jugendbewegung und politische Erziehung" (PhD diss., University of Heidelberg, 1958), 88f.

58. *Der Bannerträger*, no. 10 (1923), 103f.

59. Frank Matzke, *Jugend bekennt: So sind wir!* (Leipzig, 1930), 57; similar ideas in *Das junge Deutschland*, 1931, 398–403.

60. Helmut Lethen, *Cool Conduct. The Culture of Distance in Weimar Germany* (Berkeley, 2002), 33ff, 62f, on "masking" as a notion to cope with the confusing tension of inward (guilt) and outward (shame).

2 Fabricating the Male Bond

1. Sebastian Haffner, *Defying Hitler* (New York, 2002), 143f, 199, 290f.

2. *Kyffhäuser*, 3 Sept 1933, 614f; *Stahlhelm*, 27 Jan 1935; ibid., 29 Jan 1933 (!), "We are creating the nation!"

3. Quoted in Deborah Dwork and Robert Jan van Pelt, *Holocaust. A History* (New York, 2002), 68f.

4. Cornelia Schmitz-Berning, *Vokabular des Nationalsozialismus* (Berlin, 1998), 343–45.

5. Hitler speech, 4 Dec 1938, in Jeremy Noakes and Geoffrey Pridham, eds., *Nazism, 1919–1945. A History in Documents and Eyewitness Accounts*, 2 vols. (New York,

1983–84), vol. 1, 417; Felix Kersten, *Totenkopf und Treue. Heinrich Himmler ohne Uniform* (Hamburg, 1952), 184.

6. Yehuda Bauer, "Overall Explanations, German Society and the Jews, or: Some Thoughts About Context," in *Probing the Depths of German Antisemitism. German Society and the Persecution of the Jews, 1933–1941*, ed. David Bankier (Jerusalem, 2000), 16; Ian Kershaw, *The Nazi Dictatorship. Problems and Perspectives of Interpretation*, 4th ed. (London, 2000), 161–82 (social classes); Eric D. Weitz, *A Century of Genocide. Utopias of Race and Nation* (Princeton, 2003), 110 (slaves).

7. Shelley Baranowski, *Strength Through Joy. Consumerism and Mass Tourism in the Third Reich* (Cambridge, 2007).

8. David Schoenbaum, *Hitler's Social Revolution. Class and Status in Nazi Germany 1933–1945* (London, 1967), 76; Claudia Koonz, *The Nazi Conscience* (Cambridge, Mass., 2004), 59f, 73f, 133f, 145; Peter Fritzsche, *Life and Death in the Third Reich* (Cambridge, Mass., 2008).

9. Max Domarus, *Hitler. Speeches and Proclamations 1932–1945. The Chronicle of a Dictatorship* (Wauconda, 1992), vol. 2, 955.

10. Poster of the 1934–35 campaign, http://www.dhm.de/lemo/objekte/pict/plio3466/index.html, accessed 28 Jan 2009. See Lore Walb, *Ich, die Alte—ich, die Junge. Konfrontation mit meinen Tagebüchern 1933–1945* (Berlin, 1997), 72f; *Deutschland-Berichte der Sopade*, vol. II, 1935 (Frankfurt, 1980), 200f. (2 Feb 1935).

11. Noakes and Pridham, *Nazism, 1919–1945*, vol. 1, 437.

12. Leutloff, "Deutsche Volksbildungsarbeit," *Bericht. Weltkongreß für Freizeit und Erholung Hamburg vom 23.–30. 7. 1936* (Berlin, 1937), 586, quoted in Franz Janka, *Die braune Gesellschaft. Ein Volk wird formatiert* (Stuttgart, 1997), 253.

13. H. R. Trevor-Roper, ed., *Hitler's Table Talk, 1941–1944. His Private Conversations* (New York, 2000), 142. Contrary to what Hannah Arendt suggests (*The Origins of Totalitarianism* [New York, 2004, originally 1951], 565), these statements did not refer to the inmates of concentration camps but to the Aryan Volksgemeinschaft. Hitler's public elaborations were less cynical; Joachim C. Fest, *Hitler* (New York, 1974), 433–36.

14. *Adolf Hitler in Franken. Reden aus der Kampfzeit* (Nuremberg, 1938), 83.

15. Carl Schmitt, *The Concept of the Political* (New Brunswick, 1976), 46f and 27.

16. Otto Dov Kulka and Eberhard Jäckel, eds., *Die Juden in den geheimen NS-Stimmungsberichten 1933–1945* (Düsseldorf, 2004), Document no. 1109 (DVD). More generally, see Omer Bartov, "Defining Enemies, Making Victims: Germans, Jews, and the Holocaust," *American Historical Review* 103 (1998), 258–71.

17. Victor Klemperer, *I Will Bear Witness. A Diary of the Nazi Years, 1933–1941* (New York, 1998), 233f, 17 Aug 1937.

18. Martin Doerry, ed., *My Wounded Heart. The Life of Lilli Jahn, 1900–1944* (New York, 2004), 50f, 57, 61, 64f; Michael Wildt, *Volksgemeinschaft al Selbstermächtigung. Gewalt gegen Juden in der deutschen Provinz, 1919–1939* (Hamburg, 2007), 191–93, 202f (*Stürmer*); generally, see Saul Friedländer, *Nazi*

Germany and the Jews. The Years of Persecution, 1933–1939 (New York, 1997), and Marion Kaplan, *Between Dignity and Despair. Jewish Life in Nazi Germany* (New York, 1998); Bankier, *Probing the Depths of German Antisemitism.*

19. Doerry, *My Wounded Heart*, 77f; David Bankier, *The Germans and the Final Solution. Public Opinion Under Nazism* (Oxford, 1992), 86f; Frank Bajohr and Dieter Pohl, *Der Holocaust als offenes Geheimnis. Die Deutschen, die NS-Führung und die Alliierten* (Munich, 2006), 39–43.

20. Richard Evans, *The Third Reich in Power, 1933–1939* (New York, 2005); Ian Kershaw, *Popular Opinion and Political Dissent in the Third Reich. Bavaria 1933–1945* (Oxford, 1983); Sheila Fitzpatrick and Alf Lüdtke, "Energizing the Everyday. On the Breaking and Making of Social Bonds in Nazism and Stalinism," in *Beyond Totalitarianism. Stalinism and Nazism Compared*, ed. Michael Geyer and Sheila Fitzpatrick (Cambridge, 2009), 266–301. On "indifference" as a category to describe Germans' attitude toward anti-Jewish politics, see Carolyn J. Dean, *The Fragility of Empathy After the Holocaust* (Ithaca, 2004), 76–105.

21. Michael Burleigh and Wolfgang Wippermann, *The Racial State: Germany 1933–1945* (Cambridge, 1991), 75–197; Robert Gellately and Nathan Stoltzfus, eds., *Social Outsiders in Nazi Germany* (Princeton, 2001).

22. Hermann Göring, *Reden und Aufsätze* (Munich, 1938), 226–44; Karl Mierke, "Gefährdete Kameradschaft," *Soldatentum* 6 (1939), 138–41, 188–95; Hermann Foertsch, *Der Offizier der deutschen Wehrmacht*, 5th ed. (Berlin, 1941), 56, 67; Schulz, "Loslösung und Einfügung im Soldatenleben," *Soldatentum* 4 (1937), 2–10; Kurt Kreipe, "Versager im soldatischen Friedensdienst," *Soldatentum* 2 (1935), 79–82; Gerathewohl, "Eigenart und Behandlung des Einzelgängers," *Soldatentum* 5 (1938), 163–68; Baldur von Schirach, *Die Hitler-Jugend. Idee und Gestalt* (Berlin, 1934), 85 (stake).

23. [Erich] Ludendorff, *The Nation at War* (London, c. 1936, originally German [1935]).

24. [Horst] Buchholz, "Aufbau der Gesinnung und des Kameradschaftsgeistes," *Kongreßbericht der deutschen allgemeinen ärztlichen Gesellschaft für Psychotherapie über die Tagung in Breslau vom 3.–6. Okt. 1935* (Heidelberg, 1935), 72–77.

25. Noakes and Pridham, *Nazism, 1919–1945*, vol. 1, 417.

26. Michael Kater, *Hitler Youth* (Cambridge, Mass., 2004); Jürgen Schiedeck and Martin Stahlman, "Die Inszenierung 'totalen Erlebens.' Lagererziehung im Nationalsozialismus," in *Politische Formierung und soziale Erziehung im Nationalsozialismus*, ed. Hans-Uwe Otto and Heinz Sünker (Frankfurt, 1991), 167–202; Gerhard Kock, *"Der Führer sorgt für unsere Kinder . . ." Die Kinderlandverschickung im Zweiten Weltkrieg* (Paderborn, 1997), 144–49; Kiran Klaus Patel, *Soldiers of Labor. Labor Service in Nazi Germany and New Deal America, 1933–1945* (New York, 2005), 190ff. On the figures see also Koonz, *The Nazi Conscience*, 157; newspaper report on teacher camps from 1937 in Noakes and Pridham, *Nazism, 1919–1945*, vol. 1, 432–35. On the Wehrmacht, see chapter IV.

27. Erving Goffman, *Asylums. Essays in the Social Situation of Mental Patients and Other Inmates* (Garden City, 1961).

28. Ernst Krieck, *Nationalsozialistische Erziehung*, 4th ed. (Osterwieck, 1937), 9–13.

29. Haffner, *Defying Hitler*, 257–91. On Kracauer, see Chapter 1.

30. Arnold van Gennep, *The Rites of Passage* (Chicago, 1960); David Gilmore, *Manhood in the Making. Cultural Concepts of Masculinity* (New Haven, 1990), Chapter 7; Frank W. Young, *Initiation Ceremonies. A Cross-Cultural Study of Status Dramatization* (Indianapolis, 1965), 24–41, 63–104.

31. Victor W. Turner, *The Ritual Process. Structure and Anti-Structure* (Ithaca, 1977), 95f.

32. John Remy, "Patriarchy and Fratriarchy as Forms of Androcracy," in *Men, Masculinities and Social Theory*, ed. Jeff Hearn and David Morgan (London, 1990), 43–54; for "momma's boy" see *Das junge Deutschland* (1944), 85–90, and for pre-Nazi Germany see *Arbeiterjugend* (1926), 108, *Das junge Deutschland* (1928), 159–168; for "school of manliness" see Ute Frevert, *A Nation in Barracks. Modern Germany, Military Conscription and Civil Society* (Oxford, 2004), 162, and Patel, *Soldiers of Labor*, 216; for "wrong consciousness" see Helmut Stellrecht, *Neue Erziehung* (Berlin, 1942), 61; Max Momsen, *Leibeserziehung mit Einschluß des Geländesports* (Osterwieck, 1935), 19f.

33. Guido Knopp, *Hitler's Children* (Phoenix Mill, 2004), 139–43.

34. *Wir Mädel*, 1940–41, 812; Jesco von Puttkamer, *Deutschlands Arbeitsdienst* (Oldenburg, 1938), 24, 41.

35. Stellrecht, *Neue Erziehung*, 61.

36. F. Lehmann, *Wir von der Infanterie*, 3d ed. (Munich, 1934), 18.

37. *Wir Mädel* 1940–41, 812, 814.

38. Erich Weniger, *Wehrmachtserziehung und Kriegserfahrung* (Berlin, 1938), 118; cf. Hans von Seeckt, *Gedanken eines Soldaten* (Leipzig, 1935), 90f; for recent sociological research, see Michael S. Kimmel, "Masculinity as Homophobia. Fear, Shame, and Silence in the Construction of Gender Identity," in *Theorizing Masculinities*, ed. Harry Brod and Michael Kaufmann (Thousand Oaks, 1994), 119–41; George Herbert Mead, "The Psychology of Punitive Justice," *American Journal of Sociology* 23 (1918), 590f; Albert K. Cohen, *Deviance and Control* (Englewood Cliffs, 1966), 8f.

39. Criminal Case against Sergeant-Major Wilhelm J., 18 May 1944, Bundesarchiv-Zentralnachweisstelle Aachen-Kornelimünster, W 11/M 59.

40. Hermann Melcher, *Die Gefolgschaft* (Berg, 1990), 112f.

41. Memoirs of Kurt Kreissler (pseudonym), vol. I, 5 (author's copy); Friedrich Grupe, *Jahrgang 1916. Die Fahne war mehr als der Tod* (Munich, 1989), 66–68.

42. Author's interview with Hanns Karl Vorster (pseudonym), 1994. Cf. Erhard Steininger, *Abgesang 1945. Ein Erlebnisbericht* (Leer, 1981), 95f; Max Bauer, *Kopfsteinpflaster. Erinnerungen* (Frankfurt, 1981), 100–2.

43. Hans Lorenz, *Graubrot mit Rübenkraut. Ein zeitgeschichtliches Schicksal* (Moers, 1993), 108f, 117. Cf. Weniger, *Wehrmachtserziehung und Kriegserfahrung*, 122; Wilhelm Reibert, *Der Dienstunterricht im Reichsheer. Ein Handbuch für den deutschen Soldaten*, 6th ed. (Berlin, 1934), 96; Friedrich Altrichter, *Das Wesen der soldatischen Erziehung* (Oldenburg, 1942), 129–34; Joseph Goebbels, "Soldat im Kampf der Geister," *Das Reich*, 12 Oct 1941, front page.

44. Author's interview with Klaus Ewald, 1995; Knopp, *Hitler's Children*, 18f, 132f; Bernd Hainmüller, *Erst die Fehde—dann der Krieg. Jugend unterm Hakenkreuz—Freiburgs Hitlerjugend* (Freiburg, 1998).

45. "Verschworene Gemeinschaft," *Völkischer Beobachter*, 24 Jan 1939; Omer Bartov, "The Conduct of War: Soldiers and the Barbarization of Warfare," in *Resistance Against the Third Reich, 1933–1990*, ed. Michael Geyer and John W. Boyer (Chicago, 1994), 48f.

46. Jost Hermand, *A Hitler Youth in Poland. The Nazis' Program for Evacuating Children During World War II* (Evanston, 1997), 3, 5, 10.

47. Hitler speech at the Nuremberg Party Rally, 14 Sept 1935, in Noakes and Pridham, *Nazism 1919–1945*, vol. I, 416f; Hermand, *A Hitler Youth in Poland*, 11, 17, 50.

48. Ibid., 30.

49. Ibid., 55f.

50. For drastic eyewitness reports see Heinrich Böll, "Eine deutsche Erinnerung. Interview mit René Wintzen, Oktober 1976," in idem, *Werke. Interviews I, 1961–1978* (Cologne, 1980), 624ff, and Böll's private letters as a Wehrmacht soldier, Heinrich Böll, *Briefe aus dem Krieg 1939–1945*, 2 vols. (Cologne, 2001), vol. 1, 120, 524f.

51. Diary of Gerhard Modersen (pseudonym, author's copy), 29 Jan 1943.

52. Günther de Bruyn, *Zwischenbilanz. Eine Jugend in Berlin* (Frankfurt, 1992), 111f. Evidence is legion.

53. Hermand, *A Hitler Youth in Poland*, 53–55.

54. Justus Ehrhardt, "Cliquenwesen und Jugendverwahrlosung," *Zentralblatt für Jugendrecht und Jugendpflege* 21 (1930), 414f; Curt Bondy, "Die jugendliche Verbrecherbande als psychologisches und sozialpädagogisches Problem," *Die Erziehung* (1926), no. 3, 146–59; Albert Cohen, *Delinquent Boys. The Culture of the Gang* (Glencoe, 1955), 164 and 140; Victoria Getis, "Experts and Juvenile Delinquency, 1900–1935," in *Generations of Youth. Youth Cultures and History in Twentieth-Century America*, ed. Joe Austin and Micharl Nevin Willard (New York, 1998), 21–35; James W. Messerschmidt, *Masculinities and Crime. Critique and Reconceptualization of Theory* (Lanham, 1993); Hubert Lafont, "Changing Sexual Behaviour in French Youth Gangs," in *Western Sexuality. Practice and Precept in Past and Present Times*, ed. Philippe Aries and Andre Bejin (Oxford, 1985), 168–180.

55. Frevert, *A Nation in Barracks*, 166 (military service). See analogous considerations on gangs in Cohen, *Delinquent Boys*, 140f. Albrecht Erich Günther, *Geist der Jungmannschaft* (Hamburg, 1934).

3 Performing Genocidal Ethics

1. *Sicherheitsdienst,* the Security Service of the SS.

2. German original in the files of the trial against members of Einsatzgruppe D in the early 1960s, Staatsarchiv Munich, Staatsanwaltschaften 21672/25, fol. 672–677, and in Andrej Angrick, *Besatzungspolitik und Massenmord. Die Einsatzgruppe D in der südlichen Sowjetunion 1941–1943* (Hamburg, 2003), 389–93. On Schiwek and his poem see his testimony, 24 Jan 1962, Staatsarchiv Munich, Staatsanwaltschaften 21672/4, fol. 784–94, ditto 20 Dec 1962, ibid., 2167/5, fol. 1116–23, esp. 1121.

3. Memo Staatsanwaltschaft Munich, 6 Apr 1962, Staatsarchiv Munich, Staatsanwaltschaften 33109/4, fol. 921–25, and statement Walter G., 2 Oct 1963, ibid., 33109/7, fol. 1595f; Warren Green, "The Fate of the Crimean Jewish Communities," *Jewish Social Studies* 46 (1984), 169–76; Angerick, *Besatzungspolitik und Massenmord,* 241–50, 323–42.

4. Testimony Otto Eichelbaum, 25 June 1964, Staatsarchiv Munich, Staatsanwaltschaften 21672/8, fol 1820, quoted also in Angrick, *Besatzungspolitik und Massenmord,* 247.

5. Ernest Gellner, *Natonalism* (London, 1997), 63–65; Lynn Hunt, *Inventing Human Rights. A History* (New York, 2007).

6. Heinrich Himmler, Speech at the meeting of SS generals (SS-Gruppenführertagung) in Posen, 4 Oct 1943, Document No. 1919-PS, Nuremberg Trial, German original in *Der Prozess gegen die Hauptkriegsverbrecher vor dem International Militärgerichtshof* (Nuremberg, 1947–49), vol. 29, 110–73, quotes 122f; my translation differs slightly from *Nazi Conspiracy and Aggression,* vol. IV (Washington, D.C., 1946), 616–34; Himmler, speech to SS generals, 23 Jan 1939, quoted in Josef Ackermann, *Heinrich Himmler als Ideologe* (Göttingen, 1970), 141; Peter Fritzsche, *Life and Death in the Third Reich* (Cambridge, Mass., 2008), 93. See Ulrich Herbert, *Best. Biographische Studien über Radikalismus, Weltanschauung und Vernunft* (Bonn, 1996), 283f, 527.

7. Hannah Arendt, *The Origins of Totalitarianism* (New York, 2004, originally 1951), 475; Elke Fröhlich, ed., *Die Tagebücher von Joseph Goebbels,* part II, vol. 1 (Munich: K. G. Saur, 1996), 278 (20 Aug 1941).

8. *Justiz und NS-Verbrechen,* vol. 15 (Amsterdam, 1976), 61, quoted in Christopher R. Browning and Jürgen Matthäus, *The Origins of the Final Solution. The Evolution of Nazi Jewish Policy, September 1939–March 1942* (Lincoln, 2004), 254.

9. *Handblätter für die weltanschauliche Erziehung der Truppe,* ed. RFSS, SS-Hauptamt, no date, copy in Bundesarchiv-Militärarchiv, Freiburg, RSD 4, no. 5.

10. Ernst Klee, Willi Dressen, and Volker Riess, eds., *"The Good Old Days." The Holocaust as Seen by Its Perpetrators and Bystanders* (New York, 1991), 96f; original emphasis; translation corrected according to the German original transcript; copies in Yad Vashem Archives, Jerusalem; BA Ludwigsburg, B 162/3380; Staatsarchiv Ludwigsburg, EL 317 III, 1100.

11. Adolf Eichmann proudly declared in Jerusalem in 1961, facing a death sentence, he would not regret anything: "Repentance is for little children." Hannah Arendt, *Eichmann in Jerusalem. A Report on the Banality of Evil* (rev. ed., New York, 1965), 24.

12. Ernst Jünger, *Das Wäldchen 125. Eine Chronik aus den Grabenkämpfen 1918*, 3d ed. (Berlin, 1928), 140 (guilt); idem, *Der Kampf als inneres Erlebnis* (Berlin, 1922), 32, 74 (overcoming).

13. Klaus Theweleit, *Male Fantasies*, 2 vols. (Minneapolis, 1989); Michael Wildt, *Generation des Unbedingten. Das Führungskorps des Reichssicherheitshauptamtes* (Hamburg, 2002); Tom Segev, *Soldiers of Evil. The Commandants of the Nazi Concentration Camps* (New York, 1987), 54ff.

14. Rudolf Hoess, *Commandant of Auschwitz. The Autobiography*, trans. Constantine FitzGibbon (London, 2000), 42–45; Karin Orth, *Die Konzentrationslager-SS. Sozialstrukturelle Analysen und biographische Studien* (Göttingen, 2000), 110–12.

15. Bernhard Sauer, *Schwarze Reichswehr und Fememorde. Eine Milieustudie zum Rechtsradikalismus in der Weimsrer Republik* (Berlin, 2004), 320–26.

16. Ernst von Salomon, *The Outlaws* (London, 1931), 141, 66, 138, 261f, 62–64, 342–46, 358f, 420f.

17. Joseph Goebbels, *Das erwachende Berlin* (Berlin, 1934), 126, quoted in Sven Reichardt, "Fascist Marches in Italy and Germany: Squadre and SA Before the Seizure of Power," in *The Street as Stage. Protest Marches and Public Rallies Since the Nineteenth Century*, ed. Matthias Reiss (Oxford, 2007), 185; idem, "Vergemeinschaftung durch Gewalt. Das Beispiel des SA-'Mördersturms 33' in Berlin-Charlottenburg zwischen 1928 und 1932," in *Beiträge zur Geschichte der nationalsozialistischen Verfolgung in Norddeutschland* 7 (2002), 23 (song), 30; idem, *Faschistische Kampfbünde. Gewalt und Gemeinschaft im italienischen Squadrismus und in der deutschen SA* (Cologne, 2002), 117; J. K. von Engelbrechtchen, *Eine braune Armee entsteht. Die Geschichte der Berlin-Brandenburger SA* (Munich, 1937), 85 (storm bars); Peter H. Merkle, *The Making of a Stormtrooper* (Princeton, 1980).

18. Paul Kluke, "Der Fall Potempa," *Vierteljahrshefte für Zeitgeschichte* 5 (1957), 279–96, 283 (Hitler's telegram); Ian Kershaw, *Hitler 1889–1936: Hubris* (New York, 1999), 381–83. On the release, see Victor Klemperer, *I Will Bear Witness. A Diary of the Nazi Years, 1933–1941* (New York, 1998), 7.

19. Orth, *Konzentrationslager-SS*, 130; Hoess, *Commandant in Auschwitz*, 68; see also Martin Broszat, "The Concentration Camps 1933–45," in Helmut Krausnick et al., *Anatomy of the SS-State* (New York, 1968), 397–504, esp. 432f; Paul Martin Neurath, *The Society of Terror. Inside the Dachau and Buchenwald Concentration Camps* (Boulder, 2005), 71, 73, 76.

20. Friedrich Grimm, *Politischer Mord und Heldenverehrung* (Berlin, 1938), 29, 35, 37; testimony of a prisoner of Buchenwald Concentration Camp, in *Buchenwald. Ein Konzentrationslager. Bericht der ehemaligen KZ-Häftlinge Emil Carlebach*

et al. (Frankfurt, 1984), 109f (teacher); Yehoshua R. Büchler, " 'Unworthy Behavior': The Case of SS Officer Max Täubner," *Holocaust and Genocide Studies* 17 (2003), 409–29; Heinrich Himmler, *Geheimreden 1933 bis 1945 und andere Ansprachen*, ed. Bradley F. Smith and Agnes F. Peterson (Frankfurt, 1974), 32, speech to SS generals, 8 Nov 1938.

21. Hoess, *Commandant in Auschwitz*, 65f.
22. Klaus Michael Mallmann, "Heinrich Hamann—Leiter des Grenzpolizeikommissariats Neu-Sandez," in *Karrieren der Gewalt. Nationalsozialistische Täterbiographien*, ed. Klaus-Michal Mallmann and Gerhard Paul (Darmstadt, 2004), 104–14.
23. Testimony Salomon St., 10 Feb 1961, Bundesarchiv Ludwigsburg (BAL) 162/1370, fol. 320; judgment Landgericht Bochum, 22 July 1966, BAL 162/14273, fol. 80f; testimony Böhning, 30 Jan 1962, BAL 162/1373, fol. 1053f.
24. Judgment Landgericht Bochum, 22 July 1966, BAL 162/14273, fol. 97–102, 126, 230–34; testimony Mayer B., 25 July 1960, BAL 162/1370, fol. 450.
25. Judgment Landgericht Bochum, 22 July 1966, BAL 162/14273, fol. 90 and 382; testimony Josef Rouenhoff, 3 Nov 1961, BAL 162/1372, fol. 840.
26. Judgment Landgericht Bochum, 22 July 1966, BAL 162/14273, fol. 421ff; testimony Johann Bornholt 16 June 1961, BAL 162/1371, fol. 633.
27. Testimony Gerhard K., 4 Feb 1960, BAL 162/2512, fol. 5756ff (Heinrich Hamann); see Knut Stang, *Kollaboration und Massenmord Die litauische Hilfspolizei, das Rollkommando Hamann und die Ermordung der litauischen Juden* (Frankfurt, 1996), 153ff; Klee, Dressen, and Riess, *"The Good Old Days,"* 46ff and testimony Heinrich Schmitz, 15 Jan 1960, BAL 162/2512, fol. 5657f. (Jäger); Klaus-Michael Mallmann, Volker Rieß, and Wolfram Pyta, eds., *Deutscher Osten 1939–1945. Der Weltanschauungskrieg in Photos und Texten* (Darmstadt, 2003), 121 (pub); quote of Mertens: testimony Arthur Denkmann, 28 Jan 1964, BAL 162/2573, fol. 553, and testimony August Merten, 30 Nov 1965, BAL 162/2573, fol. 604–30; cf. Kathrin Hoffmann-Curtius, "Trophäen in Brieftaschen—Fotographien von Wehrmachts-, SS- und Polizeiverbrechen," *kunsttexte.de*, no. 3 (2002), 1–14, http://www.kunsttexte.de/download/poli/hoffmann-curtius.PDF, accessed 28 Jan 2009.
28. Judgment Landgericht Bochum, 22 July 1966, BAL 162/14273, fol. 169–83; testimony Isak G., 16 Dec 1960, BAL 162/1370, fol. 432.
29. My translation differs slightly from *Internet Modern History Sourcebook*, http://www.fordham.edu/halsall/mod/horstwessel.html, accessed 29 Jan 2009. On the Horst Wessel myth, see Jay W. Baird, *To Die for Germany. Heroes in the Nazi Pantheon* (Bloomington, 1992), 73–90; Sabine Behrenbeck, *Der Kult um die toten Helden. Nationalsozialistische Mythen, Riten und Symbole 1923 bis 1945* (Vierow, 1996), 134–48, 222f.
30. As such, they represented the "old fighter," see Theodore Abel, *Why Hitler Came into Power*, new ed. (Cambridge, Mass., 1986).

31. Judgment Landgericht Bochum, 22 July 1966, BAL 162/14273, fol. 8–16 (Hamann), 16–20 (Labitzke); 20–25 (Bornholt), 25–28 (Rouenhoff), 29–31 (Denk).

32. Testimony Rouenhoff, 3 Nov 1961, BAL 162/1372, fol. 836ff; testimony Labitzke, ibid., fol. 709 (anti-Semitism); testimony Hamann, 12 Feb 1962, BAL 162/1374, fol. 1210–13 (Galicia); testimony Hamann, quoted in judgment Landgericht Bochum, 22 July 1966, BAL 162/14273, fol. 79 (Jewish life); testimony Bornholt, 10 Sept 1963, BAL 162/1378, fol. 2388f (gold and money); testimony Reinhard, 27 Sept 1963, BAL162/1378, fol. 2540f (basement); testimony Bornholt, 1 March 1962, BAL162/ 1373, fol. 1168 (plunder).

33. Testimony Brock, 10 Oct 1961, BAL 162/1372, fol. 777f (casino); judgment Landgericht Bochum, 22 July 1966, BAL 162/14273, fol. 225, refers to testimony Rouenhoff (Lustig).

34. Order by Erich von dem Bach-Zelewski, 11 July 1941, quoted in Christopher Browning, *Ordinary Men. Reserve Police Battalion 101 and the Final Solution in Poland* (New York, 1992), 13f; idem and Matthäus, *The Origins of the Final Solution*, 258; Edward B. Westermann, *Hitler's Police Battalions. Enforcing Racial War in the East* (Lawrence, 2005), 176f.

35. Testimony Heinrich Hamann, 2 June 1962, BAL 162/1374, fol. 1451; testimony Friedrich Schröder, 22 March 1961, BAL 162/1375, fol. 1682.

36. Judgment Landgericht Bochum, 22 July 1966, BAL 162/14273, fol. 187ff; Mallmann, "Heinrich Hamann," 104f.

37. Judgment Landgericht Bochum, 22 July 1966, BAL 162/14273, fol. 191.

38. Ibid., 294, 280.

39. Ibid., 282f, 297.

40. Testimony Alois Kroll, 16 Feb 1961, BAL 162/1370, fol. 392–94, Wolfgang Sofsky, *The Order of Terror. The Concentration Camp* (Princeton, 1997), 16ff.

41. Judgment Landgericht Bochum, 22 July 1966, BAL 162/14273, fol. 15ff (base motives), fol. 158 (blame on Hamann); testimony Ernst Meierhöfer, 30 Sept 1960, BAL 162/1369, fol. 186–91 (fear of Hamann); testimony Labitzke, 13 Apr 1961, BAL 162/1371, fol. 575–77.

42. David H. Kitterman, "Those Who Said 'No!': Germans Who Refused to Execute Civilians During World War II," *German Studies Review* 11 (1988), 241–54; Herbert Jäger, *Verbrechen unter totalitärer Herrschaft. Studien zur nationalsozialistischen Gewaltkrim inialität*, new ed. (Frankfurt, 1982).

43. Testimony Gaschnitz, 23 June 1961, BAL 162/1371, fol. 678f; testimony Rouenhoff, 3 Nov 1961, BAL 162/1372, fol. 858; testimony Labitzke, 13 Apr 1961, BAL 162/1371, fol. 575f.

44. Laurence Rees, *Auschwitz. A New History* (New York, 2005), 127–33, 156f, quotations from interviews with O. G. for the BBC documentary *Auschwitz: Inside the Nazi State*.

45. Trial testimonies of Herbert Selle et al., quoted Klee, Dressen, and Riess, *"The Good Old Days,"* 108.

NOTES TO PAGES 78–83

46. Testimony Georg Ulrich, 3 Sept 1964, BAL 162/2573, fol. 569 (sardine procedure); Sofsky, *Order of Terror*, 9; Daniel Jonah Goldhagen, *Hitler's Willing Executioners. Ordinary Germans and the Holocaust* (New York, 1996), 135f, 168ff, 327ff.

47. Harold Garfinkel, "Conditions of Successful Degradation Ceremonies," *American Journal of Sociology* 61 (1956), 421. Inga Clendinnen, *Reading the Holocaust* (Cambridge, U.K., 1999), 138–55.

48. Angerick, *Besatzungspolitik und Massenmord*, 171. Cf. Goldhagen, *Hitler's Willing Executioners*, 258–62.

49. Browning and Matthäus, *The Origins of the Final Solution*, 255–60; Goldhagen, *Hitler's Willing Executioners*, 188–91; Freia Anders, Hauke-Hendrik Kutscher, and Katrin Stoll, eds., *Bialystok in Bielefeld. Nationalsozialistische Verbrechen vor dem Landgericht Bielefeld 1958 bis 1967* (Bielefeld, 2003).

50. Testimony Auerbach: http://veritas.nizkor.org/ftp.cgi/people/e/ftp.py?people/e/eichmann.adolf/transcripts/Sessions/Session-026-01, accessed 29 Jan 2009; Raul Hilberg, Stanislaw Staron, and Josef Kermisz, eds., *The Warsaw Diary of Adam Czerniakow: Prelude to Doom* (New York, 1979), 402. On the camps, see Terrence Des Pres, *The Survivor. An Anatomy of Life in the Death Camps* (New York, 1976), 60–62.

51. Klee, Dressen, and Riess, *"The Good Old Days,"* 28–32; the photographer: testimony Wilhelm Gunsilius, 11 Nov 1958, BAL 162/ 40557, fol. 40–43.

52. Jürgen Matthäus, "Key Aspects of German Anti-Jewish Policy," in *Lithuania and the Jews. The Holocaust Chapter. Symposium Presentations* (Washington, D.C., 2005), 17–32, quotes from leaflets ibid., 18.

53. Barykada [politish underground paper], no. 3, March 3, quoted in Christoph Doeckmann, Bebatte Quinkert, and Tatjana Tönsmeyer, ed., *Kooperation und Verbrechen. Formen der "Kollaboration" im östlichen Europa 1939–1945* (Göttingen, 2003), 9.

54. John A. Armstrong, "Collaborationism in World War II: The Integral Nationalist Variant in Eastern Europe," *Journal of Modern History* 40 (1968), 396–410. On the anthropology of pollution, see Mary Douglas, *Purity and Danger. An Analysis of the Concepts of Pollution and Taboo* (London, 2002), viii–xxi, 9–12, 95f, 160–68.

55. Testimony Bornholt, 16 June 1961, BAL 162/1371, fol. 633–37.

56. Klee, Dressen, and Riess, *"The Good Old Days,"* 24–27. See testimony Erich Ehrlinger, 9 Dec 1958 and 28 Apr to 21 May 1959, BAL 162/2505, fol. 2641–2705.

57. David Gaunt, Paul A. Levine, and Laura Palosuo, eds., *Collaboration and Resistance During the Holocaust. Belarus, Estonia, Latvia, Lithuania* (Berne, 2004); Martin Dean, *Collaboration in the Holocaust. Crimes of the Local Police in Belorussia and Ukraine, 1941–1944* (New York, 2000); Leonid Rein, "Local Collaboration in the Execution of the 'Final Solution' in Nazi Occupied Belorussia," *Holocaust and Genocide Studies* 20 (2006), 381–409; Tomislav Dulić , *Utopias of Nation. Local Mass Killings in Bosnia and Herzegovina, 1941–42* (Uppsala, 2005).

58. Regina Mühlhäuser, "Between 'Racial Awareness' and Fantasies of Potency: Nazi Sexual Politics in the Occupied Territories of the Soviet Union, 1942–1945,"

in *Brutality and Desire. War and Sexuality in Europe's Twentieth Century*, ed. Dagmar Herzog (Houndmills, 2009), 203 (SS meeting); Buchheim, "Command and Compliance," in Krausnick et al., *Anatomy of the SS-State*, 343–45 (Dietrich; camraderie). Buchheim, though, separates "bad" camaraderie from "good" comradeship, which is misleading.

59. Buchheim, "Command and Compliance," in Krausnick et al., *Anatomy of the SS-State*, 317.
60. Raul Hilberg, *The Destruction of the European Jews*, vol. I, 3d ed. (New Haven, 2003), 343f. See Angerick, *Besatzungspolitik und Massenmord*, 302ff, 361ff. Cf. Christian Gerlach, *Kalkulierte Morde. Die deutsche Wirtschafts- und Vernichtungspolitik in Weißrußland 1941 bis 1944* (Hamburg, 1999), 571ff.
61. Testimony Albert Hartl, 16 Jan 1957, BAL 162/2559, fol. 14054–62; Klee, Dressen, and Riess, *"The Good Old Days,"* 82ff (Thomas); Mallmann, Rieß, and Pyta, *Deutscher Osten*, 86, 153; Angerick, *Besatzungspolitik und Massenmord*, 431ff; Browning, *Ordinary Men*, 56f (Trapp).
62. Klee, Dressen, and Riess, *"The Good Old Days,"* 75–86; Browning, *Ordinary Men*, 56, 71f, 87, 102f, 118 (Hoffmann), 127–30, 185.
63. Staatsarchiv Munich, Staatsanwaltschaften 33109/18, fol. 3204f. Cf. Angerick, *Besatzungspoitik und Massenmord*, 248f.
64. Testimony Martin Mundschütz, 4 Feb 1970, Staatsarchiv Munich, Staatsanwaltschaften 33109/18, fol. 3214.
65. Browning, *Ordinary Men*, 168, refers to similar results of Philip Zimbardo's Stanford prison experiment; Mallmann, Rieß, and Pyta, *Deutscher Osten*, 119f.
66. Albert K. Cohen, *Deviance and Control* (Englewood Cliffs, 1966), 8f; Browning, *Ordinary Men*, 185f; on hierarchical masculinities, see Frank J. Barrett, "The Organizational Construction of Hegemonial Masculinity: The Case of the US Navy," *Gender, Work and Organization* 3/3 (1996), 129–42, based on R. W. Connell, *Masculinities* (Berkeley, 1995), 67–86. Cf. Harald Welzer, *Täter. Wie aus ganz normalen Menschen Massenmörder werden* (Frankfurt, 2005), 130f, 147ff, 161f; Alexander Neumann, Peter Peckl, and Kim Priemel, "Praxissemester 'Osteinsatz'. Der Führernachwuchs der Sipo und der Auftakt zur Vernichtung der litauischen Juden," *Zeitschrift für Genozidforschung* 7 (2006), 39ff; Alexander V. Prusin, "A Community of Violence: The SiPo/SD and Its Role in the Nazi Terror System in Generalbezirk Kiew," *Holocaust and Genocide Studies* 21 (2007), 1–30.
67. Wildt, *Generation der Unbedingten*, 572ff (Schulz); Angerick, *Besatzungspolitik und Massenmord*, 433; Judgment Landgericht Bochum, 22 July 1966, BAL 162/14273, fol. 316.
68. Testimony Albrecht Zöllner, 26 Apr 1962, Staatsarchiv Munich, Staatsanwaltschaften 33109/4, fol. 954 (quote), see ibid., fol. 934–79; ditto 12 and 17 Jan 1967, ibid., 33109/14, fol. 25–46, 93–108, testimony Heinz Hermann Schubert 13 Feb 1967, ibid., fol. 189f, all on Ohlendorf controlling his men's willingness to murder, yet revealing that there were still chances to dodge this responsibility.

69. Testimony Georg Ulrich, 3 Sept 1964, BAL 162/2573, fol. 572f.

70. Testimony Heinrich Schmitz, 15 Jan 1960, BAL 162/2512, fol. 5659f, 5674, the entire unit was made to shoot; testimony August Merten, 30 Nov 1965, BAL 162/2573, fol. 623f, but see testimony Franz Schwelle, 18 Feb 1960, BAL 162/2512, fol. 5797.

71. Judgment Landgericht Bochum, 22 July 1966, BAL 162/1374, fol. 1313–17 (Himmler), fol. 323 (Lindert).

72. Angerick, *Besatzungspolitik und Massenmord*, 188, 434; Westermann, *Hitler's Police Batallions*, 170.

73. Hannah Arendt, *On Violence* (New York, 1967), 67, referring to Franz Fanon, *The Wretched of the Earth* (New York, 2004), 45.

74. Affidavit of Otto Ohlendorf, 20 Nov 1945, Nuremberg Documents UK 81, in *Nazi Conspiracy and Aggression*, vol. VIII (Washington, D.C., 1946), 596–603 (my translation is corrected); affidavit of idem, 5 Nov 1945, Nuremberg Documents 2620 PS, quoted in Klee, Dressen, and Riess, *"The Good Old Days,"* 60.

75. As above.

76. Wolfram Wette, "Tötung der Opfer und der Erinnerung—Das Massaker von Babij Jar am 29./30.9.1941," in *Massenhaftes Töten. Kriege und Genozide im 20. Jahrhundert*, ed. Peter Gleichmann and Thomas Kühne (Essen, 2004), 339–60.

77. Bernward Dörner, *Die Deutschen und der Holocaust. Was niemand wissen wollte, aber jeder wissen konnte* (Berlin, 2007); Sibylle Steinbacher, *"Musterstadt" Auschwitz: Germanisierungspolitik und Judenmord in Ostoberschlesien* (Munich, 2000), 247–52.

78. Adolf Hitler, *Monologe im Führerhauptquartier 1941–1944* (Munich, 1980), 106 (25 Oct 1941).

79. Georg Simmel, *The Sociology* (Glencoe, 1950), 331f, 346f.

80. E. J. Hobsbawm, *Primitive Rebels. Studies in Archaic Forms of Social Movements in the 19th and 20th Centuries* (New York, 1965), 150–74; Anton Blok, *Honour and Violence* (Cambridge, U.K., 2001), 36–39; Jean La Fontaine, *Initiation. Ritual Drama and Secret Knowledge Across the World* (New York, 1985).

81. Büchler, " 'Unworthy Behavior,' " 417, 419, 422. See the judgment in Klee, Dressen, and Riess, *"The Good Old Days,"* 196ff.

82. Testimony Harm Willms Harms, 18 Oct 1956, BAL 162/2500, fol. 46f; see also testimony Heinrich Hippler, 11 Nov 1958, ibid., fol. 125ff. (on different photos).

83. Erik H. Erikson, *Childhood and Society*, 2d ed. (New York, 1963), 337.

84. Norman H. Baynes, *The Speeches of Adolf Hitler*, Apr 1922–Aug 1939, vol. I (London, 1942), 75. German original in [Adolf] Hitler, *Sämtliche Aufzeichnungen 1905–1924*, ed. Eberhard Jäckel and Axel Kuhn (Stuttgart, 1980), 960. Although this speech related to the Communists, the sentence nevertheless reveals Hitler's social "philosophy."

85. Primo Levi, *The Drowned and the Saved* (New York, 1988), 43; Sofsky, *Order of Terror*, 130ff. In our context is of minor relevance whether or not Levi's reference to the Mafia appropriately catches the bonding mechanisms of the Mafia, but see

James Fentress, *Rebels & Mafiosi. Death in a Sicilian Landscape* (Ithaca, 2000), and Letizia Paoli, *Mafia Brotherhoods. Organized Crime, Italian Style* (New York, 2003).

86. Pierre Bourdieu, *Distinction. A Social Critique of the Judgment of Taste* (Cambridge, Mass., 1984); idem, *Practical Reason. On the Theory of Action* (Cambridge, Mass., 1998).

87. Mallmann, Rieß, and Pyta, *Deutscher Osten*, 14. Similar comments were rather popular, see testimony of Heinrich Sieling, 15 Jan 1962, on a statement of Heinrich Hamann (other rules in Poland than in the Reich), BAL 162/1373, fol. 1001–5.

88. Cf. Keith Tester, *Moral Culture* (London, 1997), 98–112. For an application of the concept of pariah groups to larger political entities see Disk Geldenhuys, *Isolated States: A Comparative Analysis* (Cambridge, 1991).

89. Baynes, *The Speeches of Adolf Hitler*, 75.

90. Elke Fröhlich, ed., *Die Tagebücher von Joseph Goebbels*, part II, vol. 7 (Munich, 1993), 454 (2 March 1943). Cf. Bernd Wegner, "The Ideology of Self-Destruction: Hitler and the Choreography of Defeat," *Bulletin of the German Historical Institute London*, 26 (2004), 27, for the translation of these quotes.

4 Spreading Complicity

1. Charles Burdick and Hans-Adolf Jacobsen, eds., *The Halder War Diary* (Novata, CA, 1988), 446, diary entry, 3 July 1941; Minutes of a Meeting at Hitler's Headquarter, 16 July 1941, Nuremberg Document 221-L, trans. in *Documents on German Foreign Policy*, 1918–1945 (Washington, D.C., 1964), series D, vol. 13, 149–156; Karl Reddemann, ed., *Zwischen Front und Heimat. Der Briefwechsel des münsterischen Ehepaares Agnes und Albert Neuhaus* (Münster, 1996), 221; letter of Lieutenant Otto D., 30 July 1941, Bibliothek für Zeitgeschichte Stuttgart, Sammlung Sterz. More in Ortwin Buchbender and Reinhold Sterz, eds., *Das andere Gesicht des Krieges. Deutsche Feldpostbriefe*, 1939–1945, 2d ed. (Munich, 1983).

2. War Diary of Fritz Farnbacher, copy owned by author, 22–24, 30 June 1941, 1 July 1941. On the chain of military events (with no reference to the criminal dimension of the war) see Joachim Neumann, *Die 4. Panzerdivision, 1939–1943. Bericht und Betrachtung zu zwei Feldzügen und zwei Jahren Krieg in Rußland* (Bonn, 1985); on German terror see Kobrin G. Beil, "The Holocaust," in *The Book of Kobrin. The Scroll of Life and Destruction*, ed. Betzalel Shwartz and Israel Chaim Biltzki (San Francisco, 1992), 382f.

3. War Diary Farnbacher, 20 July 1941.

4. Ibid., 2, 19 July 1941, 23 June 1941.

5. The numbers amount to 87 percent in 1941, 72 percent in 1942, and still a relatively considerable 64 percent in 1943; see Burkhart Müller-Hillebrand, *Das Heer 1933–1945. Entwicklung des organisatorischen Aufbaus*, 3 vols. (Darmstadt, 1954–69), vol. 3, 65f, 217f, and Christian Hartmann, "Verbrecherischer Krieg—verbrecherische Wehrmacht? Überlegungen zur Struktur des deutschen Ostheeres 1941–1944," *Vierteljahrshefte für Zeitgeschichte* 52 (2004), 4.

6. Heinrich Böll, *Briefe aus dem Krieg 1939–1945*, 2 vols., ed. Jochen Schubert (Cologne, 2001), vol. 1, 299, letter to his fiancée, 18 Feb 1942.

7. Translation in Hans-Adolf Jacobsen, "The *Kommissarbefehl* and Mass Executions of Soviet Prisoners of War," in Helmut Krausnick et al., *Anatomy of the SS State* (New York, 1968), 532–34; original: *Verbrechen der Wehrmacht. Dimensionen des Vernichtungskrieges 1941–1944. Ausstellungskatalog* (Hamburg, 2002), 52f.

8. Translation in *Nazi Conspiracy and Aggression*, vol. III (Washington, D.C., 1946), 637–39.

9. Fedor von Bock, *The War Diary, 1939–1945*, ed. Klaus Garbet (Atglen, 1996), 217 (4 June 1941); Wolfram Wette, *The Wehrmacht. History, Myth, Reality* (Cambridge, Mass., 2006), 95; Geoffrey P. Megargee, *War of Annihilation. Combat and Genocide on the Eastern Front, 1941* (Lanham, 2006), 19–41.

10. No minutes were taken at this secret meeting; our knowledge of Hitler's speech is based on the entries in *The Halder War Diary*, 345f.

11. Felix Römer, " 'Im alten Deutschland wäre solcher Befehl nicht möglich gewesen.' Rezeption, Adaption und Umsetzung des Kriegsgerichtsbarkeitserlasses 1941–42," *Vierteljahrshefte für Zeitgeschichte* 56 (2008), 61.

12. Isabel V. Hull, *Absolute Destruction: Military Culture and the Practices of War in Imperial Germany* (Ithaca, 2005), 117–26, quotations ibid. from Julius von Hartmann, "Militärische Nothwendigkeit und Humanität," *Deutsche Rundschau* 13 (1877), 462. Cf. Manfred Messerschmidt, "Völkerrecht und Kriegsnotwendigkeit in der deutschen militärischen Tradition seit den Einigungskriegen," *German Studies Review* 6 (1983), 237–69; John N. Horne and Alan Kramer, *German Atrocities, 1914. A History of Denial* (New Haven, 2001); to be sure, there is no direct continuity from 1914 to 1941.

13. Marcel Reich-Ranicki, *The Author of Himself* (Princeton, 2001), 123.

14. Memoirs on the Campaign on Poland by Private G., quoted in Jochen Böhler, *Auftakt zum Vernichtungskrieg. Die Wehrmacht in Polen 1939* (Frankfurt, 2006), 48.

15. On the propagandistic abuse of the "Bloody Sunday" on 3 Sept 1939 in Bydgoscz (Bromberg) see Böhler, *Auftakt zum Vernichtungskrieg*, 135–40, and Alexander B. Rossino, *Hitler Strikes Poland. Blitzkrieg, Ideology, and Atrocity* (Lawrence, 2003), 61–63.

16. Lieutenant G., report from 2 Sept 1939, quoted in Böhler, *Auftakt zum Vernichtungskrieg*, 61; Rossini, *Hitler Strikes Poland*, 176 (guerilla-psychosis).

17. OKH Guidelines on Peculiarities of Polish Warfare, 1 July 1939, quoted in Rossini, *Hitler Strikes Poland*, 25f.

18. Jacob Apenslak, ed., *The Black Book of Polish Jewry. An Account on the Martyrdom of Polish Jewry Under the Nazi Occupation* (New York, 1943), 5; Böhler, *Auftakt zum Vernichtungskrieg*, 189, based on additional archival sources.

19. "Führer's Speech to the Commanders in Chief," 22 Aug 1939, in *Trials of War Criminals Before the Nuremberg Military Tribunals Under Control Council Law*

No. 10. Nuremberg, October 1946–April 1949, vol. 10 (Washington, D.C., 1951), 698–703.

20. Reich-Ranicki, *The Author of Himself*, 123, 127, 129. See also Zygmunt Klukowski, *Diary of the Years of Occupation 1939–44* (Urbana, 1993), 40–42.

21. Rossini, *Hitler Strikes Poland*, 86f, 234, 300 fn 17.

22. Ibid., 174–76; Böhler, *Auftakt zum Vernichtungskrieg*, 181–87, 224f.

23. Notes on a talk given by Blaskowitz to Brauchitsch, 6 Feb 1940, in Gerd R. Ueberschaer, ed., *NS-Verbrechen und der militärische Widerstand gegen Hitler* (Darmstadt, 2000), 159f. On Blaskowitz, see Helmut Krausnick and Hans-Heinrich Wilhelm, *Die Truppe des Weltanschauuungskrieges. Die Einsatzgruppen der Sicherheitspolizei und des SD 1938–1942* (Stuttgart, 1981), 34, 76f, 96–99, 102f, 106, 134; on Hitler's amnesty ibid., 82.

24. Raffael Scheck, *Hitler's African Victims. The German Army Massacres of Black French Soldiers in 1940* (Cambridge, U.K., 2006).

25. Alexander Hill, *The War Behind the Eastern Front. The Soviet Partisan Movement in North-West Russia 1941–1944* (New York, 2005), 43; relevant is the Barbarossa Decree, 13 March 1941, and the OKW order on the "cooperation with the Security Police and the SD," 28 Apr 1941, both in Gerd R. Ueberschär and Wolfram Wette, eds., *Der deutsche Überfall auf die Sowjetunion. "Unternehmen Barbarossa" 1941* (Frankfurt, 1991), 246–50.

26. *The Halder War Diary*, 384 (6 May 1941).

27. Memorandum on a Conference of Under-Secretaries, 2 May 1941, in *Trial of the Major War Criminals Before the International Military Tribunal, Nuremberg, 14 November 1945–1 October 1946*, vol. XXXI (Nuremberg, 1946), 84, Doc. 2718-PS. Alex J. Kay, *Exploitation, Resettlement, Mass Murder. Political and Economic Planning for German Occupation Policy in the Soviet Union* (New York, 2006).

28. OKW Order, 16 June 1941, in Ueberschär and Wette, *Der deutsche Überfall auf die Sowjetunion*, 261. See Megargee, *War of Annihilation*, 39–41.

29. Wolf-Dieter Mohrmann, ed., *Der Krieg hier ist hart und grausam! Feldpostbriefe an den Osnabrücker Regierungspräsidenten 1941–1944* (Osnabrück, 1984), 48f.

30. Christian Streit, *Keine Kameraden. Die Wehrmacht und die sowjetischen Kriegsgefangenen 1941–1945*, new ed. (Bonn, 1997), 244ff; Reinhard Otto, "Sowjetische Kriegsgefangene. Neue Quellen und Erkenntnisse," in *"Wir sind die Herren dieses Landes." Ursachen, Verlauf und Folgen des deutschen Überfalls auf die Sowjetunion*, ed. Babette Quinkert (Hamburg, 2002), 124–35.

31. Wette, *The Wehrmacht*, 113f. Cf. Hartmut Rüß, "Wer war verantwortlich für das Massaker von Babij Jar?" *Militärgeschichtliche Mitteilungen* 57 (1998), 483–508. At large: Dieter Pohl, *Die Herrschaft der Wehrmacht. Deutsche Militärbesatzung und einheimische Bevölkerung in der Sowjetunion 1941–1944* (Munich, 2008).

32. On the 707th divison, see Christian Gerlach, *Kalkulierte Morde. Die deutsche Wirtschafts- und Vernichtungspolitik in Weißrußland 1941 bis 1944* (Hamburg, 1999), 620; quotes in Hannes Heer, "Killing Fields. The Wehrmacht and the Holocaust

in Belorussia, 1941–42," in idem and Klaus Naumann, *War of Extermination. The German Military in World War II, 1941–1944* (New York, 2000), 62f. Heer's assumption notwithstanding, such brutality was not typical for the "common soldier."

33. Letter of Heinrich K., 18 July 1942, Bibliothek für Zeitgeschichte Stuttgart, Sammlung Sterz (sausages).

34. Redemann, *Zwischen Front und Heimat*, 222, Neuhaus to his sister Johanna, 15 June 1940; Letter of Helmut Wißmann, privately owned, 24 July 1941; Letters of Franz Wieschenberg, Kempowski-Archiv Nartum, Nr. 3386, 3 Aug 1941, and 22 July 1940. Singing that song was "not just thoughtlessness" but signaled "that, at least in Germany, there was no longer a place for Jews," as Werner Mork states in a memoir on his time as a twenty-year-old Wehrmacht soldier around 1940, http://www.dhm.de/lemo/forum/kollektives_gedaechtnis/318/index.html, accessed 4 May 2008. On German soldiers' anti-Semitism see Omer Bartov, *Hitler's Army. Soldiers, Nazis, and War in the Third Reich* (New York, 1991); Alf Lüdtke, "The Appeal of Exterminating 'Others': German Workers and the Limits of Resistance," *Journal of Modern History* 64 suppl. (1992), S46–S67; Sven Oliver Müller, *Deutsche Soldaten und ihre Feinde. Nationalismus an Front und Heimatfront im Zweiten Weltkrieg* (Frankfurt, 2007); Michaela Kipp, "The Holocaust in the Letters of German Soldiers on the Eastern Front (1939–44)," *Journal of Genocidal Research* 9 (2004), 601–15.

35. Letter of Corporal W. F., 22 Aug 1941, in Buchbender and Sterz, *Das andere Gesicht des Krieges*, 79; Horst Fuchs Richardson, ed., *Your Loyal and Loving Son. The Letters of Tank Gunner Karl Fuchs*, 1937–41 (Washington, D.C., 2003), 118f, 121, letters to his wife and parents, 3 and 15 Aug 1941.

36. Letter of an anonymous corporal, 10 July 1941, in Buchbender and Sterz, *Das andere Gesicht des Krieges*, 74; Fuchs Richardson, *Your Loyal and Loving Son*, 121, 138f, 141, letters from 3 Aug 1941, 15 Oct 1941, and 20 Oct 1941; letter of theology student Günther H., 19 Aug 1941, Historisches Archiv des Erzbistums Köln, Collegium Carolinum Bonn (CLB), Kriegsbriefe Zweiter Weltkrieg; letter of Helmut Wißmann, 16 Aug 1941, 13 Oct 1941; letter of Stefan Schmidhofer to his wife, 30 Sept 1941, privately owned.

37. Letter of sergeant-major Christoph Banse, 7 July 1941, quoted in Martin Humburg, *Das Gesicht des Krieges. Feldpostbriefe von Wehrmachtsoldaten aus der Sowjetunion 1941–1944* (Opladen, 1998), 198; see Walter Manoschek, ed., *"Es gibt nur eines für das Judentum: Vernichtung." Das Judenbild in deutschen Soldatenbriefen 1939–1944* (Hamburg, 1995), 33. On the NKVD massacres and the German reaction in general see Bogdan Musial, *"Konterrevolutionäre Elemente sind zu erschießen." Die Brutalisierung des deutsch-sowjetischen Krieges im Sommer 1941* (Berlin, 2000).

38. Herbert Johannes Veigel, *Christbäume. Briefe aus dem Krieg* (Berlin, 1991), 60, letter, 6 July 1941; Udo von Alvensleben, *Lauter Abschiede. Tagebuch vom Krieg* (Frankfurt, 1971), 195, diary entry, 16 Aug 1941.

39. Minutes of a meeting at Hitler's Headquarters, 16 July 1941, Nuremberg Document 221-L, translated in *Documents on German Foreign Policy, 1918–1945* (Washington, D.C., 1964), series D, vol. 13, Document 114, 149–56.

40. Directive from 25 Sept 1941, quoted in Walter Manoschek, " 'Coming Along to Shoot Some Jews?' The Destruction of Jews in Serbia," in Heer and Naumann, *War of Extermination*, 43 (my translation is revised); idem, *"Serbien ist judenfrei." Militärische Besatzungspolitik und Judenvernichtung in Serbien 1941/42* (Munich, 1993), 60 (Böhme), 87 (returning soldier). Cf. Erich Kuby, *Mein Krieg. Aufzeichnungen aus 2129 Tagen* (Munich, 1975), 228f.

41. *Verbrechen der Wehrmacht. Dimensinen des Vernichtungskrieges*, 89; Krausnick and Wilhelm, *Die Truppe des Weltanschauungskrieges*, 258–61; Wette, *The Wehrmacht*, 95–98, also on similiar orders issued by commanders Erich von Manstein and Hermann Hoth.

42. Facsimile in *Verbrechen der Wehrmacht. Dimensionen des Vernichtungskrieges*, 515. Translation in *Nazi Conspiracy and Aggression*, vol. III (Washington, D.C., 1946), 597–99. See Timm C. Richter, "Die Wehrmacht und der Partisanenkrieg in den besetzten Gebieten de Sowjetunion," in *Die Wehrmacht. Mythos und Realität*, ed. Rolf-Dietrich Müller and Hans-Erich Volkmann (Munich, 1999), 837–57.

43. Case studies on the execution of these orders and the escalation of brutality: Mark Mazower, *Inside Hitler's Greece. The Experience of Occupation, 1941–1944* (New Haven and London, 1993), 155–261; Michael Geyer, "Civitella della Chiana on 29 June 1944: The Reconstruction of German 'Measure,' " in Heer and Naumann, *War of Extermination*, 175–216; Madelon de Keizer, *Razzia in Putten. Verbrechen der Wehrmacht in einem niederländischen Dorf* (Cologne, 2001).

44. Theodor W. Adorno, *Minima Moralia* (Frankfurt, 1987), 51.

45. Helmuth Groscurth, *Tagebücher eines Abwehroffiziers 1938–40. Mit weiteren Dokumenten zur Militäropposition gegen Hitler*, ed. Helmut Krausnick and Harold C. Deutsch (Stuttgart, 1970), 534–42; Ernst Klee, Willi Dressen, and Volker Riess, eds., *"The Good Old Days." The Holocaust as Seen by Its Perpetrators and Bystanders* (New York, 1991), 137–54.

46. "Report of 691st Infantry Regiment on 1 to 7 October 1941," facsimile in *Verbrechen der Wehrmacht. Dimensionen des Vernichtungskrieges*, 585.

47. According to statements made by Sibille and other witnesses interrogated in the early 1950s. See letter Sibille, 2 Feb 1953, Hauptstaatsarchiv Darmstadt, H 13 Darmstadt, 979, Ks 2/54 against Nöll, Zimber and Magel, 207–10, and verdict from 10 March 1956, ibid., 756f. On the Krutscha murder see also Thomas Kühne, "Male Bonding and Shame Culture: Hitler's Soldiers and the Moral Basis of Genocidal Warfare," in *Ordinary People as Mass Murderers. Perpetrators in Comparative Perspectives*, ed. Olaf Jensen, Claus-Christian W. Szejnmann, and Martin L. Davies (Houndmills, 2008), 55–77.

48. Erich Schwinge, *Militärstrafgesetzbuch nebst Kriegssonderstrafrechtsverordnung*, 2d ed. (Berlin, 1944), 100–9.

49. The verdict of the appeals court from 10 March 1956 assumed a minimum number of fifteen men and women, Hauptstaatsarchiv Darmstadt, H 13 Darmstadt, 979, Ks 2/54 against Nöll, Zimber, and Magel, 756. Numbers between fifty and two hundred fifty victims were given in witness statements.

50. Statement of Wilhelm W., 11 Dec 1953, ibid., 386; statement of Hans W., 28 Aug 1953, ibid., 336f; Statement of Adolf Z., 24 Sept 1953, ibid., 360; similar Karl B., 5 Dec 1953, ibid., 379. *Frankfurter Rundschau*, 3 March 1956, 32. On Józefów see Chapter Three and Christopher Browning, *Ordinary Men. Reserve Police Battalion 101 and the Final Solution in Poland* (New York, 1992).

51. Peter Lieb, "Täter aus Überzeugung? Oberst Carl von Andrian und die Judenmorde der 707. Infanteriedivision 1941/42," *Vierteljahrshefte für Zeitgeschichte* 50 (2002), 523–57, esp. 529 and 537–43, quotations from Andrian's personal diary. On the 707th Infantry Division, see Gerlach, *Kalkulierte Morde*, 609–28.

52. Wilm Hosenfeld, *"Ich versuche jeden zu retten." Das Leben eines deutschen Offiziers in Briefen und Tagebüchern*, ed. Thomas Vogel (Munich, 2004), 286 (letter to his wife, 10 Nov 1939), 302 (note, 14 Dec 1939), 455 (letter to his son, 7 March 1941), 538 (note, 14 Oct 1941), 626–28 (diary entry and letter to his wife, 23 July 1942), 641 (diary entry, 13 Aug 1942), 486 (letter to his wife, 25 May 1941), 834 (letter to his wife, 23 Aug 1944). On Szpilman see ibid., 108–13, 972–74, and Władysław Szpilman, *The Pianist. The Extraordinary True Story of One Man's Survival in Warsaw, 1939–1945* (New York, 1999), 209–22, epilogue by Wolf Biermann.

53. Hosenfeld, *"Ich versuche jeden zu retten,"* 304 (note, 15 Dec 1939), 345 (letter to his wife, 10 May 1940), 722 (diary entry, 23 June 1943).

54. Helmut Schmidt, "Politischer Rückblick auf eine unpolitische Jugend," in idem et al., *Kindheit und Jugend unter Hitler* (Berlin, 1994), 232; letter of Kurt Kreissler, 23 May 1943, privately owned. See also Günter Kießling, *Versäumter Widerspruch* (Mainz, 1993), 54f; Sigrid Bremer, *Muckefuck und Kameradschaft. Mädchenzeit im Dritten Reich. Von der Kinderlandverschickung 1940 bis zum Studium 1946* (Frankfurt, 1988), 40; Hartmut Soell, *Fritz Erler—Eine politische Biographie*, 2 vols. (Berlin, 1976), vol. 1, 50f; Bryan Martin Rigg, *Hitler's Jewish Soldiers. The Untold Story of Nazi Racial Laws and Men of Jewish Descent in the German Military* (Lawrence, 2002).

55. Jochen Klepper, *Überwindung. Tagebücher und Aufzeichnungen aus dem Kriege* (Stuttgart, 1958), 157 (diary entry, 2 Aug 1941), 132 (diary entry, 8 Aug 1941), 211 (diary entry, 23 Sept 1941).

56. Klepper, *Überwindung*, 206 and 213, diary entries, 20 and 25 Sept 1941; see also 160, entry from 23 Aug 1941. Cf. Manoschek, *"Es gibt nur eines für das Judentum: Vernichtung,"* 25.

57. Jochen Klepper, *Unter dem Schatten Deiner Flügel. Aus den Tagebüchern der Jahre 1932–1942* (Stuttgart, 1955), 969f, 992, 1029, 1133; Rita Thalmann, *Jochen Klepper. Ein Leben zwischen Idyllen und Katastrophen* (Munich, 1977).

58. Wilhelm Reibert, *Der Dienstunterricht im Reichsheer*, 3d ed. (Berlin, 1934), 96.

59. Alfred Götze, ed., *Trübners Deutsches Wörterbuch*, vol. IV (Berlin, 1943), 84; judgment of the *Volksgerichtshof* (National Court) against Kurt Huber, 28 Apr 1943, Bundesarchiv Berlin, NJ 1704, vol. 7, f132 (thanks to Detlef Bald, Munich, for providing me with this material); Detlef Bald, *Die "Weisse Rose." Von der Front in den Widerstand* (Berlin, 2004); David Raub Snyder, *Sex Crimes Under the Wehrmacht* (Lincoln, 2007), 37.

60. Quotes from testimonies and trial statements during and after the war in Heinrich Walle, *Die Tragödie des Oberleutnants zur See Oskar Kusch* (Stuttgart, 1995), 37, 46, 75, 93; ibid., 370–78, judgment, 31 Jan 1944.

61. Norbert Haase and Gerhard Paul, eds., *Die anderen Soldaten. Wehrkraftzersetzung, Gehorsamsverweigerung und Fahnenflucht im Zweiten Krieg* (Frankfurt, 1995); Manfred Messerschmidt and Fritz Wüllner, *Die Wehrmachtjustiz im Dienste des Nationalsozialismus. Zerstörung einer Legende* (Baden-Baden, 1987); Sigbert Stehmann, *Die Bitternis verschweigen wir. Feldpostbriefe 1940–1945* (Hannover, 1992), 245–47.

62. Hans and Sophie Scholl, *Briefe und Aufzeichnungen*, ed. Inge Jens, rev. ed. (Frankfurt, 1988), 99, compare ibid., 98, 324f.

63. Hosenfeld, *"Ich versuche jeden zu retten,"* 349 (letter to his son, 22 May 1940), 395 (letter to his wife, 23 Sept 1940), compare 569 (letter to his son, 2 Jan 1942) on the need to join in anyway.

64. Letters of Schmidhofer, 22 and 30 Dec 1940; letters of Wieschenberg, 20 June 1940, 25 Aug 1940, 20 Oct 1940; letter of Helmut Wißmann, 29 Oct 1940; Willy Peter Reese, *A Stranger to Myself. The Inhumanity of War: Russia, 1941–1944*, ed. Stefan Schmitz (New York, 2005), 7f, 12f, 17, 23.

65. Letter of Franz Wieschenberg, 29 July 1941. Compare letters of Helmut Wißmann, 19–25 Feb 1941; Reddemann, *Zwischen Front und Heimat*, 343, letter of Albert Neuhaus, 6 Nov 1941.

66. Letters of Franz Wieschenberg, 15 Aug 1941, 6 Sept 41, 16 Jan 1942; letters of Helmut Wißmann, 30 Sept 1941; Reddemann, *Zwischen Front und Heimat*, 343, 352, 354, letters of Neuhaus, 6, 14, and 17 Nov 1941, see also 516, 670, 748.

67. War Diary Farnbacher, 9 Oct 1941, 6 Nov 1941 (Napoleon); letter of Franz Wieschenberg, 28 March 1943 (bunker tantrum); Reddemann, *Zwischen Front und Heimat*, 599, letter of Neuhaus, 29 Aug 1942.

68. Letters of Helmut Wißmann, 1 Dec 41, 6, 11, and 29 Sept 1942, 7 Oct 1942, 10 and 22 Nov 1942, 3 Dec 1942; letters of Kurt Kreissler, 31 Aug 1941, 11 Sept 1941, 23 Oct 1941, 2 Dec 1941; memoirs of Kurt Kreissler (a type of diary in manuscript, c. 1943–44, privately owned), vol. II, 16–20, 76f. Compare Friedrich Grupe, *Jahrgang 1916. Die Fahne war mehr als der Tod* (Munich, 1989), 189f, 279, 293; Walter Bähr and Hans W. Bähr, eds., Kriegsbriefe *gefallener Studenten 1939–1945* (Tübingen, 1952), 81f, 211f, 297ff.

69. Letters of Kurt Kreissler, 27 Jan 42, 2 March 42, 28 March 43, 10 July 43; memoirs of Kurt Kreissler, vol. II, 76f, 80; letters of Helmut Wißmann, 8 Oct 1942;

Reese, *A Stranger to Myself*, 41. See also Klaus Latzel, *Deutsche Soldaten —
nationalsozialistischer Krieg? Kriegserlebnis — Kriegserfahrung 1939–1945*
(Paderborn, 1998), 40–99.

70. Letter of Franz Wieschenberg, 17 Feb 1942, 10 March 1942 (fallen comrades);
Reddemann, *Zwischen Front und Heimat*, 599, diary entry of Neuhaus, 21 July
1942 (crowd). See also Bähr and Bähr, *Kriegsbriefe gefallener Studenten*, 457f, and
Joachim Dollwet, "Menschen im Krieg, Bejahung — und Widerstand? Eindrücke
und Auszüge aus der Sammlung von Feldpostbriefen des Zweiten Weltkrieges im
Landeshauptarchiv Koblenz," *Jahrbuch für Westdeutsche Landesgeschichte*
13 (1987), 289–92.

71. *Die Feldpostbriefe des Adelbert Ottheinrich Rühle 1939–1942. Briefe und Gedichte
eines Frühvollendeten* (Heusenstamm, 1979), 74f.

72. War Diary Farnbacher, 18 and 25 Apr 1942 (sugar mommy); Bähr and Bähr,
Kriegsbriefe gefallener Studenten 1939–1945, 193–95, letter of Kurt Reuber, 25 Dec
42 (Stalingrad). This interpretation contradicts Bartov, *Hitler's Army*, 12–58, who
links the "demodernization of the front" to the "destruction" (rather than the
strengthening) of the primary groups.

73. Iring Fetscher, *Neugier und Furcht. Versuch mein Leben zu verstehen* (Hamburg,
1995), 68f; Martin Schröter, *Held oder Mörder? Bilanz eines Soldaten Adolf Hitlers*
(Wuppertal, 1991), 47; War Diary Farnbacher, 25 Dec 1941.

74. War Diary Gustav Krieg (pseudonym), privately owned, 29 Nov 1942, 24 Jan 1943,
30 Jan 1943, 3 Feb 1943, 8 March 1943, 24 Sept 1943.

75. True masculinity: "Man and Woman in Wartimes," *Der Stoßtrupp. Deutsche
Frontzeitung*, no. 607/608 (June 1942); Edward Shils and Morris Janowitz,
"Cohesion and Disintegration in the Wehrmacht in World War II," *Public
Opinion Quarterly* 12 (1948), 298. Demianova: Regina Mühlhäuser, "Between
'Racial Awareness' and Fantasies of Potency: Nazi Sexual Politics in the
Occupied Territories of the Soviet Union, 1942–1945," in *Brutality and
Desire. War and Sexuality in Europe's Twentieth Century* ed. Dagmar Herzog
(Houndmills, 2009), 201. See also Wendy Jo Geertjejanssen, "Victims,
Heroes, Survivors: Sexual Violence on the Eastern Front During World
War II," PhD diss., University of Minnesota, 2004; Birgit Beck, *Wehrmacht
und sexuelle Gewalt. Sexualverbrechen vor deutschen Militärrichtern 1939–1945*
(Paderborn, 2004).

76. War Diary Farnbacher, copy of a letter, 16 Feb 1943.

77. Bremer, *Muckefuck und Kameradschaft*, 40, quoting her father.

78. Letter of Franz Wieschenberg, 10 Nov 1941; Günther Cwojdrak, *Kontrapunkt.
Tagebuch 1943–1944* (Berlin, 1989), 49, diary entry, 6 Oct 43; Heinrich Boll, *Brief
an einen jungen Katholiken* (Cologne, 1961), 15f, 28; Kuby, *Mein Krieg*, 186, letter
of Kuby's father, 13 Sept 1941.

79. Reese, *A Stranger to Myself*, 18, 44; Birke Mersmann, *"Was bleibt vom
Heldentum?" Weiterleben nach dem Krieg* (Berlin, 1995), 34f.

80. War Diary Farnbacher, 24–25 Nov 1941 and 7 Dec 1941; see already 27 Oct 1941. In general, see Alexander Hill, *The War Behind the Eastern Front. Soviet Partisans in North-West Russia, 1941–1944* (New York, 2004); Ben Shepherd, *War in the Wild East. The German Army and Soviet Partisans* (Cambridge, Mass., 2004).
81. War Diary Farnbacher, 30 Dec 1941.
82. Ibid., 21 Feb 1942, 7, 18, and 21 March 1942; outcast: ibid., 21 Dec 1941; foray: ibid., 27 March 1942.
83. Letters of Werner Gross (pseudonym), 28 July 1942, 25 Sept 1942, 4 Apr 1943, Landeshauptarchiv Koblenz, Best. 700,153, no. 286–91.
84. Shepherd, *War in the Wild East*, 129–218; Gerlach, *Kalkulierte Morde*, 859–1036; Theo J. Schulte, *The German Army and Nazi Policies in Occupied Russia* (Oxford, 1989); Hartmann, "Verbrecherischer Krieg—verbrecherische Wehrmacht?" 24–29, 54–64.
85. Reese, *A Stranger to Myself*, 51–53 (Russia); idem, *Mir selber seltsam fremd. Die Unmenschlichkeit des Krieges. Russland 1941–44*, ed. Stefan Schmitz (Berlin, 2004), 242f (poem not in the English edition).
86. Reddemann, *Zwischen Front und Heimat*, 431, Neuhaus to his wife, 28 Feb 1942; Reese, *A Stranger to Myself*, 135. Case study: Christoph Rass, *"Menschenmaterial": Deutsche Soldaten an der Ostfront. Innenansichten einer Infanteriedivision 1939–1945* (Paderborn, 2003), 348–402.
87. Kuby, *Mein Krieg*, 228f, diary, 25 March 1942, cf. 250, 23 May 1942.
88. Ibid., 37, diary, 15 May 1940. On German soldiers' plundering, see Götz Aly, *Hitler's Beneficiaries. Plunder, Racial War, and the Nazi Welfare State* (New York, 2006), 98–117, and *Latzel, Deutsche Soldaten—nationalsozialistischer Krieg?*, 133–56.
89. Kuby, *Mein Krieg*, 125, 373f, diary, 10 July 1941, 11 Dec 1943.
90. Ibid., 228f, diary, 25 March 1942.
91. Wolfgang Oleschinski, "Ein Augenzeuge des Judenmords desertiert. Der Füsilier Stefan Hampel," in Wolfgang Wette, *Zivilcourage. Empörte, Helfer und Retter aus Wehrmacht, Polizei und SS* (Frankfurt, 2004), 51–59; Hampel's autobiographical statement, 11 May 1943, penned for the court-martial, and the sentence in Norbert Haase, *Deutsche Deserteure* (Berlin, 1987), 112–19.
92. Reese, *A Stranger to Myself*, 137, 148, 154.
93. Diary of Paul Riedel, 7 May 1942, Bibliothek für Zeitgeschichte Stuttgart.
94. Hosenfeld, *"Ich versuche jeden zu retten,"* 302–4 (diary, 14 Dec 1939), 607 (17 Apr 1942), 628–30 (23–25 July 1942), 799f (letter to his wife, 25 March 1944).
95. Benjamin Ziemann, "Fluchten aus dem Konsens zum Durchhalten. Ergebnisse, Probleme und Perspektiven der Erfrschung soldatischer Verweigerungsformen in der Wehrmacht 1939–1945," in Müller and Volkmann, *Die Wehrmacht*, 589–613; the deserters were embarrassed about what the Nazi regime did to them as Aryan Germans rather than what the Nazis did to those who were persecuted as non-Aryans. Hampel was an exception.

96. Hosenfeld, *"Ich versuche jeden zu retten,"* 301f (note, 14 Dec 1939), 653 (diary entry, 6 Sept 1942), 714 (letter to his wife, 9 May 1943).

97. Diary of Paul Kreissler, 22 Jan, 8 Feb, 3 March, 20 Sept 1943; Reese, *Mir selber seltsam fremd,* 240, 242, quotes from his diary and cynical poems; Hosenfeld, *"Ich versuche jeden zu retten,"* 782 (diary, 28 Dec 1943), cf. 302, 628–30, 653, 714, 782, 799f.

98. Hosenfeld, *"Ich versuche jeden zu retten,"* 628 (diary, 23 July 1942), 697 (diary, 19 Feb 1943), 637 (diary, 7 Aug 1942).

99. Göring speech, 4 Oct 1942, in Walter Roller and Suanne Höschel, eds., *Judenverfolgung und jüdisches Leben unter den Bedingungen der nationalsozialistischen Gewaltherrschaft,* vol. 1, *Tondokumente und Rundfunksendungen, 1930–1946* (Potsdam, 1996), 217f; Jeffrey Herf, *The Jewish Enemy. Nazi Propaganda During World War II and the Holocaust* (Cambridge, Mass., 2006), 168f.

100. *Der Führer,* 17 May 1943, quoted in Peter Longerich, *"Davon haben wir nichts gewußt!" Die Deutschen und die Judenverfolgung 1933–1945* (Berlin, 2006), 278f.

101. Kölnische Zeitung, 3 Feb 1943, quoted in Bernward Dörner, *Die Deutschen und der Holocaust. Was niemand wissen wollte, aber jeder wissen konnte* (Berlin, 2007), 461.

102. Letter of Private Heinz S., 20 May 1942, quoted in Müller, *Deutsche Soldaten und ihre Feinde,* 223; letter of Alfred N., 29 May 1943, Bibliothek für Zeitgeschichte, Sammlung Sterz; Kuby, *Mein Krieg,* 263, letter, 28 June 1942.

103. Letter of Helmut Wißmann to his wife, 26 Jan 1943. See letter of Lieutenant Paul D., 31 Jan 1943, Bibliothek für Zeitgeschichte, Sammlung Sterz.

104. Müller, *Deutsche Soldaten und ihre Feinde,* 162, and Dollwet, "Menschen im Krieg," 293, letter of anonymous soldier, 24 Nov 1943.

105. Letter of Hans A., 24 March 1943, quoted in Müller, *Deutsche Soldaten und ihre Feinde,* 152f.

106. Letter of Private Hans H., 12 June 1943, Buchbender and Sterz, *Das andere Gesicht des Krieges,* 117.

107. Wieschenberg to his wife, 28 Aug 1944.

108. Rüdiger Overmans, *Deutsche militärische Verluste im Zweiten Wektkrieg* (Munich, 1999), 237–40, 276–84.

109. Andreas Kunz, *Wehrmacht und Niederlage. Die bewaffnete Macht in der Endphase der nationalsozialistischen Herrschaft 1944 bis 1945* (Munich, 2005).

110. Letters of Franz Wieschenberg, 26 Aug and 3 Sept 1944; Buchbender and Sterz, S. 154; Bartov, *Hitler's Army,* 118–25, 145–57, 166–79; Stephen G. Fritz, *Frontsoldaten. The German Soldier in World War II* (Lexington, 1995), 215f, 241f; Müller, *Deutsche Soldaten und ihre Feinde,* 138–42. Statistical evidence on the soldiers' belief in Hitler is provided by American opinion polls among German POWs, M. I. Gurfein and Morris Janowitz, *Trends in Wehrmacht Morale* (New York, 1951).

111. Leonidas E. Hill, ed., *Die Weizsäcker-Papiere, 1933–1950,* (Berlin, 1974), 337; *Hitlers politisches Testament. Die Bormann Diktate vom Februar und April 1945* (Hamburg,

1981), 121–25; Bernd Wegner, "The Ideology of Self-Destruction. Hitler and the Choreography of Defeat," *Bulletin of the German Historical Institute London* 26 (2004), 18–33; Michael Geyer, "Endkampf 1918 and 1945. German Nationalism, Annihilation, and Self-Destruction," *No Man's Land of Violence. Extreme Wars in the 20th Century*, ed. Alf Lüdtke and Bernd Weisbrod (Göttingen, 2006), 37–67.

112. Letter of Franz Wieschenberg, 28 Aug 1944; letter of Helmut Wißmann, 9 Aug 1943. See Buchbender and Sterz, *Das andere Gesicht des Krieges*, 141–48, also to the soldiers' reaction to the failed July-complot against Hitler.

113. Dollwet, "Menschen im Krieg, Bejahung—und Widerstand?" 318.

114. Memoirs of Kurt Kreissler, 149, 153–58.

5 Watching Terror

1. Diary of Felix Landau, 2 Aug, 8 July, 21 July, 6 Aug 1941, in Ernst Klee, Willi Dressen, and Volker Riess, eds., *"The Good Old Days." The Holocaust as Seen by Its Perpetrators and Bystanders* (New York, 1991), 94, 100, 105f; translation corrected by the author. On Landau see chapter III.

2. Judgment Landgericht Stuttgart on Felix Landau, 16 March 1962, BAL 162/3380; testimony of Marjan Nadel, 24 Aug 1959, Staatsarchiv Ludwigsburg, EL 317 III, Bü 1089, fol. 283–85; on Trude's table dance see testimony of Jakob Goldsztein, 30 July 1959, ibid., fol. 273–76; T. Friedmann, ed., *Die Taetigkeit der Schutzpolizei, Gestapo und ukrainische [sic] Miliz in Drohobycz 1941–1944. Dokumentensammlung* (Haifa, 1995); Gudrun Schwarz, *Eine Frau an seiner Seite. Ehefrauen in der "SS-Sippengemeinschaft"* (Hamburg, 1997), 201–6.

3. Ida Blom, Karen Hagemann, and Catherine Hall, eds., *Gendered Nations. Nationalisms and Gender Order in the Long Nineteenth Century* (Oxford, 2000). But see Lora Wildenthal, *German Women for Empire, 1884–1945* (Durham, 2001).

4. Birthe Kundrus, "Gender Wars. The First World War and the Construction of Gender Relations in the Weimar Republic," in *Home/Front. The Military, War and Gender in Twentieth-Century Germany*, ed. Karen Hagemann and Stefanie Schüler-Springorum (Oxford, 2002), 159–79.

5. Quotations from Alfred Rosenberg's *Der Mythos des XX. Jahrhunderts* (1930) and from Joseph Goebbels's *Michael* (1929) in George L. Mosse, *Nazi Culture. Intellectual, Cultural and Social Life in the Third Reich* (New York, 1966), 40f.

6. Hitler speech to the National Socialist Women's Congress in 1935, quoted in Mosse, *Nazi Culture*, 40. Claudia Koonz, *Mothers in the Fatherland. Women, the Family, and Nazi Politics* (New York, 1987), has focused on women's support of Nazi crimes by emotional and reproductive work in the family; cf. Atina Grossmann, "Feminist Debates About Women and National Socialism," *Gender & History* 3 (1991), 350–58, and Elizabeth D. Heineman, *What Difference Does a Husband Make? Women and Marital Status in Nazi and Postwar Germany* (Berkeley, 1999).

7. See, e.g., Elisabeth von Barsewitsch, *Die Aufgaben der Frau für die Aufartung* (Berlin, 1933); Michelle Mouton, *From Nurturing the Nation to Purifying the Volk. Weimar and Nazi Family Policy, 1918–1945* (New York, 2007).

8. Quotations from speeches of Reich Minister Rudolf Hess in 1936, SS Chief Group Leader Jeckeln in 1937, and from an article from *Der Angriff* from 1936, all quoted in Mosse, *Nazi Culture*, 41–45.

9. Luise Fick, *Die deutsche Jugendbewegung* (Jena, 1939), 180.

10. Hanna Rees, *Frauenarbeit in der NS-Volkswohlfahrt* (Berlin, 1938), 30–35. Cf. Rebekah McFarland-Icke, *Nurses in Nazi Germany. Moral Choice in History* (Princeton, 1999).

11. Jill Stephenson, *Women in Nazi Germany* (Harlow, 2001), 176f.

12. Vandana Joshi, *Gender and Power in the Third Reich. Female Denouncers and the Gestapo (1933–45)* (Houndmills, 2003), 16, 44–47, 93, 99, 169, 185f. Based on his research of Gestapo files in Düsseldorf, Joshi estimates that up to 37 percent of the denouncers were female. Previous researchers such as Gisela Diewald-Kerkmann, *Politische Denunziation im NS-Regime oder die kleine Macht der 'Volksgenosssen'* (Bonn, 1995), have underestimated the female share; Matthew Stibbe, *Women in the Third Reich* (London, 2003), 49, 159–62. In general, see Robert Gellately, *Backing Hitler. Consent and Coercion in Nazi Germany* (Oxford, 2001).

13. Quoted in Gisela Bock, "Ordinary Women in Nazi Germany: Perpetrators, Victims, Followers, and Bystanders," in *Women in the Holocaust*, ed. Dalia Ofer and Leonore J. Weitzman (New Haven, 1998), 91.

14. Jeremy Noakes and Geoffrey Pridham, eds., *Nazism, 1919–1945. A History in Documents and Eyewitness Accounts*, 2 vols. (New York, 1983), vol. 1, 421; Stibbe, *Women in the Third Reich*, 108–27; Stefan Bajohr, "Weiblicher Arbeitsdienst im 'Dritten Reich.' Ein Konflikt zwischen Ideologie und Ökonomie," *Vierteljahrshefte für Zeitgeschichte* 28 (1980), 347.

15. Nori Möding, " 'Ich muß irgendwo engagiert sein—fragen Sie mich bloß nicht, warum.' Überlegungen zu Sozialisationserfahrungen von Mädchen in NS-Organisationen," in *"Wir kriegen jetzt andere Zeiten." Auf der Suche nach der Erfahrung des Volkes in nachfaschistischen Ländern*, ed. Lutz Niethammer and Alexander von Plato (Berlin, 1985), 262–64 (RAD girls); Dagmar Reese, *Growing Up Female in Nazi Germany* (Ann Arbor, 2006), 92–95 (BDM girls); Jutta Rüdiger, "Der Bund Deutscher Mädel in der Hitler-Jugend," in *Das Dritte Reich im Aufbau*, vol. 2, ed. Paul Meier-Benneckenstein (Berlin, 1939), 400; Lore Walb, *Ich, die Alte—ich, die Junge. Konfrontation mit meinen Tagebüchern 1933–1945* (Berlin, 1998), 109, diary, 6 Nov 1938; cf. Lisa Pine, "Creating Conformity: The Training of Girls in the *Bund Deutscher Mädel*," *European History Quarterly* 33 (2003), 367–85.

16. Interview, 25 Feb 1995, quoted in Michelle Mouton, "Sports, Song, and Socialization. Women's Memories of Youthful Activity and Political Indoctrination in the BDM," *Journal of Women's History* 17 (2005), 71 and 65; Lisa Kock, "Man

war bestätigt und konnte was!" Der Bund Deutscher Mädel im Spiegel ehemaliger Mädelführerinnen (Münster, 1994), 138.

17. Baldur von Schirach, *Revolution der Erziehung. Reden aus den Jahren des Aufbaus*, 3d ed. (Munich 1942), 46, speech, 19 Apr 1938; Möding, "Ich muß irgendwo engagiert sein," 268f.

18. Eva Jantzen and Merith Niehuss, eds., *Das Klassenbuch. Chronik einer Frauengeneration 1932–1976* (Weimar, 1994), 107, diary entry, 7 Apr 1938.

19. Melita Maschmann, *Account Rendered. A Dossier on My Former Self* (London, 1964, German original 1963), 54, 10, 23, 35f. On Maschmann's exculpatory strategies see Joanne Sayner, " 'Man muß die Bunten Blüten abreißen': Melitta Maschmann's Autobiographical Memories of Nazism," *Forum of Modern Language Studies* 41 (2005), 213–25.

20. Maschmann, *Account Rendered*, 86; Walb, *Ich, die Alte—ich, die Junge*, 108, diary, 18 Oct 1938; Jantzen and Niehuss, *Das Klassenbuch*, 107, entry in a circulating "class diary," 7 Apr 1938; Ute Frevert, *Women in German History. From Bourgeois Emancipation to Sexual Liberation* (Oxford, 1989), 240–44.

21. Quoted in Nicole Kramer, "Mobilisierung für die, 'Heimatfront.' Frauen im zivilen Luftschutz," in *Volksgenossinnen. Frauen in der NS-Volksgemeinschaft*, ed. Sybille Steinbacher (Göttingen, 2007), 72, see ibid., 69–92.

22. *Völkischer Beobachter*, 19 July 1939, 7.

23. Martha Moers, "Berufswahl nach weiblicher Art," *Das junge Deutschland* 37 (1943), 46–50.

24. Bernhard Rieger, "Hanna Reitsch (1912–1979): The Global Career of a Nazi Celebrity," *German History* 26 (2008), 383–405; Gerhard Bracke, *Melitta Gräfin Stauffenberg. Das Leben einer Fliegerin* (Munich, 1990).

25. Maschmann, *Account Rendered*, 56f.

26. Elizabeth Harvey, *Women and the Nazi East. Agents and Witnesses of Germanization* (New Haven, 2003), 16, analyzes impressions as given by Maschmann, *Account Rendered*, 57–135.

27. Maschmann, *Account Rendered*, 118–20, 95, 68, 65. More generally, see Harvey, *Women and the Nazi East*, 14–19, 89–95, 118, 128–36, 141–46, 174–80, and 270–82.

28. Hilde Zimmermann, "Wie auf Eis gelegt," in *Ich geb Dir einen Mantel, daß Du ihn noch in Freiheit tragen kannst. Widerstehen im KZ. Österreichische Frauen erzählen*, ed. Karin Berger et al. (Vienna, 1987), 19; Daniel Patrick Brown, *The Beautiful Beast. The Life & Crimes of SS-Aufseherin Irma Grese* (Ventura, 1996); Susanne Heschel, "Does Atrocity Have a Gender? Feminist Interpretations of Women in the SS," in *Lessons and Legacies VI. New Currents in Holocaust Research*, ed. J. M. Diefendorf (Evanston, 2004), 300–21; Simone Erpel, ed., *Im Gefolge der SS: Aufseherinnen des Frauen-KZ Ravensbrück* (Berlin, 2007).

29. Quoted in Mallmann, Rieß, and Pyta, *Deutscher Osten*, 120; see Franz W. Seidler, *Frauen zu den Waffen? Marketenderinnen, Helferinnen, Soldatinnen* (Koblenz, 1978), 175–202.

30. Speeches of Heinrich Himmler in Vienna, 1939, and to SS generals in 1937, excerpts of both in Heinrich Himmler, *Geheimreden 1933 bis 1945 und andere Ansprachen*, ed. Bradley F. Smith and Agnes F. Peterson (Berlin, 1974), 50 and 61. On the SS Sippengemeinschaft, see Schwarz, *Eine Frau an seiner Seite*, 17–98, ibid., 24 and 30, the quotes from the 1931 Himmler order and *Das Schwarze Korps*.

31. Hans-Joachim Schneider, "Der Totenkopfsturmbann Stutthof," *Dachauer Hefte* 10 (1994), 115f; Hoess, *Commandant of Auschwitz*, 113, 156; Alexandra Przyrembel, "Transfixed by an Image. Ilse Koch, the 'Kommandeuse of Buchenwald,' " *German History* 19 (2001), 369–99; Schwarz, *Eine Frau an seiner Seite*, 208.

32. Bock, "Ordinary Women in Nazi Germany," 94; Tom Segev, *Soldiers of Evil. The Commandants of the Nazi Concentration Camps* (New York, 1987), 155.

33. Seidler, *Frauen zu den Waffen*, 59–174; Ursula von Gersdorff, *Frauen im Kriegsdienst 1914–1945* (Stuttgart, 1969); Franka Maubach, "Expansion weibliche Hilfe. Zur Erfahrungsgeschichte von Frauen im Kriegsdienst," in Steinbacher, *Volksgenossinnen*, 93–111; Brigitte Penkert, *Briefe einer Rotkreuzschwester von der Ostfront*, ed. Jens Ebert and Sybille Penkert (Göttingen, 2007).

34. Ilse Schmidt, *Die Mitläuferin. Erinnerungen einer Wehrmachtsangehörigen* (Berlin, 1999), 11, 15, 17f, 37f, 41–45, 47f, 59, 64, 74–76, 81, 171f.

35. Walb, *Ich die Alte, Ich, die Junge*, 42, 218–21, 234, 239; Möding, "Ich muß irgendwo engagiert sein," 273–76; Christel Beilmann, *Eine katholische Jugend in Gottes und dem Dritten Reich. Briefe, Gedrucktes 1930–1945* (Wuppertal, 1989), 135, 154; Michael Sager, *Jugend in der Mühle des Kriege. Russlandfeldzug und Gefangenschaft 1941–1949* (Munich, 2001), 87f; letter of R. B. to Elmar Roth, 29 Oct 1943, photocopy owned by author; diary of Gerhard Modersen, report on 1936; Fritz Klatt, "Geschlechtliche Gruppierung der Jugend," *Das junge Deutschland* 24 (1930), 166–69.

36. Inge Marszolek, " 'Ich möchte Dich zu gern mal in Uniform sehen.' Geschlechterkonstruktionen in Felpostbriefen," *WerkstattGeschichte* 22 (1999), 41–59; Klara Löffler, *Zurechtgerückt. Der Zweite Weltkrieg als biographischer Stoff* (Berlin, 1999); letters of Edith to Helmut Wißmann, 3 and 11 March 1941, privately owned.

37. Quote from a letter from 1942, Susanne zur Nieden, *Alltag im Ausnahmezustand. Frauentagebücher im zerstörten Deutschland 1943 bis 1945* (Berlin, 1993), 113–17.

38. Lieselotte Orgel-Purper, *Willst Du meine Witwe werden? Eine deutsche Liebe im Krieg* (Berlin, 1995), 175.

39. Schmidt, *Die Mitläuferin*, 20; Otto Dov Kulka and Eberhard Jäckel, eds., *Die Juden in den geheimen NS-Stimmungsberichten 1933–1945* (Düsseldorf, 2004), 412, 416f.

40. Report of NSDAP district Göttingen, 19 Dec 1941, ibid., 481f, no. 3400; Frank Bajohr and Dieter Pohl, *Der Holocaust als offenes Geheimnis. Die Deutschen, die NS-Führung und die Alliierten* (Munich, 2006), 46–49; Victor Klemperer, *I Will Bear Witness. A Diary of the Nazi Years, 1942–1945* (New York, 1999), 254 (17 Aug 1943).

41. Joshi, *Gender and Power in the Third Reich*, 185f.
42. Statement of Goebbels's Ministry of Propaganda in Sept 1941, quoted in Peter Longerich, *"Davon haben wir nichts gewußt!" Die Deutschen und die Judenverfolgung 1933–1945* (Berlin, 2006), 172; Ursula von Kardoff, *Berliner Aufzeichungen 1942 bis 1945* (Munich, 1994), 72, 3 March 1943.
43. Nathan Stoltzfus, *Intermarriage and the Rosenstrasse Protest in Nazi Germany* (New York, 1996); Elisabeth Noelle-Neumann, *The Spiral of Silence. Public Opinion — Our Social Skin*, 2d ed. (Chicago, 1993).
44. Ludwig Eiber, " 'ein bißchen die Wahrheit.' Briefe eines Bremer Kaufmanns von seinem Einsatz beim Reserve-Polizeibatallion 105 in der Sowjetunion 1941," 1999. *Zeitschrift für Sozialgeschichte des 20. und 21. Jahrhunderts* 6, no. 1 (1991), 71–73.
45. Correspondence between Hilde and Franz Wieschenberg, 30 March and 19 Apr 1942, see chapter 4; Bernward Dörner, *Die Deutschen und der Holocaust. Was niemand wissen wollte, aber jeder wissen konnte* (Berlin, 2007), 336–40.
46. Ibid.
47. Hannah Arendt, "Organized Guilt and Universal Responsibility," in *Collective Responsibility. Five Decades of Debate in Theoretical and Applied Ethics*, ed. Larry May and Stacey Hoffman (Savage, 1991), 274, 277 (first published in spring 1945); in this essay, Arendt furthermore presents ideas about the Nazis' totalitarian control over Germans and their "conscience cleared through the bureaucratic organization" (280), which anticipated her subsequently published famous works on totalitarianism and on Adolf Eichmann. More recent scholarship, including this book, renders more account to the agency of even ordinary Germans and to their subjectivity, which *during* the Nazi period was just not (or only insufficiently) "cleared" through anonymous organizations, although perpetrators and bystanders *later* certainly referred to such mechanisms for exculpatory purposes. Even less acceptable is Arendt's escape into the idea of "universal responsibility" for the Nazi crimes. On Germans' knowledge of the Holocaust, see also Ian Kershaw, *Hitler, the Germans, and the Final Solution* (New Haven, 2008), 139–234; Peter Fritzsche, *Life and Death in the Third Reich* (Cambridge, Mass., 2008), 225–307.
48. Herbert and Sibylle Obenaus, eds., *"Schreiben, wie es wirklich war!" Aufzeichnungen Karl Dürkefäldens aus den Jahren 1933–1945* (Hannover, 1985), 108, 106, 110f, 113f, 117, 127, summarized in Kershaw, *Hitler, the Germans, and the Final Solution*, 142f; Klemperer, *I Will Bear Witness*, 371 (24 Oct 1944), 377 (26 Nov 1944).
49. Max Domarus, *Hitler. Speeches and Proclamations 1932–1945 and Commentary by a Contemporary. The Chronicle of a Dictatorship* (Wauconda, 1992), vol. 4, 2681f.
50. See, e.g., Walb, *Ich, die Alte — ich, die Junge*, 246–351.
51. Diary entry, 25 Aug 1944, in Heinrich Breloer, ed, *Mein Tagebuch. Geschichten vom Überleben 1939–1947* (Cologne, 1984), 220.
52. See chapter 4 for Göring's Oct 1942 speech; Fritzsche, *Life and Death in the Third Reich*, 286. Detailed on the propaganda: Jeffrey Herf, *The Jewish Enemy. Nazi*

Propaganda During World War II and the Holocaust (Cambridge, Mass., 2006); Dörner, *Die Deutschen und der Holocaust*, 485 (Mosel inn; Wurm); Paulheintz Wantzen, *Das Leben im Krieg 1939–1946. Ein Tagebuch. Aufgezeichnet in der damaligen Gegenwart* (Bad Himburg, 1999), 1094, diary, 9 May 1943 (Rosenberg).

53. Quoted in Gellately, *Backing Hitler*, 253f.

54. See, e.g., Neil Gregor, "A *Schicksalsgemeinschaft?* Allied Bombing, Civilian Morale, and Social Dissolution in Nuremberg, 1942–1945," *The Historical Journal* 43 (2000), 1051–70, without reference to the uniting effect of the knowledge of the Holocaust—which made the *Schicksalsgemeinschaft.*

Conclusion

1. Cornelia Brink, *Ikonen der Vernichtung. Öffentlicher Gebrauch von FotograWen aus nationalsozialistischen Konzentrationslagern nach 1945* (Berlin, 1998), 73.

2. Charles S. Maier, "Collective Guilt? No . . . But:" *Rechtshistorisches Journal* 16 (1997), 681–86. See, more generally, Larry May and Stacey Hoffman, eds., *Collective Responsibility. Five Decades of Theoretical and Applied Ethics* (Savage, 1991). Gesine Schwan, *Politik und Schuld. Die zerstörerische Macht des Schweigens* (Frankfurt, 1997). Brief accounts on Germany's coping with the past, summarizing the broad range of literature, are in Bernhard Giesen, "The Trauma of Perpetrators. The Holocaust as the Traumatic Reference of German National Identity," in *Cultural Trauma and Collective Identity*, ed. Jeffrey C. Alexander et al. (Berkeley, 2004), 112–54, and Robert G. Moeller, "The Third Reich in Post-war German Memory," in *Nazi Germany. The Short Oxford History of Germany*, ed. Jane Caplan (Oxford, 2008), 246–66.

3. Philip Gourevitch, *We Wish to Inform You That Tomorrow We Will Be Killed with Our Families. Stories from Rwanda* (New York, 1998), 95. Cf. Keith Doubt, *Understanding Evil. Lessons from Bosnia* (New York, 2006), and Donald Bloxham, *The Final Solution. A Genocide* (Oxford, 2009), 261–99.

4. G. W. F. Hegel, *The Phenomenology of Mind* (New York, 1977), 474.

5. Ute Frevert, "Nation, Krieg und Geschlecht im 19. Jahrhundert," in *Nation und Gesellschaft in Deutschland*, ed. Manfred Hettling and Paul Nolte (Munich, 1996), 151–70, 151 for the Treitsche quotation. Cf. Jörn Leonhard, *Bellizismus und Nation. Kriegsdeutung und Nationsbestimmung in Europa und den Vereinigten Staaten 1750–1914* (Munich, 2008).

6. Benedict Anderson, *Imagined Communities. Reflections on the Origin and Spread of Nationalism*, rev. ed. (London, 1991), 6–7.